Advertising Campaign Planning

Developing an Advertising-Based
Marketing Plan
4th Edition

by
Jim Avery

Advertising Campaign Planning:
Developing an Advertising-Based Marketing Plan

© 1993, 1997, 2000, 2010 Jim Avery
All Rights Reserved. Published 2010.
First edition published 1993. Second edition 1997. Third edition 2000.
Fourth edition 2010
Printed in the United States of America
19 18 17 16 15 14 13 12   4 5

ISBN: 978-1-887229-41-8

Published by The Copy Workshop
A division of Bruce Bendinger Creative Communications, Inc.
2144 N. Hudson • Chicago, IL 60614
773-871-1179 • thecopyworkshop@aol.com

Editor: Bruce Bendinger
Production Editor: Patrick Aylward
Cover Design: Gregory S. Paus
Producer: Lorelei Davis Bendinger

Photo credits—xiii: Jef Richards; 184: Tiara Williams.

To George Barrus—
For teaching me to believe in advertising.

Table of Contents:

Planning Points

The Marketing Planning Document

DDB Worldwide Communications Group Inc.
437 Madison Avenue
New York, NY 10022 USA
Telephone 212-415-3169 Fax 212-817-699

Greg Taucher
Director, Worldwide Accounts & Contracts
and Chief People Officer

Dear Reader,

Jim Avery asked me to write the forward for the latest edition of his book.

I said yes.

While I have a relentless pursuit for reading as many industry related books, periodicals, articles, case studies and abstracts as I can put my hands on, I haven't actually read an advertising, marketing or marketing communications textbook since I was in graduate school at Northwestern University. That was a long time ago.

I read Jim's book on a recent flight back the U.S. from London. It's an excellent read. It's a very well written, well organized, well constructed and comprehensive guide for the "real world" of advertising-based marketing campaign planning and implementation. Key words: real world.

It's solid. It's really solid. And while pragmatic, Jim provides the reader with excellent balance in his outlined approach to campaign development and the management of the process. It speaks directly to the power and value of consumer information, insight and perspective. And in today's challenging operating environment, this is where the battle for market share and category leadership is fought, won and hopefully not lost. And what I enjoyed most, Jim's book does not read or feel like a textbook ... this book more like a "campaign" development owner's manual than a textbook.

And while not even Google or Bing could dredge up how many books have been written on the subjects of advertising and marketing and campaign planning, Jim's book continues to be an excellent resource for students and professionals alike. Enjoy the read ....I did.

Greg Taucher

Preface:

"Walking ten thousand miles is better than reading ten thousand books."

—Old Chinese saying

Our Mission.

As publishers of advertising and marketing textbooks, our mission is to publish books that actually teach you something about marketing and advertising.

Sounds simple. But it isn't.

Printing books is easy. But finding books that can help you develop skills for a business world that gets tougher every day is … tough.

To publish special books, you need special people.

Jim Avery, Ad Executive/Professor/International Consultant.

A True Story:

After succeeding at some of the toughest minded ad agencies in America, Jim Avery, now Professor Avery (or just 'Avery' to most) chose to make a transition. He moved from helping marketers and agencies develop advertising and marketing plans to helping students to understand that process.

He has done exactly that. He is now a full-professor holding the Gaylord Professorship in strategic communication at the University of Oklahoma.

His teaching now has international scope, starting with a series of seminars for DDB university in Singapore. His professional development seminars for advertisers, government groups, and advertising associations have ranged from Beijing, Belgrade, Bucharest, Budapest, Dublin, Hangzhou, Helsinki, Ho Chi Minh City, Hong Kong, Istanbul, Kuala Lumpur, Ljubljana, Macau, Milan, Prague, Shanghai, Singapore, Sofia, Vienna, Warsaw, to Zagreb, as well as in North America.

He has also shared his approach and experience with the following agencies: J. Walter Thompson, DDB, Hal Riney, TBWA, ADK, Associated,

Richards Group, VML, Euro RSCG, Publicis, Grey, McClainFinlon, FCB, Propaganda3, Third Degree, Brandz Group, Leo Burnett, Ogilvy, Carat, Weber Shandwick, and many others.

His philosophy has always been to continually work to improve each situation. While he has taught the advertising campaign class for nearly two decades, each semester he has found new ways to improve the course. This book is a summary of the updates and improvements he has made in recent years.

—The Copy Workshop

Author's Notes:

This is the Fourth Edition of a book intended for anyone who wants to know how to write an advertising based marketing plan.

The first three editions did a good job. Some of you have used them.

This Fourth Edition will do it a little better. We've changed it for a changing world. And just in time.

Because, quite frankly, the world is different. The US is no longer the natural leader in worldwide advertising. London dominates the account planning function. Asia is the master of BTL (Below-the-Line) and award-winning creative comes from everywhere—from Hamburg to Rio.

This book will try to incorporate at least some of those changes including complete marketing communication or TTL (through-the-line), incorporating idea-driven planning.

But many of those ideas will still be driving advertising programs. Because even with all the new challenges and new media, the paid media messages of an advertising-driven program are what it takes to get the job done. Advertising remains the primary marketing communication tool for a wide variety of marketers.

We will try to keep all the changes in a changing world from getting in the way of developing the advertising and the complimentary marketing programs that will increase your effectiveness. This book is about focusing on what it takes to get the job done. It's not intended to define terms or explain everything or analyze why something works the way it does. If you need to know more, I will refer you to a few books at the end of each chapter, just in case ...

For Professionals, Entrepreneurs, and Students.

If you're a working professional or entrepreneur, hopefully this book can help you get to the next level.

If you're a student, this book assumes you've already taken courses like Principles of Advertising, Advertising Management, Media Planning, Advertising Creativity, and possibly even Advertising Research. If you haven't taken those courses, you may need to supplement your knowledge. Your instructor should be able to help you find the necessary additional information.

This gets to the point.

It provides a detailed action outline for writing a marketing plan. That said, it is, however, only one way to do it. It is a good way—but not the only way. Please do not construe this to be holy writ. The method presented here is just one way to do it. There are probably as many different methods for writing a marketing planning document as there are companies that write them.

Still, I believe this is a very good method—it is one with great clarity and it encourages a certain intellectual discipline. Finally, it is easily adaptable to other formats or philosophies of marketing planning. Remember the title, this is a method for an advertising based marketing plan.

Three Major Sections.

This book is divided into three major parts—Planning Points, The Plan, and The Presentation.

The first part, called Planning Points, helps a student agency or group from a campaign class get organized and lists other information you need to get started. If you are a business person, this section can also aid you to organize your information.

The middle section—the main part—takes you through the outline of the marketing planning document itself—The Plan. It is the heart of the book. It contains practical advice on the thing that can make or break a student marketing plan.

Finally, the third part covers The Presentation. This may be a contest (like the AAF/NSAC), a presentation to the client for your campaigns class, or one of those real world events (like a presentation to potential investors). This part is a moving target, with computer-based presentation techniques and technology evolving all the time. In addition, there can be great variation in the presentation environment itself.

I personally recall presenting a media and creative plan to seventeen hundred Midas franchisees at an island resort in Florida. We had a fourteen foot tall screen to help make the plan clear. Today, this seldom happens. Most presentations are made in too-small conference rooms with six or eight people. Sometimes they are made to one very important person. If you are competing in the AAF/NSAC, you will be in a fairly large room with a large audience comprised of teams from competing schools—and three judges.

The Book That Feels Like a Marketing Plan...

One of the challenges you will have is working with people who don't think the way you do. If you're an account manager, that means creative people—art directors and copywriters who will look for creative ways to address marketing issues. That's the way this book evolved.

Overall, we tried to make this book feel like a marketing plan—it's intended to look like a planning document... except for the subheads that call out what we are doing.

The subheads are there because Bruce (Bendinger... editor, et al), insisted we have subheads not just to help organize the material but to make the information more accessible. I fought him on this at first, but he's right. The book is better for having the subheads.

But realize that while they'll help you learn the subject, they should not be in a marketing planning document.

In the majority of cases, your planning document will not have introductions and subheads. But with these exceptions, it will be constructed very much like the middle portion of this book.

Some Words of Thanks.

There are a lot of people to thank:

People like Bill Impey and Larry Carroll—for insisting on excellence in the marketing planning I provided to them when they were my clients.

People like Jim Johnson and Peter Parsons—for teaching me, and Larry Singer—for trusting me.

All the students who survived this book in lecture form before it was written—and helped me refine it. People like Bob Rickert and Bruce Rowley and Cello Vergara and Dave Peacock and Mark Strickler and A.P. Loevenguth and Robin Lanahan and Stu Redsun and Rob Siltenan and … and …

People like Tim Bengtson and Mike Kautsch—for encouraging me to begin my writing. And Ann Maxwell and Jim Marra—for their positive reinforcement.

To my father—for teaching me the value of work, which is what this book is all about. And to my mother… for at least thirty years of correcting my grammar and always encouraging me. I am sure she is looking down at me now and thinking, "No, I taught you better… don't use ellipses, the dash would be better."

To Bruce Bendinger of The Copy Workshop—for hounding me for no less than three years to write this book.

And to Michelle Faulker, now at Mindshare in Chicago, and Amanda Plewes, now at Click Here in Dallas, both past students who helped me to understand Digital Media.

But most of all I have to thank my wife Janet—my love, my first editor, and my partner forever.

Thanks also to Wells Rich Greene—for developing some of these systems before I ever went to work there. It's an agency we all miss.

The Interactive Advertising Bureau for the use of their definitions—see the appendix.

And thanks to The Association for Education in Journalism and Mass Communications (AEJMC)—for teaching me how to make the transition from professional to professor.

Thanks to all of you for all your help and the lessons learned.

And to those of you about to embark on this journey, remember that sharing what you know can not only make the world a better place, it makes each of us a better person.

—Jim Avery

About The Author

Jim Avery • University of Oklahoma.

Jim Avery began an academic career after seventeen years with ad agencies in New York and Chicago. He was Senior Vice-President Management Supervisor on Midas International at Wells Rich Greene/Chicago. Today we would call that position a world-wide account director. He has won both creative and marketing awards.

He has been at University of Oregon, University of Kansas, Penn State, and the University of Alaska/Anchorage. He now holds the Gaylord Chair in strategic communications at the University of Oklahoma. He is a full, tenured professor and head of the strategic communications area in the Gaylord College of Mass Communication.

Avery-coached student advertising teams have taken first and second nationally in the American Advertising Federation's National Student Advertising Competition (AAF/NSAC). A high percentage of the winning teams, both regionally and nationally, have used this book.

Avery served as head of the *Advertising Division of AEJMC*. He continues to be a member of AEJMC, is a member of the *American Academy of Advertising* and the *International Advertising Association*. He is an active marketing and advertising consultant and writes a syndicated newspaper column, *"The Advertising Workshop."*

In 1996, he was appointed to the *National Advertising Review Board (NARB)*, an industry group founded by the *American Advertising Federation, American Association of Advertising Agencies, Association of National Advertisers,* and the *Council of Better Business Bureaus,* where he served for eight years.

The Planning Document
Getting Started

*Faster, faster until the thrill of speed
overcomes the fear of death.*
—Hunter S. Thompson

Introduction.

Start Today.

Herb Leiberman at Grey used to say, "Make it happen."

Now you're ready to start. You have your systems and organization set, and you're anxious to get on with it.

You have a large task ahead. So you need to start today. Now.

If you wait a week because you have other projects or classes to deal with, you'll be a week behind everyone else. Then, you'll have to find a way to make up that time. And there's never enough time.

The Marketing Planning Document.

Simply put, this book is about How To Do It.

On the following pages we will start to track you through the writing of a Marketing Planning Document. (Notice I said we. There isn't anyone here writing this but me, but in marketing and advertising, everything is we. Never assume credit in the singular.)

There are several good textbooks on advertising campaigns. This includes Don Parente's book and an older one by Don Schultz and Beth E. Barnes. Kotler is a good author on marketing as are the Belches. O'Guinn does a great job on below-the-line ...

But even though these books work to educate you on what an advertising campaign is and expand your advertising and marketing vocabulary, none of them explains how to do it. This one does. Ready?

First ...

Get a pencil, put it behind your ear or in your pocket—wherever it's handy. Then, sit down with this book and read at least through Situation Analysis or Research. Be ready to make notes in the margin. Mark the stuff that applies to you. Add thoughts and questions. Come to think of it, you may want some Post-It® notes as well.

Don't worry, you aren't going to sell this book back anyway. It is your book, I don't care what your mother said about defiling books. It's time to adopt the Nike philosophy of market planning ... Just do it.

You will be reading most of this book more than once. Might as well start now. Follow the directions that start on the following page. Plant those seeds.

Planning Points

Things to know before you start ...

Before you begin writing your marketing planning document, there are a number of areas we should cover:

1. **Target Audience:**

   It is important to realize that the single most important information you will ever gather relates to understanding who will buy or use your Brand. This is the essence of Account Planning.

   The more you understand about the people you intend to reach with your advertising message, the better that advertising will be.

   For this reason, marketing should be done with a point of view that places the consumer, or the target group, first and foremost.

   This book was written with that point of view.

   Therefore, this section had to appear first.

2. **Working Procedures:**

   This next planning point will provide direction on how to help your group run more smoothly. It might be a student group or a planning team in business.

   It covers organization of an advertising agency team—so you can create a similar pattern for yourselves.

   It also includes reporting procedures and formats—plus a few housekeeping hints for your agency.

3. **Writing Style:**

   Business writing is quite a bit different from the writing style that may have served you well in your English class or even in Creative Writing courses. Business writing is different.

   This planning point will cover some quick tips that can help move your writing in the right direction. Keep working on it.

4. **Computer Considerations:**
   The computer will be a critical resource for your ad agency team.

   a. Most of your agency documents will be done on some sort of word-processing program—perhaps with your agency logo on the letterhead.

   b. Your Plans Book, a critical document which presents your Marketing Plan, will be prepared using some sort of desktop publishing program, integrating text, graphics, and charts. Graphs and charts are good things because they help communicate a point faster.

   c. Your Presentation will probably be prepared in PowerPoint or some similar program, like Keynote—the one I prefer. Demand a good level of skill with this type of program.

   d. You may use other computer-based resources as well if you produce print ads or videos, prepare a media plan, or develop a direct-mail program.

As you develop your marketing plan, some of you may find yourselves developing new skills on the computer. If you already have these skills, you will find yourself a valuable member of the team as you put those skills to good use.

5. **The Outline:**
   This is the framework for your Marketing Planning Document. Take a bit of time to absorb it.

   Try to keep this overall organizational structure and discipline in mind as you move from chapter to chapter. It will help you maintain focus as you concentrate on the details in each section. You may find it helpful to refer back to it from time to time and use it for a guide as you plan and develop your own campaign.

A Starting Point.

The outline listed in this book should be considered as a starting point. You'll be using a proven framework.

However, remember that, if there's a good reason, you can change anything you want and it will be just fine. For example, you may change the presentation sequence to suit your audience. Just remember, to change anything you'll need to defend your reasons for the alterations. When you're done, you may find yourselves thinking a whole new way—like marketers.

Target Audience of This Book

*If you can't turn yourselves into a consumer, then you
shouldn't be in the advertising business at all.*
—Leo Burnett

Introduction.

In one of the original advertising textbooks, *Advertising Media Planning*, Jack Sissors and Linc Bumba defined Target Audience as *"the desired or intended audience for advertising as described or determined by the advertiser."*

We all need to think in terms of targets. I think there are two major groups of people who will be interested in this book—entrepreneurs and students.

They are the Target Audience of this book.

The reason for telling you the target audience of this book is a little like giving you the objective for the book. Once you know for whom the book is intended, you understand why it was written. And, when it's time to craft your message, you will have a clearer idea of your own audience.

The target audience for your ad campaigns will be the people who buy, use, or influence the buying or using of whatever it is you intend to sell.

A. **Entrepreneurs:**

People who invent businesses and then try to make them grow usually need a little help with their advertising, including marketing. If you are one of these people, there is a strong probability that you do not always trust the people from whom you get advice.

This book will tell you how to write a Marketing Plan by yourself so your bank will give you a loan, or so that you can actually use the information to market what you sell.

If you are a very small entrepreneur, then you will likely do the work yourself, or you will convince your brother-in-law, who has been sponging off you for the past six months, to do some work.

This book will show you how to write a Marketing Plan on a step-by-step basis. However, please note that it will not help you write the entire business plan. This is a key part of that whole plan—some would say *the* key part—but there are often matters that must be addressed, such as your overall budget, not just your marketing budget. However, this book will help you with your overall planning.

From National to Local.

If you are an entrepreneur with a local business idea (at least to start with), you might have to do a little interpretation because this book will mostly be written with a national skew. That is, most examples will be for advertisers who advertise on a national basis.

However, even knowing that, this book will likely be quite a bit clearer than others you may find. Just remember that you will have to translate some of the nationally oriented information to your local or regional marketing area.

If you're a larger entrepreneur, this book will provide you with an understanding of what your marketing and advertising people are doing—or supposed to be doing. If you use an advertising agency, it will give you a chance to see what they do to earn their keep.

There is also some chance that the book may lead you to discover that those who say they are working on your advertising are incompetent fools who need to be fired. On that basis, the price of this book may be the best investment you've ever made.

B. **Students:**
   Three Target Groups.

   There are potentially three different groups of students that may be interested in this book:

   1. Students in an Advertising Campaigns class.
   2. Students competing in the AAF (American Advertising Federation) National Student Advertising Contest or AAF/NSAC.
   3. Students who work at student-run advertising agencies.

In general, all advertising students will find this book useful.

In the main, this book was written for students in an Advertising Campaigns class that has been designed to be a "capstone" class. That means you take the class after you've taken Principles of Advertising, Advertising Copywriting, Advertising Media Planning, Advertising Management, Advertising Research, etc.

For that reason, this book will not attempt to explain every detail of every element in the campaign planning process. This book is intended to explain how to do it once you've learned the theory in another class and how to put the various disciplines together in an orderly and effective way.

It's written with the Advertising Campaigns class in mind, but this is virtually the same as preparing for the AAF/NSAC.

Finally, If you're in a student-run advertising agency, you will most likely be working on smaller, pro-bono clients. They'll often have unique problems and unique limitations. For those reasons, you'll find the book requires you to make an interpretation from time to time. Nonetheless, I still think it will be the most useful guide you will find.

For more information, please also read:

At the end of each chapter will be a list of other books you may read to get more information on the subject.

Here are three that may prove useful in addition to this book:

1. Don E. Schultz and Beth E. Barnes. *Strategic Brand Communication Campaigns*. 5th ed. (McGraw-Hill, 1999).
   This book is quite comprehensive and will be referred to from time to time as a primary resource. Even though this book is over ten years old, the principles still hold. You should try to have at least one copy available for your team.

2. Lisa Fortini-Campbell. *Hitting the Sweet Spot*. (Chicago: The Copy Workshop, 1991).
   Another classic. This book will be particularly useful in areas related to your Target Audience and the Account Planning function. You should own your own copy.

3. Al Ries and Jack Trout. *Positioning: The Battle for Your Mind.* (New York: McGraw-Hill, 1986).

   Another book you should own. It's available as an inexpensive paperback. It's even cheaper used—and well worth it. You should get it and read it—at least the first nine chapters.

Working Procedures

The secret of life is honesty and fair dealing.
If you can fake that, you've got it made.
—Groucho Marx

Introduction.

Welcome to Advertising Campaigns. This will be the most difficult, painful, time-consuming, and frustrating class of your university career.

It will also be the most fun, the most rewarding, and likely the one from which you will learn the most.

As noted, we assume that you have already taken several other classes in advertising and understand the axioms of basic advertising, copywriting, media planning, etc. This book will not seek to educate you in any of those disciplines—after all, you have already survived those classes and conquered the principles of each.

However, it may give you a little different perspective on these disciplines as you see how they all work together.

This book will help you to know what to do when you write a marketing plan or document and give a presentation.

In fact, that is the reason for this book's being.

Housekeeping Issues.

But before we get into how to write a marketing document, there are some housekeeping issues that need to be addressed.

First, we will assume that you are working in a group of four to six people. You will be judged by what you do as a group, and the work should be considered a joint project.

As such, you are all responsible for one another's grade, but more important, you are all responsible for one another's work.

The quality of the final work and the learning what goes with it are much more important than a mere grade.

As you begin, consider these aspects:

A. Agency Organization:

Most traditional advertising agencies are organized into the functions of account management, creative, media, research, and/or account planning. Each has their own resources and computer expertise. If you follow the changes in ad agency organization, you know that most of the large multi-national advertising agencies have unbundled media to form media agencies. Another change—the resulting media agencies now have account managers.

In most circumstances, I recommend that you organize your student group to match that of a typical advertising agency, and add in media. This will increase your translatable learning. I've recorded a quick outline of agency job descriptions here as a reference.

1. Account Manager:

We used to call these people account executives, but to avoid confusion with sales people in real estate, insurance, and brokerage houses who are also called account executives, we have changed the name to account managers.

It's their responsibility to work with their clients outside the agency and manage the account inside the agency. In most cases, they're actually running a small business—such as the Epson business at Grey in Hong Kong, or the Barilla business at Euro RSCG in Chicago, or the Chio Chips business at Scholz & Friends in Budapest.

The account manager should consider himself or herself responsible for the major marketing on the Brand. Their job is identical to that of a brand manager at the client, except the product they produce shows up in the media, not on the retailer's shelf. Let me say that again. The job of account manager at a good advertising agency is virtually identical to the job of brand manager at a good company. You both work to increase sales. In many of the best agency-client relationships, the two work together as a team.

In your student group, the account manager will take control of meetings, issue conference and status reports, and probably be responsible for the marketing objectives and marketing strategy.

The account manager will also have major input into the remainder of the document, including creative strategy, media strategy, sales promotion strategy, etc.

2. **Creative:**

In most advertising agencies, creative people are divided into copywriters, art directors, and producers.

They may have input into the creative platform, blueprint, or brief, but their major responsibility is to create brilliant advertising.

The creative people in your student group have the same charge.

With the growth of Internet-based activities, you might also include areas like interactive and web design. Often, the creatives take the lead in the design and production of the presentation— although it makes more sense to me to have the planner do that.

3. **Media:**

Advertising agency media departments are usually independent entities and are sometimes married with marketing services.

For the purposes of this book, we will assume they are independent, with account management handling the marketing services. These departments estimate costs, plan media, and buy media.

In your student group, the person you choose should have an affinity for numbers. They don't need to understand those Texas Instruments calculators that some professors require in statistics, but they do need to know how to use programs like Excel or Numbers, and you might need a good $3.99 calculator from Walmart. They will have to be able to determine not just what medium to use, but also where and when to advertise. Importantly, they will defend those decisions.

There has been explosive growth in media options, and, while many have audiences that are too small to generate marketing impact, you still need to have your media antennae tuned to new opportunities.

4. **Research:**

The gathering of information is the responsibility of the advertising agency research department and your student group researcher.

As you will see, this function is particularly critical in the development stage of your planning. In fact, it is common for every agency member to become part of the research during development.

5. **Account Planning:**

This somewhat new function has aided advertising agencies to do a much better job of targeting the advertising for their client and understanding that client. The account planner is the consumers' advocate at the agency. His or her major contribution is to identify consumer insight and to write the creative strategy or brief. It is the result of intense interaction with the consumer, as well as other members of the agency team. At your student agency, you will also want to choose an account planner.

6. **Presentations, IT, Computer Skills:**

Call it what you will, your team will need good computer skills to put together a winning presentation. "IT," or Information Technology, is one aspect. Knowing what to do when the hard drive crashes is another.

Within your team, you will have varying degrees of computer skills. This is one more area in which you will be judged as a group, so you should discover your strengths.

Even though it is not a traditional agency job, many teams appoint someone as the Chief Computer Guru. This job may be in addition to one of the jobs discussed previously. For example, your Media Director may also be the resident PowerPoint expert.

B. **Record Keeping:**

The Campaigns class is a very much like a business. The better records you keep, the better the quality of your work will be.

Peter Drucker once said, "What gets measured, gets managed."

There are two kinds of records you need—a library and reports.

But first you need ... The Box.

1. **The Box:**

    The very first thing you need to do when you start this campaign is to get a box. It can be a physical box, in which case it should be wide and tall enough to hold a file folder. It can be a file drawer, a fruit box, or a plastic or cardboard box designed to hold files. Or, it can be a folder on an Internet site. Make certain it has enough capacity to store some large files. And, of course, be sure you have back up in place.

    Appoint a Librarian.

    Write "Library" on the outside of The Box or the Internet file, then appoint someone to be Librarian. Anytime a group member finds an article in *AdWeek* or in a newspaper or anywhere else that has anything to do with the campaign, it should be filed in The Box.

    There are at least three reasons for this:

    a. **The quality of your work will be evaluated by judges.**

        If this is for an Advertising Campaigns class, your client will most likely attend your presentation. There will be time for that client to ask you questions at the end of that presentation. Your professor may have a question or two as well.

        If you are in an AAF/NSAC group, then you will be evaluated by three to five professionals. They will most certainly ask questions after your presentation.

        Finally, this could be for a student advertising agency. In this case, every time you make a presentation to your client, they will ask questions. You need a resource to keep the answers to these questions.

        When they are going to ask questions, have The Box nearby, because it will impress them, and second, because it will aid you to find the answer if you cannot remember.

The latter is not usually reality however, because if you're not bright enough to remember the answer, you're probably not bright enough to remember where you filed the information.

The first reason for The Box is showmanship.

b. **Since there are several of you working on this campaign, each of you will want to keep information in a different place.**

The copywriter will want all the information on how people make purchase decisions at his or her apartment. The media planner will also want to have all the information on rates and costs within easy access.

The Box is the answer.

Everything goes in The Box, and if anyone wants to use it overnight or over the weekend, they can just sign it out. If they lose it, they will lose face with the remainder of the group, because everyone will know that they lost it.

So the second reason for The Box is it's a place to store information and reduce arguments.

And, yes, you can certainly make a copy of documents for your own specific use—but there needs to be a "Box Copy."

c. **The Box will become a symbol that the group is now working—kind of like the legislature is in session:**

The Box makes meetings official. That is the third reason.

Learn to use The Box, because if it does not have everything that needs to be in it, it will not serve its function.

2. **Reports:**

Next, you need to start writing Conference and Status reports. These reports will record your progress.

A copy of these reports should be provided for each member of your group and for your class instructor. This will allow a group member who missed a meeting to know what happened and what they need to do to catch up.

Conference Reports also provide a method to keep your instructor posted on your agency team's progress.

a. **Conference Reports:**

These will provide a review of what happened at each meeting (or conference). You should report who was there, what was discussed, what agreements were reached, and what needs to be accomplished before the next meeting.

Each of these items is important, especially in a student advertising campaign class or in a student group.

Consider the flake who has been assigned to your group—the person who will not do anything that is required, often with a ready excuse. You have already decided that you cannot let him or her have a significant assignment because you know s/he won't do it.

If you include in the Conference Report the fact that this flake didn't even bother to show up, then you know that the instructor also knows—and you didn't need to tattle. Your mother will be proud of you.

All you had to do was write the weekly Conference Report.

The Conference Report will also serve as a record of who, when, why, and what was discussed.

If you need to know when a specific strategy was agreed to, just check the past conference reports.

An example of a student Conference Report can be found on page 21.

b. **Status Report:**

This is a record that allows you to see what has been done and what needs to be finished. It records who is responsible and when it is due. An example of a Status Report is on page 22.

Notice that the left-hand column (project) identifies the category of what needs to be done.

As the semester, or year, progresses this column will contain more and more information.

When you're working on the media segment of the planning document, it is likely that there will be an overall heading for "Media Plan" followed by a subhead of "strategies."

Then there will be a notation that you are working on the seasonality strategy. As you look across the page you will find the status—that it's due next week. Everyone will know.

The Status Report should be distributed to every member of the group—and to the class instructor. Whether it is on paper or sent electronically is up to you. I would expect a status report to have a cover memo outlining the most pressing issues for the next week.

This report will also allow you to identify the person who chooses to skate by with as little work as possible because you will simply not change the due date when someone doesn't complete a project on time.

This will help the instructor notice that this person did not hand in the research interviews when everyone else had completed their work ten days earlier.

C. **Financial Considerations:**

A good presentation will require a financial investment. The development of your campaign, including the planning document and the presentation, will cost a bit of money. But the money will not be needed until the end of the term when everything starts to come together.

You might want to check with someone who took the class at your school last term, but as of the writing of this book, the average group spends about $500 to complete the class.

Many programs have established policies—ranging from class fees and client contributions to fairly aggressive fund-raising programs. Much of this cost is for photocopying. You will need to make copies of weekly reports, status reports, conference reports, and you will need to duplicate your research questionnaires.

The cost of your presentation can be expensive due to all the trinkets and trash you will develop and present—T-shirts, an embroidered hot pad holder, an etched cookie jar, whatever. The slides are no cost, but duplicating them in a color leave-behind can be expensive. A CD will usually be sufficient. If you choose to show creative mounted on foam core, it can take a few bucks. If you need software, it is usually not cheap.

Appoint a Treasurer.

If you are like most groups, $500 does not just appear out of thin air. I recommend that you tax yourselves each week or month.

Appoint a Treasurer and make him or her responsible for collections. Meanwhile, make projections and find ways to earn money.

If you're an AAF group getting ready to compete in the regional contest, you might want to raise some money by getting donations. These donations may require you to provide some work in exchange for funding. Travel costs vary, but unless the contest is in your home town, meals and hotel should be in your budget.

If you're an AAF Finalist and go to the nationals, congratulations. Now you will also have more money to raise. You can double the costs above and add money for more travel, hotel, and meals.

Use Your Skills to Make Money.

Some programs have ongoing ways to make money. Ball State students assist with parking at Indianapolis Colts games. And, of course, there's the bake sale.

Another way to raise money for your team is to earn the money using your advertising knowledge. Here are a few ways:

Campus Coupon Book.

Students at the University of Alaska created a coupon book to be distributed to students. Group members then sold coupons in the book to retail establishments. By the way, the student newspaper was not happy.

Radio Station Raffle.

Another group of students asked radio stations for contributions of time. They traded the time to an auto dealer for a car, then they raffled the car.

Sell Advertising Textbooks.

The company that publishes this book (The Copy Workshop) allows their advertising textbooks to be sold through your student ad club. The ad club then keeps the 20% that normally goes to the campus bookstore. Other companies may have similar offers.

These are just three ideas. You may have more. In fact, you should. Use what you have learned about advertising, marketing, and sales promotion. It beats going to Costco, getting some muffins, and sitting at a card table all morning.

Spend some time thinking about ways to make money to pay for your advertising campaign. In some ways, it's similar to the thinking you'll need to develop a winning campaign.

D. Responsibilities:

Be specific. Every member of the group will have a specific area of responsibility.

This should be assigned by the group.

It is likely that your class instructor asked you to be in a specific group because your skills complement the skills of others in the group.

That's all well and good. But, remember…

Desire Is Good. Capability Is Better.

You probably have someone who wants to work in media, someone who wants to be a copywriter, someone who wants to be a planner, and someone who wants to be an account manager. That is good, and a great way to start.

But you need to remember that just because someone *wants* to be a copywriter doesn't make them a copywriter. Desire is good, but capability is better. Being able to write copy makes someone a copywriter.

Sometimes you'll have someone who wants to write copy and you'll want them to write for another group because if they work for someone else you will have a better chance of winning.

Welcome to the real world. You will always find people who are incompetent. Often, for reasons that are hard to understand, they are working in good jobs. Sometimes you'll be able to get rid of them, but sometimes you'll just have to put up with them.

If you have one of these people in your group, find a way that they can feel responsible and contribute without destroying your work.

The best way to deal with these people, however, is to not have them in your group to begin with.

Good Advice for Bad Students.

If you are a person who doesn't want to work, or if you aren't very capable, your goal in the first week of class should be to find a very good group, and then find a way to weasel your way into it.

After all, if you get in the group and do enough to get by, you can have a pretty easy semester—if everyone else in your group is working.

Now, this wouldn't work if I were the class instructor—for two reasons. First, I pick the groups—so there is no way for you to do your weaseling. Second, I allow groups to fire people.

It gets better. If you get fired by your group, you have to do the entire project on your own, find another group to hire you, or drop the class. (Hint: there's a zero percent probability that if one group fires you another group will offer you a job.) But on a more positive note, if you are someone who gets it done, you will not have to worry about this.

Good Advice for Good Groups.

In general, you should not actually assign individual responsibilities until you are almost finished with the Situation Analysis.

This gives all of you a little time to work out how you will work with one another and to establish a kind of working relationship. You need to discover who will work, who is reliable, and who will become the object of your collective hostility.

Finally, make people accountable for specific tasks. Put someone in charge of every section and every element of the project. You may decide that everyone is going to work on the Situation Analysis and as a result, you really don't need someone to be in charge. Wrong.

When everyone is responsible, no one is responsible.

So put someone in charge and let them do it. Yes, you can assign certain sections to individuals, but be careful that you don't organize it so that person B can't do their job until person A finishes their job. Hold their feet to the fire if they don't, and congratulate them when they do a good job.

Hint: If you're an American Advertising Federation group, don't select your presenters until the very last possible moment. Once you decide on those five people, just about everyone else will quit working.

Blue Group Conference Report

Present for agency:	Anderson, Sue
	Chiu, Sally
	Smith, Bill
	Taylor, Jennifer
	Wilsinski, Fred
Present for client:	No one
Meeting place:	Room K-136
Date of meeting:	January 27, 2010
Date of report:	January 28, 2010
Written by:	Bill Smith

The purpose of this meeting was to establish the ground rules to be followed by the Blue group in the *Advertising Campaigns* class.

Discussion:

Sally Chiu outlined what she judged to be the major goal for the semester. Fred Wilsinski embellished those ideas by stressing the importance that everything be creative.

The remainder of the discussion centered on finances.

Agreements:

It was agreed that the group would find examples of creative advertising and bring them to each group meeting. It was further agreed that the group would seek a disciplined approach to the new campaign. The group resisted the temptation to make initial assignments.

It was also agreed that the Agency may write a recommendation to change any aspect of *Advertising Campaigns.*

Agency further agreed to participate in each class period.

Action:
1. Bill Smith agreed to buy an online subscription to *AdWeek,* no later than January 29.
2. Jennifer Taylor and Fred Wilsinski agreed to share the cost of the *CA Advertising Annual.* They will bring it to the next meeting.
3. Everyone agreed to meet Saturday morning at Sue Anderson's apartment at ten o'clock.

Example: Status Report

Project Status Report
Advertising Campaigns Class

Project	Status	Next Steps	Due Date	Who
Groups	In process	1. Prepare memorandum designating one team member responsible for group assignments	9/01	Student
		2. Make group assignments	9/09	Instructor
AdWeek	Subscribe to	Be prepared to discuss in detail in class	9/02	Student
Conference Report	In process	One due each week from each group	9/16	Group
Case Book	In process	1. Write and publish	TBD	Instructor
		2. Study and prepare for quiz	TBD	Student
Research	In process	Prepare questions for client meeting	TBD	Student
Presentation	In process	1. Review procedure with photo lab	TBD	Student
		2. Rehearsal for final presentation	TBD	Group
		3. Final presentation	TBD	Group

WS
8/31/10

Writing Style

Advertising is a craft executed by people who aspire to be artists,
but [is] assessed by people who aspire to be scientists.
I cannot imagine any human relationship more perfectly
designed to produce total mayhem.
—John Ward

Introduction.

Rules Happen.

That said, you should understand that writing style is dictated more by corporate philosophy than by what is right and what is wrong.

For example, the Associated Press maintains an entire book so the writers who work for A.P. will know what style to use.

As time goes on, the rules become more and more numerous. And they may well differ depending on who you're writing to—your target audience. In this case, your target audience will have a business/marketing mindset, not an academic or literary perspective. So the writing style that might have earned you an "A" in literature or creative writing might not be the style you'll want to use in this discipline.

Personally, I think A.P.'s book is too much in its entirety, but here are a few things to keep in mind when you write.

Fifteen Good Guidelines.

Here is a short list of rules that students should follow:

1. **Use the shortest possible set of words.**
   Flowery adjectives and adverbs are out of place in business writing. Use the shortest possible set of words to communicate your point.

2. **Use the shortest word when you have a choice.**
   Use "use" instead of "utilize" whenever you can. How often do you utilize the bathroom? Always use the shortest word when you have a choice.

3. **Always spell words correctly.**
   Use spell check and use your dictionary. Proofread your work for incorrectly used words that are spelled correctly. Both "manager" and

"manger" are words. I would guess that your project would not be using an account manger—except perhaps in the Christmas display.

By the way, if you are in my class, you will be fired if you misspell the brand name or the name of your client.

4. **Use good grammar.**
Remember: if you make mistakes in spelling or grammar, the reader will assume that you are uneducated and that there will be no reason to believe or respect your point of view.

The only other interpretation the reader may assume is that you do not care enough about this communication to check it.

5. **Tell the most important thing first.**
Get to the point. Put it up front. Don't make the reader wade through a lot of minutiae to find the good stuff.

6. **Use topic sentences.**
Always make the first sentence of a paragraph the topic sentence. In English Composition class you may have learned that you should vary the topic sentence to add interest to your writing. This thinking does not apply in business writing.

7. **Never start a paragraph with a dependent clause.**
If you put a dependent clause at the start (like this), then your reader has to wait to get to your point or desired action. The reader will get your point faster if you put that phrase later in the paragraph.

8. **Do not start sentences with prepositional phrases.**
Again, the reader will get your point faster. However, this is a harder rule to follow.

In less formal writing (such as this paragraph), prepositional phrases at the beginning of a sentence seem to make the sentence friendlier. Still, in business writing, and especially in formal planning documents, do not start sentences with prepositions.

9. **"The purpose is…"**
When you start a memorandum or letter, you should clearly communicate your purpose in the first sentence. It is common to write *"The purpose for this letter is…."* I quite often have students start all written communication with the word *"this"*:

"This provides...,"
"This responds to your request for...,"
"This requests...," or
"This recommends...,"

are all examples of this usage.

"This" forces you to write the purpose in the first sentence.

When you are about to graduate, you will write letters to potential employers. Keep this writing style in mind.

It will communicate to your potential new employer that you are familiar with how business people communicate. If you want to communicate that you're creative, clever, or speak seven languages, that's good. But don't waste people's time with your writing. Get to it.

10. Never end a sentence with a preposition.

Winston Churchill once wrote to his staff, *"This is something up with which I shall not put."* There is no preposition at the end of that sentence. Churchill knew how to be smart, a bit humorous, and make his point.

11. Use the tabs and indent settings on your typewriter or computer.

a. Make decimals line up under one another.

Most computers have a decimal tab. Learn to use it.

b. Make numbers or bullet points stand out.

Look at this section. The "U" in "Use" lines up over the "a." The "Ms" in "Make" and "Most" line up.

Using tabs makes it easier for the reader to see when there is another point to be communicated. It helps keep the reader organized. It helps keep you organized.

12. Never start a sentence with an Arabic number.

Write it out. Twelve is the number of this point.

13. Be specific.

If you want the reader to believe what you are writing, do not simply write *"Research indicates that ..."*

This kind of statement often creates more questions than it answers. What research? When was it conducted? Under what circumstances?

"MRI data for 2010 indicates that…" is better. "A small sample set of on-campus interviews…" is, perhaps, not as strong—but it doesn't make it seem like you're faking it, either.

14. Write as short as you can to communicate the point.
We all have more to read than we have time to read. Give us a break.

15. Avoid superlatives.
In business documents, overstatement and "hype" are viewed with suspicion. What may be appropriate for the advertising or sales promotion may not be appropriate for the advertising and marketing plan.

Three More Tips from The Copy Workshop.

The Copy Workshop Workbook deals with contemporary copywriting style in advertising, which is not the same as the proper style for business documents.

However, they suggest three more tips that can improve your business writing.

1. Write in the active voice.
Every sentence with a passive verb should be examined critically. Wait, that's in the passive voice. How about, "Examine every sentence with a passive verb." Better yet, "Try to get rid of every sentence with a passive verb."

2. Parallel construction can help build clarity.
Parallel construction organizes your communication.

Parallel construction makes facts easier to follow.

Parallel construction builds stronger arguments.

You are often communicating a series of complex thoughts. Try to organize your language as well as your thinking.

3. Don't overdo the marketing jargon.
You're about to dive into a world of powerful concepts—strategy, tactics, interactivity, consumer insight.

Sometimes the words themselves can feel like they have almost mystical power.

"This consumer insight will motivate a paradigm shift in the target audience purchase behavior." A little over the top, don't you think?

If the marketing concepts you'll be developing are strong and smart, you'll be able to make the point without using every marketing catchphrase. As we said, don't overdo it.

Writing as a Group.

There is a good business writing style. You should stick to it. But you can all make minor decisions within your group as you work to develop a consistent style and tone of voice for your team.

The finished document should look as if one person wrote it.

Most important, it should look as if your entire future career depends on how good your document looks. After all, it does.

Good Writing and Good Design.

Good writing *looks* good.

You have great control over the look of your writing with computer-based word processing and desktop publishing programs.

Unfortunately, these programs won't usually tell you the difference between good typography and bad typography, they merely do what you tell them to do.

So, it seems worth mentioning that either you should know what you're doing or you should copy someone who knows what they're doing. This is not as strange as it sounds. If you find some graphic formats that really work—that are easy to read and have an appealing design—while you should certainly try to do better, don't feel like you've failed if you follow a format developed by a top professional.

Here's what the legendary art director Helmut Krone had to say, *"I'd like to propose a new idea for our age: Until you've got a better answer, you copy. I copied Bob Gage for five years. I even copied the leading between his lines of type. And Bob originally copied Paul Rand, and Rand first copied a German typographer named Tschichold."*

These are some of the finest art directors and designers in the history of advertising. They followed formats developed by others. So don't feel you have to invent a whole new graphic format. You've got enough to deal with. Or should that be you've got enough with which to deal.

One more book to consider.

You might want to pick up a copy of *What Do You Mean I Can't Write? A Practical Guide to Business Writing for Agency Account Managers* by Norm MacMaster. This little book was a well-thumbed stack of pages passed around on the bottom run of top agencies. It's exactly what it says it is—with sixty-some easy-to-read pages that will help you improve your business-writing style even further.

You can get a copy through Amazon.

Somebody took my copy.

Computer Considerations

The adage that 20% of the people do 80% of the work is totally bogus.
Ten percent of the people do 90% of the work!
—Jay Chiat

Introduction.

A. Hardware and Compatibility:

In many ways, we're only as good as our tools—mental and physical. For your ad agency team, this means your computers.

You should make an assessment of who has what.

You should know what is available at your university's computer lab.

You should have compatible programs and either be able to store information in a file online or send the files to each other as e-mail attachments. Ask if there is storage space available at the University website.

The Need for Backup.

There is an unconfirmed rumor that your computer knows when the deadline is approaching. This rumor gets confirmed every semester—right around deadline time.

This, of course, can drive up the cost of printing your planning document. Your nearest copy shop probably charges more for a rush order.

Back up on a regular basis and have a backup plan in place for when (not if) some key piece of equipment decides to test your stress tolerance.

B. Software and Ability:

As we've mentioned, desire doesn't make a good copywriter, ability makes a good copywriter. The same goes for computer skills.

What can take one person the better part of an evening can be done by another in less than half an hour. Who do you want?

Put your ego on hold and evaluate who is best at doing what. If you find that you have some weaknesses—maybe more than one—figure out what you have to learn and who has to learn it. Or, figure out who you have to recruit.

Commonly Used Software.

These are some of the programs and their uses:

Word Processing and e-mail Software:

Every member of your team should be proficient. This is how you and your team will communicate. Almost everyone uses Word. However, I should confess, this was written in Pages, a program I prefer.

Desktop Publishing and Graphic Software:

You will need to use this software for your Plans Book and for preparation of print materials. Once, Quark was the favorite, but now most use InDesign. The key is that a few in your group are confident on one or the other. Everyone will have to know how to scan and use an image manipulation program. Someone should master Photoshop and maybe Freehand or Illustrator.

You will need a good selection of fonts and access to printing in black and white and color. You may find that some pieces need to be printed in larger sizes.

Spreadsheet and Database Software:

Your Media Director will need to be able to use this type of software for preparing your media plan and budgets. I seem to get along with Numbers, but Excel is more widely used. You may also need to access some specialized media planning software.

Some of the information you will need will be available over the web, so good searching capabilities on the Internet will also be useful, and everyone in the group should be capable of that.

Presentation Software and Hardware:

PowerPoint used to reign supreme. I am no longer convinced. I prefer Keynote, but that research is from a sample of one.

Whichever you choose, learn to use them well. More and more presentations are using Flash animation and showing websites with dancing hamsters and interactive social media applications.

Projection capabilities are also critical with this type of software, and you should find out as early as possible what equipment you will be able to use for your presentation.

And More...

Your plan may call for a website. You may create an audio logo. You may produce and edit a TV commercial. Did we mention buttons, hats, and, of course, T-shirts?

Each of these tasks has their own specialized software and, sometimes, specialized suppliers. As you identify your needs, try to identify who, what, and how you will meet them.

There's only one type of software to avoid—games. You've got a lot to do, try to keep those far, far away from your computer.

The Outline

It is up to us to decide what to do with the time that is given us.
— Gandalf

Introduction.

This section will provide an outline for your planning document.

It is reasonable to assume that if you know what you are going to write and know where it is going, it will be easier for you to write it.

Many good outlines exist. The outline found here is only one example. But it is also the outline for this book. Step by step, it takes you through the development of a marketing planning document.

The First Part.

The first part has three sections.

Section I (Situation Analysis) and Section II (Research) contain a review of what you have learned. This material will help give you the expertise to write the marketing document.

Section III (Problems and Opportunities) summarizes what you have learned that may be actionable in the coming year. Some prefer a S.W.O.T. format. This stands for Strengths, Weaknesses, Opportunities, and Threats. We will also address this format briefly in Chapter 3, Problems and Opportunities.

The Second Part.

The second part sets the constraints for your Marketing Plan— Section IV (Marketing Objective) and Section V (Budget).

The Plan.

The remainder, starting with Section VI (Marketing Strategy), is the plan itself. The marketing strategy should be considered a summary of the plan.

The major segments of the plan are Section VII (Creative), Section VIII (Media), Section IX (Below-the-line), Section X (Evaluation), and Section XI (Testing).

The Outline begins below. Follow it in preparing your Marketing Plan, your ad campaign, and other MarCom activities. The more detail you provide, the better the information.

If you can add a new segment or two, you will add dimension to the plan.

You will notice that this outline follows the structure of the book. It is very similar to the Table of Contents, though not identical.

As you begin to develop your presentation, you will find that this outline is a useful structure for your presentation as well—though you will naturally need to condense and dramatize as necessary. You may need to know every detail of the situation analysis, but your audience won't. These days, the final presentation will not include all of this information—though it will be available. We will continue the discussion of the presentation later.

Marketing Planning Document Outline:

- I. Situation Analysis
  - A. Current Users
  - B. Geographical Emphasis
  - C. Seasonality
  - D. Purchase Cycle
  - E. Creative Requirements
  - F. Competitive Sales
  - G. Competitive Media

- II. Research
  - A. Objectives
  - B. Strategies
  - C. Method
  - D. Summary of Findings

- III. Problems & Opportunities

- IV. Marketing Objective
  - A. Number
  - B. Rationale

- V. Budget

- VI. Marketing Strategy
  - A. Promotion
    1. Advertising

         a.   Creative
         b.   Media
         c.   Production
     2.   Sales Promotion
         a. Consumer
         b. Trade
     3.   Public Relations
         a. Publics
         b. Tactics
     4.   Direct Marketing
         a. Direct Response Media
         b. Telemarketing
     5.   Event Marketing
         a. Consumer Events
         b. Trade Events
     6.   Miscellaneous
         a. Personal Selling
         b. Packaging
         c. Merchandising
         d. Promotional Products
  B. Product
  C. Pricing
  D. Distribution (Place)
  E. People
  F. Rationale

VII.   Advertising Creative
  A. Target Audience
  B. Objective
  C. Strategy
  D. Support
  E. Consideration
  F. Tone
  G. Rationale
  H. Tactics

VIII. Advertising Media
  A. Objectives

  1. Target Audience
  2. Geography
  3. Seasonality
  4. Continuity, Flighting
  5. Creative Constraints
  6. Reach versus Frequency
 B. Strategies
  1. Media Mix and Types
  2. Media Format or Classes
  3. Geographic Use of Media
  4. Seasonal Use of Media
  5. Flighting versus Continuity
 C. Rationale
  1. Support of Strategy
  2. Support of Delivery and Efficiency
 D. Tactics

IX. Below-the-line
 A. Consumer Promotion
  1. Current Situation
  2. Objectives
  3. Strategies
  4. Rationale
  5. Tactics (Events)
  6. Payout
 B. Trade Promotion
  1. Current Situation
  2. Objectives
  3. Strategies
  4. Rationale
  5. Tactics (Events)
  6. Payout
 C. Public Relations
  1. Current Situation
  2. Objectives
  3. Publics
  4. Strategies

        5. Rationale

    D. Direct Marketing
        1. Current Situation
        2. Objectives
        3. Target Audience
        4. Strategies
        5. Rationale

    E. Event Marketing
        1. Current Situation
        2. Objectives
        3. Target Audience
        4. Strategies
        5. Rationale

    F. Miscellaneous

X.   Evaluation (Research)
    A. Current Situation
    B. Objective
    C. Strategy
    D. Tactics (Method)

XI.   Testing
    A. Objective
    B. Strategies
    C. Tactics (Method)
    D. Rationale
    E. Evaluation

Additional Sections.

It may be appropriate to add a section. For example, in Section VI, Marketing, you may wish to emphasize or delete as needed. A secondary target audience might motivate its own special section.

Example: Hispanic Section.

The US Census Bureau estimates the Hispanic population of the US is approaching fifty million people. That is about seventeen percent of the entire population, the largest and fastest growing ethnic/race minority. It will be an unusual national marketing or advertising plan that does not address this significant market. If your Brand is Kellogg's Corn Flakes, it's likely that you will have a Hispanic Section.

The Hispanic Section would have creative, media, and promotion within the one section.

It would also be acceptable to put a Hispanic Section in the creative section, in the media section, and in the promotion section or, as suggested, have these as part of the Hispanic section.

There could be any number of other sections added to this outline, or you may choose to eliminate one of these sections.

Customize the Plan to Fit Your Brand.

This outline is intended to provide a view of the general marketing planning document. It is expected that each plan will be customized to fit that individual Brand.

Do not, however, construe this to give you permission to eliminate information—that could make this marketing planning document for your advertising campaign less valuable.

It is now your outline and your plan. Organize it in a way that makes sense to you and your team, and in a way that will make sense to the decision-makers who will see it—one more important target audience.

Situation Analysis

When I have new information, I change my conclusions. What do you do, Sir?
—John Maynard Keynes, when accused of inconsistency

Introduction.

The First Step—Know Where You Are.

The first step in advertising planning is to determine what you know. Jon Steel talks about triangulation in his book, *Truth, Lies and Advertising*. It is a term from geography. If you are lost, and can mark two spots on a map, you can triangulate where you are. The same is true of advertising and the encompassing marketing. If you can discover relevant facts, you can improve your ability to understand where you are—your current situation.

Advertisers and students alike are often surprised to learn either how little they know at the beginning or how much knowledge they already have. You need to know where you are before you can determine where you'll need to take the business.

When all this information is assembled in one location, it's called a Situation Analysis. Simply put, it's about understanding where you are. Though, unlike a specific location on a map, your situation may be a bit more complex. All the more reason why you need a Situation Analysis.

If the Brand is a new one, then there may be little or no information available concerning the history of the Brand or even the category.

This doesn't make the Situation Analysis impossible, just challenging. You still have to triangulate—find some reference points. For example, you may have to rely on organizations such as trade associations or the government for the information you seek.

You may have to work to manage a massive amount of information and condense it into a few useful insights. Or you may have to search far and wide to accumulate even a minimal amount of necessary information.

Either way, you'll have a better document, and you'll know what the challenges are ahead, if you get the information outlined here. Along the way, you may become an expert in the use of the library, Google, and Yahoo. Sleuthing is good. Sometimes it's like pigs and truffles—you just have to dig around and see what comes up. But, as David Ogilvy said, "It helps to know that they are found in oak forests."

If you're a professional advertising agency pitching a new client, sometimes that client doesn't choose to share everything with you.

In this case, you'll win points—big time—if you are able to find information that isn't readily available. The best possible situation is if you're able to give that client (or even a current client) some piece of information they didn't already know. Then again, just giving yourself an ample supply of information is certainly a good beginning.

"Background Review."

Writing all of this information down in one place results in a document that is sometimes called a Background Review. This is another name for a Situation Analysis. As you move through the business world, you will often find that different organizations may have different terms for what are, essentially, the same basic documents or procedures. But, whatever you call it, the key point is this: as your document expands to fill the formal outline, we undoubtedly learn something that we did not know.

The information for this Background Review, or Situation Analysis, will continue to be more and more important as time goes on.

These additional bits of information will help get us moving. But, whatever we call this document, it's purpose is to discover what we know—so that we can also discover what it is that we don't know and need to know to make the best informed decision. It's necessary to formalize what we do know so we can ask the appropriate questions in the next section (Research) where we will get answers to the questions we currently do not know.

Seven Segments.

The purpose of the Situation (never situational) Analysis is to provide a complete outline of everything currently known that will contribute to the marketing of the Brand. It commonly has seven segments.

First Four Segments.

The first four segments deal with the people who use the product or, in the case of a new product, the people we expect to use it.

These first four segments are:

- **Current Users**
- **Geography**
- **Seasonality**
- **Purchase Cycle**

As we examine Current Users, where they live (Geography), when they buy (Seasonality) and how often (Purchase Cycle), we should remember that the world has changed. It has become more and more difficult to motivate a mass audience to do something. Stuart Smith, director of account planning for Wieden & Kennedy in London no longer defines an audience using solely demographics. It may be that the era of defining the target group for a brand of yogurt as women 18 to 54 is gone.

Some of you reading this book are in a school or college of mass communication. It would not be difficult to argue that the name should be changed to be something more narrow ... the school of targeted communication, for example. The discipline of Integrated Marketing Communications (IMC) endorses a program of reaching fewer and fewer people in a group. This narrowing of the target audience requires discipline in identifying specific groups of users.

Last Three Segments.
The last three segments of the background review give some detailed pieces of information about the history of the marketing of the Brand and of the category.

The last three segments are:

- **Creative Requirements**
- **Competitive Sales**
- **Competitive Media**

These seven segments make up the Situation Analysis and should address the current situation and any issues surrounding a given piece of information. However, it is perfectly acceptable to add another segment if you judge it to be important.

Example: Dannon Yogurt.
For example, in the first paragraph of the analysis labeled "Current

Users," if the Brand is Dannon Yogurt, we will identify 25 to 54 year-old adults. We choose this age as the primary for Dannon because 62.9 percent of women 25 to 54 have used yogurt in the past six months. (See Note A, page 66.)

Only identify what is happening with the Brand at this point in time, never identify future opportunities in the writing of the Current User analysis. Even if we may be giving consideration to a campaign designed to address women 50+ who are concerned about osteoporosis. Do not reveal future strategy in the situation analysis.

Save Your New Ideas.

Take care not to reveal a new campaign idea or the key elements of the plan in this section. Only point out those issues that have been raised prior to the writing of the plan.

The new ideas should be saved for the strategy segments of your marketing plan, or they might be generated in the Problems and Opportunities section. (Some people call this the SWOT Analysis—Strengths, Weaknesses, Opportunities, and Threats. It differs in that Problems are turned into two categories—Weaknesses and Threats—and Opportunities are listed as Strengths and Opportunities.)

The New Idea File.

Most marketing plan authors have a file, or a special yellow pad, or a folder on the hard drive, dedicated to new ideas.

Keep all your new ideas in the file or on the pad.

In the very beginning, it is likely that you have not had sufficient time or space to develop the right attitude or the right credibility with the client to sell these new concepts. Wait until you know a little more. This will likely be in the segment dedicated to the subject for your recommendation, or for the presentation.

Convincing "The Keeper of the Money."

Remember, a key reader of your Marketing Plan is usually a bean counter… the keeper of the money. In a packaged goods company this person will probably be a division president or a CMO (Chief Marketing Officer). They are experienced. They are hard-nosed. They've seen a lot of presentations.

They are unlikely to approve the plan until they have been convinced that it will work.

Creating a Logical Flow of Information.
The discipline of revealing what we knew in the past (Situation Analysis) and what we learned this year (Research) creates a logical flow of information. Once that is established, we reveal what we intend to do (Marketing Objectives) and how we intend to do it (Marketing Strategies) Some people call it a logic track. (Check the notes in Chapter Seven for more information.)

If the author of the marketing planning document starts to tell what is intended for the coming year in the Situation Analysis, then the natural order of the plan is destroyed; therefore, there is no opportunity to build the proper environment to sell the plan. I hope I have made my point—save your new ideas for later.

"The Brand."
For multi-brand marketers, their advertising is most often for a given brand. For example, General Mills advertising is most often seen for Wheaties, Bisquick, or Betty Crocker Cake Mix.

In some cases, there may be more than one product in a Brand—such as Aunt Jemima Pancake Mix and Aunt Jemima Pancake Syrup, the five sauces in the Ortega Sauce line, or the various types of Tide in the detergent section.

It is even more rare to see advertising that features the manufacturer, like General Mills, and if there ever is this type of advertising, generally it will be found in the *Wall Street Journal,* not in the media directed to the end consumer. This has been true for years—so we were a bit surprised to see a corporate campaign for Procter & Gamble in the Olympics. However, in general, the rule still holds. The purpose of the advertising is to sell product. Therefore...

Your Marketing Plan, including the Situation Analysis, will be on behalf of a brand, not the corporation that owns the brand.

Once the brand has been clearly established, it is common to refer to Bisquick, Wheaties, or Betty Crocker Pie Crust as the Brand, in the marketing document or plan.

A style point. When we are discussing brand work in general it is lowercase, but when we use Brand as a substitute for Bisquick, it is capitalized.

(This same general rule is followed for other topics. The situation analysis, in general, is not capitalized. Your Situation Analysis and your Marketing Plan are capitalized.)

We will also use the terms brand manager and product manager interchangeably, because some companies call them brand managers (Procter & Gamble, for example) while others call them product managers (General Mills or Kraft General Foods are two). As we said, it's common for essentially the same thing to have differing names within different business organizations.

Other Businesses.

In most cases, services and retail businesses can be treated the same way as products. Banks have product managers in charge of credit cards, checking, and loans—even though these are really more services than they are tangible products.

Major department stores have buyers in charge of a department in the same way a brand manager is responsible for marketing a brand.

In general, you will find the procedures for developing your Situation Analysis to be very similar whether you are working on the marketing of Dannon Yogurt, men's shoes at Bloomingdales, or checking accounts for CitiBank. Though, as we said, sometimes the names have changed.

A more detailed, step-by-step, how-to-do-it guide follows.

A. Current Users:

Understanding Who Buys the Product.

This portion of the situation analysis has historically been called the target audience section, but it is really a review of the current users. Understanding who buys the product is key to successful marketing.

If we can thoroughly understand who the current users are, then it's likely we can find new users who are similar to our current users.

This group could end up being our target audience, but we are not yet ready to make that decision. We will save that decision for the Marketing Strategy segment of your planning document.

In most cases, it is safe to assume that users are knowledgeable about the product. They know its good points and its weaknesses.

Knowledge about competing brands will aid this section as well.

Midas Muffler Shops' greatest competitor is probably CarX even though CarX is located in only a small portion of the United States. Both Midas and CarX sell replacement mufflers engineered to fit each car precisely, while Sears and Meineke sell less expensive mufflers that are universal, i.e., one muffler will fit several different car makes and models.

It is probably easier for Midas to compete with CarX, where the customers are similar, than it is for Midas to convert Meineke users— where the primary reason for purchase motivation is price. In this case, learning about the CarX user will aid the Midas marketing plan more than learning about the Meineke user.

Demographics and Psychographics.
The two key points to review about the current users are the demographics and the psychographics of the users.

1. Demographics:
There are two primary methods for verifying the demographics of the current users of the Brand and the category.

The first method is secondary research and the second method is primary research.

This may seem backward, to do secondary first and primary second, but it has to do with the root of the definitions.

Secondary research is information that has been gathered by someone else and published. You will first want to search these sources to discover what knowledge already exists—in order to avoid repeating someone else's work. You are the second user of the information.

In some cases, you may need to do primary research, which is research that you conduct and pay for yourself to answer specific questions. You are going directly to the user, or your target audience—you are asking the questions. You are the primary user of the information. Obviously, this is more expensive and time-consuming. So we first want to do a thorough job on our secondary research.

a. Secondary Research:

MRI, now GfkMRI, and Simmons Market Research Bureau (SMRB) are good sources of secondary information concerning the demographics of the users of specific Brands and their respective categories. If neither of these companies audit the category in which your brand competes, then you may have to rely on primary research.

Though there are other sources. For example, Technomics does similar work in the restaurant category.

Be sure to investigate both sources because while MRI and SMRB audit many of the same categories, there are some that each audit unto themselves. As noted, there are other sources of demographic information, but these two are the best places to start. See Note A at the end of this chapter for more detail.

b. Primary Research:

The second method of determining or verifying information, such as the current user profile, is primary research.

When you gain information for your marketing plan by asking direct questions to current and potential users of the Brand or category, you're doing primary research.

This primary research can be used to determine usage patterns for those members of the target group who have acknowledged using the Brand.

For example, if you wanted to know more about the demographics of your user base, ask demographic questions of your respondents. Then correlate this information to the usage questions. You will start to get a grasp of the demographics of that user group.

Remember, however, that you will probably only interview a few hundred people in your primary research.

The information contained in MRI or SMRB has many times that in its sample. So if MRI tells you the demographic profile of the current user is Men 25 to 34 and your survey says it's Women, you better work very hard to convince me. Because to start with, I don't believe you.

Factors that Motivate Purchase Behavior.

It is also likely that primary research can be used to determine the factors that motivate purchase behavior in your category (what people use to make up their minds about which brand they will buy). This is a key consideration.

When this characteristic or set of characteristics has been identified, pay close attention. It can be the vehicle for identifying the demographic and psychographic characteristics of the current users. It can even be used to determine what the user group perceives to be unique about the Brand.

This will be discussed further in Chapter Two.

2. Psychographics:

The second key point to review in the Current Users section is the psychographics of those key users.

There are a variety of companies that group consumers in typologies. VALS II, put out by SRI, uses eight typologies to classify Americans.

Prism, Kube, and LUVS are other systems that will provide equally useful information. Psychographics will provide insightful information about the way your users and audience think.

This will allow you to write better, more targeted, harder hitting, and, ultimately, more effective advertising.

The marketing director for a performing arts center once explained the value of psychographics to me with the following statement: *"If you tell me that my target audience is made of females between the ages of 25 and 54, earning over fifty thousand dollars a year, with at least a college education, I do not know as much about her as if you tell me she is more likely to be a vegetarian."*

He convinced me that psychographics is important to understanding to whom you are writing the advertising. Obviously, psychology can be quite complex. However, for our purposes, the most important elements of psychographics will be usage and behavior.

B. Geographical Emphasis:

Find Out Where Current Users Live.

The purpose for this geography section of the Situation Analysis is to provide information on where the current users live.

If, for example, we know that more mufflers are purchased in the area around the Great Lakes than are purchased in the Southwest, then we know something more about our customers—such as the fact they drive in areas where the states use salt on the roads in winter.

If we know the geographic skew to our Brand sales, then we not only know where our customers live, but we also start to accumulate useful related information about this important group of people.

For example, if you learn that the users skew to metro or urban areas, you are beginning to understand something more about the people who buy and consume your product.

Past sales by district, region, state, DMA (Nielson's Designated Marketing Area) will give you a good start on where past users live.

This geographical information will not only generate information for the geographic section of the situation analysis, when you are making media decisions, it will also begin to provide the basis for the allocation of media dollars (to be discussed in Chapter Eight). Finally, it will provide additional insight into the Current User segment of the document.

Brand Development Index (BDI).
Brand Development Index (BDI) is the next step. It is a very useful measure of sales per person. BDI will give you a quantitative measure of the Brand's history of relative success for each marketing area. It will tell you where you are doing well. It will also require sales numbers for each of those marketing areas by geography: district, region, state, or DMA.

BDI is calculated using geographic sales and the population for the area under consideration:

$$\text{Area BDI} = \frac{\% \text{ sales in this area} \times 100}{\% \text{ population in this area}}$$

BDI can also be used in other ways—for example, demographics. In addition to geographical variations, it is not uncommon for certain brands to be more popular with Hispanics, with certain age groups, or some other key characteristic. We could calculate a racial BDI, which would be different, yet similar to the geographic BDI.

BDI and BPI.

Past performance can be a relatively useful indicator of future performance. There are quite a number of packaged goods companies that allocate media dollars based on where sales came from last year.

If the advertising case rate is one dollar, and the Brand sold 10,000 cases in the Casper/Riverton DMA, then the Brand will spend $10,000 in media in Casper/Riverton.

The problem is that the Brand has been spending $10,000 in Casper/Riverton since it was introduced. Does the Brand sell the 10,000 cases because that is the proper potential of the Brand, or has it all become a self-fulfilling prophesy as the advertising has created the market?

It could be that we'd have greater sales if some of the Casper/Riverton money was spent in Presque Isle, but we have no evidence of this.

A BDI profile will give you a picture of where the Brand's strong markets are, and which ones are weak.

This can become the basis for strategy—do you want a defensive strategy to spend where you are strong, or do you want an offensive strategy to spend where you need help?

Most advertising dollars allocated in the marketplace are defensive dollars. There must be a reason why we've been able to sell 10,000 cases in Casper/Riverton. If we take that money and allocate it to Presque Isle, sales may increase in Maine, but decrease in Wyoming.

Most marketers would rather have the bird in the hand in Wyoming than gamble on the bird in the bush in Maine. Then again, it is usually true that dollars spent in high-BDI areas work better than those spent in low-BDI areas. And, as you will see, it is not only where, but when.

Determining the Greatest Sales Potential.

Later we will discuss how to determine sales potential.

This sales potential will allow us to know exactly where to allocate advertising media dollars.

If a brand development index is not available, then some regional information can be found in MRI or SMRB.

This may have to be enough if more exact information can't be found.

See Note A at the end of Chapter Eight for more detail.

C. Seasonality:

Determining Key Selling Periods.

Sales in a given month when compared to other times of the year provide information about when marketing should take place.

This is a type of BDI, and could be construed to be a Seasonality Development Index, but it is usually simply called Seasonality.

This segment of the Situation Analysis will provide detail on when sales happen throughout the year. Christmas lights and other decorations may have the highest level of seasonality of any category of products. The greeting card industry is quite aware of seasonality.

Milk, at the other extreme, is used almost equally in every week of the year. There are other examples of products we use virtually every day.

In most cases, the Brand will have a seasonality to its sales, and that seasonality will impact your planning.

The Seasonality section of the Situation Analysis should define the key selling period. There should be an exhibit that shows percent of sales per month and an index of that percent to the average month. (Usually this seasonality chart is found in the exhibits at the end of the media plan.)

Most packaged goods manufacturers skew advertising to those months when the greatest sales take place.

In fact, a great number of companies maintain a precise spending philosophy, i.e., if 13.2% of sales take place in March, then 13.2% of the advertising will be in March.

Make certain there should be 13.2% of sales in March, and that it's not a function of many years of advertising at high levels. The average month will have 8.3% of sales.

In other words, are the sales in March there because people want to consume more of the Brand at that time, or is it because the Brand has always advertised in March since that's when the annual sales meeting takes place, and the Brand tends to be on special during that period?

If the Brand has been advertising for a long period of time, it is not always possible to determine which is taking place.

Offensive or Defensive.

This can also be construed to be an offensive versus a defensive issue. If you support each month as a function of the percent of sales in that month, you'll be using a defensive strategy. Basically, you're seeking to defend sales you've achieved in the past.

If you heavy-up spending in months when sales have been weak in the past, then you're using an offensive strategy.

Remember, as you did in the Geography segment of the plan, that you can only spend the money once.

If you spend it in an historically weak month you may not spend it to support a traditionally strong month.

Sometimes this works, sometimes it doesn't. Two examples.

First, Mondays in the restaurant business tend to be slow days—some even close on Mondays. Can you "fix" Monday with extra spending, or is it the nature of things? Might you be better off encouraging weekend business, when people are more inclined to go out?

Second, winter for cookies. Archway Cookies, a small brand in the Midwest, discovered that its larger competitors (like Nabisco) were not promoting much during winter months. They perceived this as an opportunity for them to get in-store displays—a key factor in cookie sales, often an impulse buy. In this case, it worked. Even though these were slower periods for cookie sales, the smaller Archway brand was not able to promote effectively when the larger companies were promoting. So they were able to make this "slow" time one of their stronger sales periods.

D. Purchase Cycle:

How Often...

This section of your marketing document will help you understand how often your target group (or groups) use the brand.

It is useful because it helps you understand how much media weight is needed. Sometimes the media weight is simply a function of budget, but the levels can be adjusted through the use of flighting and pulsing.

Purchase cycle will aid the reader of the marketing document to put frequency into perspective—frequency of usage and frequency in media.

It helps to define how often the brand should be advertised.

Purchase cycle is defined as the number of days between the purchase of a standard unit in a given category.

In the Yogurt category, a cup is the standard unit. It can be calculated from the information in either MRI or SMRB. Look in Note A for detail on MRI (page 60).

Calculating Purchase Cycle.
Calculate the total number of cups of yogurt eaten and divide by the number of people.

The number of cups in 30 days will be your answer. Set it up like this:

Yogurt Purchase Cycle:

Frequency	'000	Total Cups
10.0	4,561	45,610
8.0	893	7,144
7.0	2,198	15,386
6.0	2,756	16,536
5.0	2,138	10,690
4.0	3,895	15,580
3.0	3,343	10,029
2.0	4,920	9,840
1.0	3,565	3,565
	28,269	134,380

Now we know that 134 million cups of yogurt are purchased every seven days by 28 million female homemakers (or their families). That works out to 4.75 cups purchased in a seven day period, or seven-tenths of a cup every day.

If we compared this to the same information from ten years earlier, we'd find that 49 million adults purchased 288 million cups of yogurt in that same 30-day period.

That would translate to a purchase of 5.88 cups and a purchase cycle of 5.1 days. The result is that fewer adults eat yogurt, but individually, they eat about the same amount of it and with about the same frequency.

Other Considerations.

The great majority of products can never use purchase cycle information because it is not possible to get sufficient exposures within the purchase cycle or because the purchase cycle is so long the numbers become meaningless. The average car owner replaces a muffler every 42 months.

The standard thinking calls for three exposures during a purchase cycle. However, if you are the marketing manager for Midas Muffler and Brake shops does that mean you advertise with a frequency of once per year? Of course not.

However, this information is valuable to most packaged good products. Even if it is not immediately actionable, it is still a good professional discipline to calculate purchase cycle.

Windows of Opportunity.

For other businesses, like restaurants or retailers, there are best times of the month, week, and year to place the advertising. Pay days, for example, are good days for advertising. Mondays, as we mentioned, are usually not.

In Alaska, the state is a major employer and pays people every two weeks on Friday, unlike most businesses, which pay employees twice a month. This change requires advertisers of some products, like mid-level restaurants or electronic appliances to schedule their advertising in line with when people are paid.

Following this line of thinking, most newspapers in the United States have developed a time when family purchasing agents look for grocery advertising in the newspaper. This is called BFD—Best Food Day. Usually, it is either Wednesday or Thursday, but it can vary by market in the United States.

Understanding the User.

Remember: this purchase cycle segment of the marketing planning document is part of our effort to understand the user.

We want to get a handle on how often the product is used. But, since we don't know exactly when they use it, we make the assumption that if we know when they buy it, that will be close to when they use it.

A demographic and psychographic description of the user, where this user exists, when they use, and this last description of how often the user uses all contribute to our overall understanding of the consumer.

E. Creative Requirements:

Initial Input.

The purpose of this segment of the Situation Analysis is to outline what is needed. It is not likely at the initial writing of this document that you will be able to answer that question, but there is some initial input you can provide. And that can be useful.

For example, if you are working on Bisquick, it is likely that the Brand will require print vehicles that provide very high quality appetite (visual) appeal of food prepared with the Brand.

Bisquick may also require a vehicle that will disperse coupons.

Look for Needs and Opportunities.

If the assignment is to write the Creative Requirements segment of the marketing document for a new ultra low-fat food, it may be that you want a medium and vehicle that will give a high level of credibility to the Brand. In this case, you might eliminate outdoor and go with magazines dedicated to health or special-expert talk shows on television.

Try to Be Helpful, Not Confining.

This segment need not be long, but it should consider history and any expected future developments. Take care at this stage not to provide too much constraining information here. You want to be helpful, but not limiting. Understanding that Bisquick will need a coupon delivery system is helpful.

While it is possible to write the plan so that you are required to use television, you should try not to write it in that fashion.

It is better to outline that the Brand will need strong visual support and appetite appeal or to write whatever else might be important, but you don't want to restrict the thinking in the media plan or the creative development.

F. Competitive Sales:

What's Working? What's Not Working?

This is a review of the current business situation for both the Brand and for all the competitors in the category.

There are a number of analysis techniques available to determine good markets and poor markets, where advertising is working and where it isn't, where sales promotion is working and where it's not, and a variety of other parameters.

The goal is to learn which elements of both the Brand, and its competitors' marketing plans are working and those that aren't.

Analysis Techniques.

Here are a few analysis techniques to consider:

1. **Provide Brand sales as they relate to last year's plan, or the last two years if possible:**
   The more detail in which this information is presented will allow the Brand a greater capability to make good decisions. Ideally, the sales figures should be presented by geographic area—DMA, state, sales region, etc.—provided on a quarterly basis. Be sure to show totals in both directions (across and down) if you are using a table.

   Once you have all the numbers in clear, easy-to-follow columns showing sales this year versus last year for all 210 DMAs, this is a good place to use indices to show the increase of sales from one year to the next. The following is a format for this chart using DMAs as the basis for the geographic description.

Exhibit A

ABC Brand
Sales History FY 10
(Index versus year ago)

	Q1	Q2	1st Half	(Index)	Q3	Q4	2nd Half	(Index)	FY 10	(Index)
Abilene-Sweet										
Albany, GA										
Alb-Schen-Troy										
Albuquerque										
Alexandria, LA										
Alexandria, MN										
Alpena										
Amarillo										
Anniston										
Total										

This chart should be continued through the remaining 200+ DMAs.

Tracking Change.

You can look at the DMAs where the greatest change took place, either in a given six-month period, a quarter, or for the total year.

Then look at last year's plan to see what happened in those markets that was different from the other markets, which may explain the unusual increase in the year-to-year change in sales for whatever time period you've used.

If the Brand has one major competitor, you might want to show this same detail for the competition as well.

The Procter & Gamble group at Saatchi in New York used to divide the markets into three groups, the good, the average, and the weak. It was called a tertile analysis. The next step is easy. What did we do differently in the top group than we did in the bottom group.

Factor Analysis.

You might also try separating the markets that received a given promotion or other element of the marketing plan.

For example, if you are working on Tide and you know that the Brand ran a trade allowance of $2.50 per case for a display allowance for a five-week period during the second quarter, and that this allowance was offered in St. Louis, Denver, Louisville, and Albany, then you might look at these markets as a total to see if you can determine the effect this program had on sales.

Suppose that in total, these markets had an increase of 12.5% in the total year, and an increase of 4.4% last year. Compare these market totals in the second quarter with similar markets that didn't have the trade allowance to determine the difference in sales.

If the non-allowance markets had an increase similar to the allowance markets in the year prior to the year when the allowance markets received the extra promotion monies, we can assume that the markets aren't usual for some other reason.

Then we need to record the percent change in sales in the non-allowance markets.

ABC Brand
Display Allowance Analysis
(percent change versus year ago)

	FY 2010	FY 2009
Display allowance areas	+12.5%	+4.4%
Areas w/o display allowance	+5.8	+4.7%
Change attributable to allowance	+6.7%	-0.3%

The table above shows a useful format to illustrate the effect that the promotion actually had.

It is now safe to assume that the display allowance created an increase of 6.7% in sales. Or, a 7.0% increase if we consider the difference from the loss in FY 2009.

Next, we need to know if this is enough to pay for the increase in funds allocated to the display allowance.

2. **Show sales for the total U.S. for all competitors in the category:** Show these sales by quarter with totals for the year and for the six-month periods. This is another opportunity to use an index so the reader can quickly see the percentage increase for the period under consideration from the same time period a year ago.

The following is an example of how that chart might look:

Exhibit C

Category Sales History FY 2010
(Index versus year ago)

	Q1	Q2	1st Half	(Index)	Q3	Q4	2nd Half	(Index)	FY 10	(Index)
ABC Brand										
Brand D										
Brand E										
Brand F										
Brand G										
Brand H										
All Others										
Total										

Take care to label these charts clearly. A continuation of these charts can be found in Chapter Eight; these two charts (Exhibits A and C) will get you started.

G. Competitive Media:

Find Out Who Spent What.

This is a review of the funds spent on marketing the different brands in the category during the past year.

The media spending chart might look like the one below:

Exhibit D

ABC Brand
Category Media Review
(Index versus year ago)

	Television			Radio	Mags	News	Outdoor	Transit	Internet
	Net	Spot	Cable						
Brand ABC									
-Dollars									
-Index									
Brand D									
-Dollars									
-Index									
Brand E									
-Dollars									
-Index									
Brand F									
-Dollars									
-Index									
Brand G									
-Dollars									
-Index									
All Others									
-Dollars									
-Index									
Total									
-Dollars									
-Index									

Finding this information can be difficult. If you are a professional working for a major advertising agency, it will be readily available in Nielsen AdViews for everything except digital. AdRelevance is the source for on-line information.

If you are a student at a university that does not subscribe to either of these services, then you will have to do some sleuthing. Check old copies of Competitive Media Reporting that may be available in the library. Search through Google to see what you can find. There may be an article in *AdAge* or some other professional publication.

Promotion Spending.
Information Resources, Inc. (IRI) is a source for information on promotional spending. You may give consideration to developing a chart to report promotion spending, or you might integrate the information into the Competitive Media Review chart (Exhibit D).

The spending can be analyzed to determine which brand is spending the most money and what impact that spending is making on sales. This is valuable information as you start to think of what tools you will use to market the Brand in the coming year.

Share of Expenditures and Share of Voice.
If you develop a chart showing the share of spending each competitor within a category has within a given time period, then this is called a Share of Expenditures chart.

If you go to the work to translate those expenditures into Gross Rating Points (GRPs) then the chart would be called a Share of Voice.

Share of Voice would be more useful than Share of Expenditures because your user group does not see dollars, they see GRPs, and you are trying to ascertain your power in the marketplace.

However, as good as that idea may be, the systems available to gather this information are not accurate enough to translate this information from dollars to delivery.

Then again, it is somewhat unlikely that an advertiser would be inefficient—resulting in a high share of expenditures and a low share of voice. For these reasons...

Most advertising agencies and their clients believe Share of Expenditures is good enough.

Usually you would like to have three years of history on these charts to determine the long-term effect of a spending strategy.

Case Rate and Percent of Sales.
Another consideration is a case rate or percent of sales analysis. There are many comparisons between this area and Chapter Eight. Percent of Sales is one example.

The case rate information is contained in Chapter Eight, but it could just as easily be presented here. A chart is usually helpful.

The case rate chart for the category will make it easy to recognize those brands that are spending the most on a per-unit basis.

Summary.
The outline that has just been presented will help the marketing plan author understand the people who will buy or use the brand.

If the business requires significant additional information, this outline should be altered to provide that input.

Part of the fun and part of the challenge is to find new ways to look at the information that reveal what others have not discovered.

For more information, please also read:
1. Lisa Fortini-Campbell. *Hitting the Sweet Spot.* (Chicago: The Copy Workshop, 1991).
   The total book is valuable for the situation analysis. Chapters 10, 11, and 14 are particularly applicable

2. Don E. Schultz and Beth E. Barnes. *Strategic Advertising Campaigns.* 5th ed. (McGraw-Hill, 1999).
   This book is quite comprehensive and will be referred to from time to time as a primary resource. You should try to have at least one copy available for your team.

MRI

Since when did ignorance become a point-of-view.
— Dilbert

Introduction.

The Internet is quickly becoming the key source of information of all kinds. Advertising and marketing are not exceptions to this trend.

However, MRI and Simmons will continue to be key sources of demographic and product usage information. This segment is intended to help you understand how to use that information. We will discuss primarily MRI, but similar information can be found using Experian Simmons. Previously it was known as SMRB, Simmons Market Research Bureau.

Primary Sources for Secondary Research.

GfkMRI, previously Mediamark Research & Intelligence, LLC (or simply MRI), is in business to report consumption patterns of both products and media. That is, they report on how we use products and how we use media.

Consumption patterns for both products and media can be found in the Mediamark Reporter. This in turn is found in MRI Plus online.

A. Category Demographics:

Number of Users and Incidence.

There are a variety of category demographic information to be gleaned from GfkMRI*, so let's start with the number of users and the incidence of their usage.

The number of users can be found in the total column. If there is an asterisk, then there are too few people for MRI to stand by the numbers. Try to avoid those, but, quite frankly, sometimes it is all you have.

The incidence numbers are the most valuable when trying to identify a target group. Look for the rows where the numbers are large in each demographic profile. In the chart at the end of this explanation (page 66) is the demographic information for Yogurt users.

Notes on How to Do It.

Before you start, look at the top of page 66 to understand who is being

---

*We will use the term MRI as a shortening of GfkMRI throughout this book because it is commonly expressed in that way.

discussed. In this case, we are looking at principal shoppers, or more accurately stated, "those who buy." Think about each number to see if it makes sense.

1. There are approximately 140,993,000 principal shoppers in the U.S. You will notice that the number is the sum of the age groups:

Age 18-24	12,397
Age 25-34	25,534
Age 35-44	27,948
Age 45-54	28,785
Age 55-64	21,545
Age 65+	24,784

That makes sense. Also note that the same is true by gender. All the men aged 18-34 and the number of women of the same age add to the number of adults in the same age group.

Men 18-49	25,324	31.3
Women 18-49	55,458	68.7
Adults 18-49	80,782	100.0

This indicates that there are a little over twice as many women principal shoppers as there are men. Or, stated another way, men make up only 31.3 percent of all US principal shoppers... at least for the 18-49 age category. You could check for yourself to see if it is the same for all age groups.

2. There are 76,431,000 principal shoppers who have used yogurt in the past six months (see the MRI reprint). Users represent 54.2% of all principal shoppers. This is the base, against which all other demographic incidence numbers will be compared.

3. There are 12,397,000 principal shoppers between 18 and 24. Of these, 6,155,000 used Yogurt during the past six months.

4. These users who are 18-24 represent 8.1% of all principal shoppers who are the same age.

5. Now go back to the Pct Across column. This is the incidence of usage. These 18-24 year old yogurt users are 49.6% of the number of all principal shoppers in the age/gender group. Or, the incidence of usage for 18 to 24 year olds is 49.6%. Or, 49.6% of all people 18 to 24 purchase yogurt. Note that this percentage, or incidence of usage, is less than that for all principal shoppers at 54.2%. So 18 to 24 year olds use less yogurt than the average principal shopper. It is 8% less, or it has an index of 92. An index is a ratio of one number to another when the average is 100. Since the index is 92, it is 8% less than national average.

6. Now look at women principal shoppers 18 to 49. There are over fifty-five million of them. Almost thirty-five million of these female principal shoppers (34,334,000) have used yogurt in the past six months. The incidence of usage is 61.9%, which is 14% higher than the national average. It is likely an age group of female principal shoppers we will consider to be in our target audience.

7. Now look for the Index on the far right. The index is 114. To understand this, remember, once again, that an index is a ratio of one number to another when the base is 100. So this 114 index shows us that a female principal shopper between the ages of 18 and 49 is 14% more likely to purchase yogurt than is the average female principal shopper in the United States.

8. Scan down the page. You can see that members of the user base who have children between the ages of 2–5 are 20% more likely to purchase yogurt than the average principal shopper who uses yogurt (index 120).

Sell Where the Incidence is Highest.
Note we did not seek the target group with the absolute largest number of people. We sought the demographic with the highest incidence of usage.

If you were going to try to sell twenty-five sweatshirts that had "ΔΔΔ" silkscreened across the chest, would you go downtown where there are a lot of people, or would you sit in front of the Tri-Delt sorority house at the university where you might only see a hundred people all day? The answer should be obvious—go to the university. It is easiest to sell where the incidence of users, or potential users, is highest.

Now that you understand what to look for in the age parameter, the next issue is how much spread in age there should be. There is no rule.

Look for where the similarities end, and when you add a new age segment, be certain they are more alike than they are different. In the yogurt example, the age parameter is likely 25 to 44, or even 54.

Next, you need to do the same thing for education, employment, professional status, marital status, race, income, household size, and anything else you can find.

B. Heavy Users:

Notice that the demographics of the heavy users show the same pattern. On the MediaMark Reporter site, go back to the target box on the left of the page and click on heavy users. The information shows us the same pattern, but the numbers change because they are based on heavy users.

Discovering Differentiation.

We have been looking at category information, but there is also information available for the Brand. This time, turn to the MRI page on Heavy Users (page 68). Use the box on the left of the page, identified as Heavy User (if you were online, you would click on Heavy User), but scan down to "Dannon Blended Yogurt (Homemakers)." This is also based on principal shoppers who have purchased the brand in the past six months.

You will notice in the far left column that there are still 140,993,000 homemakers in the US, including 55,458 who are women in the 18 to 49 age category. But, there are only 3,395 women principal shoppers 18 to 49 who purchase Dannon Blended. You can make all the other comparisons based on the brand and compare those to Breyers, Columbo, Yoplait and so on.

Careful organization and analysis will help you to get a firm grip on who uses yogurt and the differences between brands.

Dannon Incidence of Purchase

	Blended	Light & Fit	Fruit on Bottom
Women 18-49	6.1	5.6	4.8
HHI 150 K +	6.4	7.8	5.6
County Size: A	5.5	5.9	5.8
Child 2 to 5 years	6.8	4.0	4.8

This helps us to understand more about the current users, and consequently, about our target group. This quick look at the numbers shows us that Light & Fit probably appeals to people who are upper income and live in big cities. It shows us that Blended appeals to moms with children 2 to 5 years old.

If you continue the analysis with competing brands and with more demographic parameters like race, MRI will help you to paint a clear picture of the user base for the brand.

C. Media Consumption Based on Product Usage:

If you were to keep scrolling down page 71 you would come to a listing of magazines. These pages are not found here in the book, but may be provided by your instructor or located in the Café section of AdBuzz. com. Download the file "DannonBlended.pdf" and use the pages headed "Used in last 6 months Dannon Blended Yogurt (Homemakers)."

Scroll down the page to the alphabetical listing of magazines. The numbers in the five columns to the right will help you to understand which magazines are used by Yogurt users.

For example, there are 30,940,000 users of *Better Homes and Gardens*. About 24.5% (1751) of the total number of Dannon Blended Yogurt users (7,155). If you place an advertisement in *BH&G*, 5.7% of Dannon Blended Yogurt users will have the OTS the ad. Think of the 5.7 as being reach. That compares to a reach of 0.5 for your ad in *Bassmaster* or a 3.3 reach for an ad in *Car and Driver*.

These are all based on yogurt users.

D. Media Consumption Based on Demographics:

You can also find similar information based on demographics, instead of product consumption by going back to the MediaMark Reporter. This time you choose Media instead of Product when you choose a Report volume. Then choose "Demographics - Head of Household: Head of Household Age - Summary." Choose Female as the base, and 18-49 as the Target.

Again, this information can be provided by your instructor or located in the Café section of AdBuzz.com (MediaDemographics.pdf).

Scroll down the page to *Better Homes & Gardens*. There 313,302,000 people who read *Better Homes & Gardens*. Of those, 14,452,000, or 46.2% are Females between the ages of 18 and 49. Of all women 18 to 49, 24.3% read *Better Homes & Gardens*. Think of this as reach.

E. Analysis:

Category Review and Trend Analysis.

Your analysis of this MRI information should include a review of the category, including heavy and light users, and the Brand.

This is also a good opportunity to conduct a trend analysis. Show three years history of MRI or SMRB to show how consumption is changing.

MRI Materials:

The following eleven pages are from the MRI Reporter, found at: *http://www.mriplus.com/site/index.aspx*

- **Total Homemakers: 66–67**
- **Heavy Users: 68–69**
- **Dannon Blended Yogurt: 70–71**
- **Dannon Light & Fit: 72–73**
- **Dannon Fruit on the Bottom: 74–75**
- **Brand Share of Users and Volume: 76**

Go to MRI Plus, then click on MRI Reporter, then select the year. While there are a variety of reports listed, I find it quicker to just type in the name of the category I want, in this case Yogurt. Make sure you select the correct yogurt category and you will find the information we discussed on pages 60 through 64.

These pages were provided courtesy of GfkMRI.

Note: This section uses the term "principal shopper." MRI continues to use the term "homemaker," but in the last few years, have begun adopting "principal shopper" as the term to describe the household/homemaker questions. The primary reason for this change by MRI is that homemaker has a connotation of June Cleaver or Harriet Nelson i.e. stay-at-home Mom. Clearly the role of the homemaker has evolved, as evidenced by the data showing a 70/30 split between females/males in the role of principal shopper.

10+ years ago, the number was closer to 80/20. Either term is correct, but this text seeks to use the terms that are more accurate.

Fall 2008 Product
Household Products - Food products

Yogurt
Used in last 6 months Total (Homemakers)
Base: Total Homemakers

Stub	Total '000	Proj '000	Pct Across	Pct Down	Index
Total	140,993	76,431	54.2	100.0	100
Educ: graduated college plus	38,550	25,541	66.3	33.4	122
Educ: attended college	38,336	21,041	54.9	27.5	101
Educ: graduated high school	43,853	21,303	48.6	27.9	90
Educ: did not graduate HS	20,254	8,546	42.2	11.2	78
Educ: post graduate	12,277	8,475	69.0	11.1	127
Educ: no college	64,107	29,849	46.6	39.1	86
Age 18-24	12,397	6,155	49.6	8.1	92
Age 25-34	25,534	14,672	57.5	19.2	106
Age 35-44	27,948	16,626	59.5	21.8	110
Age 45-54	28,785	16,058	55.8	21.0	103
Age 55-64	21,545	11,805	54.8	15.4	101
Age 65+	24,784	11,115	44.8	14.5	83
Adults 18-34	37,931	20,827	54.9	27.2	101
Adults 18-49	80,782	45,982	56.9	60.2	105
Adults 25-54	82,267	47,356	57.6	62.0	106
Men 18-34	12,764	5,792	45.4	7.6	84
Men 18-49	25,324	11,647	46.0	15.2	85
Men 25-54	25,173	11,616	46.1	15.2	85
Women 18-34	25,167	15,034	59.7	19.7	110
Women 18-49	55,458	34,334	61.9	44.9	114
Women 25-54	57,094	35,740	62.6	46.8	115
Occupation: : Professional and Related Occupation: s	20,830	13,821	66.4	18.1	122
Occupation: Management, Business and Financial Operations	12,575	7,895	62.8	10.3	116
Occupation: Sales and Office Occupation: s	23,516	13,639	58.0	17.8	107
Occupation: Natural Resources, Construction and Maintenance Occupation: s	5,457	1,962	36.0	2.6	66
Occupation: Other Employed	23,290	11,439	49.1	15.0	91
HHI150,000+	12,517	8,819	70.5	11.5	130
HHI$75,000-$149,999	34,466	21,821	63.3	28.6	117
HHI$60,000-$74,999	14,424	8,173	56.7	10.7	105
HHI$50,000-$59,999	11,273	6,334	56.2	8.3	104
HHI$40,000-$49,999	12,881	6,532	50.7	8.5	94
HHI$30,000-$39,999	14,667	7,262	49.5	9.5	91
HHI$20,000-$29,999	15,880	7,420	46.7	9.7	86
HHI<$20,000	24,885	10,070	40.5	13.2	75
Census Region: North East	26,299	15,805	60.1	20.7	111
Census Region: South	51,576	25,019	48.5	32.7	89
Census Region: Midwest	31,491	17,003	54.0	22.2	100

Fall 2008 Product
Household Products - Food products

Yogurt
Used in last 6 months Total (Homemakers)
Base: Total Homemakers

Stub	Total '000	Proj '000	Pct Across	Pct Down	Index
Census Region: West	31,627	18,603	58.8	24.3	109
MediaMarkets: Top 5	29,022	16,686	57.5	21.8	106
MediaMarkets: Next 5	13,921	7,862	56.5	10.3	104
County Size: : A	57,179	33,132	57.9	43.3	107
County Size: B	42,317	23,130	54.7	30.3	101
County Size: C	21,396	11,081	51.8	14.5	96
County Size: D	20,102	9,087	45.2	11.9	83
Marital Status: Never Married	33,055	15,391	46.6	20.1	86
Marital Status: Now Married	71,417	43,930	61.5	57.5	113
Marital Status: Engaged	6,850	3,279	47.9	4.3	88
Marital Status: Widowed/Divorced/Legally Separated	36,521	17,110	46.9	22.4	86
Child age: <12 months	5,849	3,620	61.9	4.7	114
Child age: 12-23 months	5,005	3,106	62.1	4.1	114
Child age: <2 years	10,569	6,524	61.7	8.5	114
Child age: <6 years	25,515	16,379	64.2	21.4	118
Child age: 2-5 years	19,676	12,776	64.9	16.7	120
Child age: 6-11 years	23,710	15,109	63.7	19.8	118
Child age: 12-17 years	24,722	15,206	61.5	19.9	113
Years At Present Address: <1 year	24,089	12,297	51.0	16.1	94
Years At Present Address: 1-4 Years	43,656	24,207	55.4	31.7	102
Years At Present Address: 5+ Years	73,190	39,915	54.5	52.2	101
Home: Owned	93,677	53,638	57.3	70.2	106
Home value: $500,000+ Dollars	11,275	7,839	69.5	10.3	128
Home value: $200,000-$499,999	36,302	22,606	62.3	29.6	115
Home value: $100,000-$199,999	27,245	15,281	56.1	20.0	103
Home value: $50,000-$99,999	12,520	5,477	43.7	7.2	81
Home value: <$50,000	6,337	2,435	38.4	3.2	71
Race: White	110,029	61,773	56.1	80.8	104
Race: Black/African American	16,487	6,441	39.1	8.4	72
Race: American Indian or Alaska Native	1,228	705	57.4	0.9	106
Race: Asian	3,263	1,992	61.0	2.6	113
Race: Other	11,786	6,618	56.2	8.7	104
Race: White only	108,736	60,963	56.1	79.8	103
Race: Black/African American only	16,080	6,189	38.5	8.1	71
Race: Other Race: /Multiple Classifications	16,177	9,279	57.4	12.1	106
Spanish spoken in home (most often or other)	19,123	10,766	56.3	14.1	104

Fall 2008 Product
Household Products - Food products

Yogurt
Containers/Last 7 Days Heavy (4+) (Homemakers)
Base: Total Homemakers

Stub	Total '000	Proj '000	Pct Across	Pct Down	Index
Total	140,993	37,694	26.7	100.0	100
Educ: graduated college plus	38,550	11,916	30.9	31.6	116
Educ: attended college	38,336	10,542	27.5	28.0	103
Educ: graduated high school	43,853	10,639	24.3	28.2	91
Educ: did not graduate HS	20,254	4,598	22.7	12.2	85
Educ: post graduate	12,277	3,999	32.6	10.6	122
Educ: no college	64,107	15,237	23.8	40.4	89
Age 18-24	12,397	2,625	21.2	7.0	79
Age 25-34	25,534	6,976	27.3	18.5	102
Age 35-44	27,948	8,322	29.8	22.1	111
Age 45-54	28,785	8,537	29.7	22.6	111
Age 55-64	21,545	5,602	26.0	14.9	97
Age 65+	24,784	5,634	22.7	14.9	85
Adults 18-34	37,931	9,601	25.3	25.5	95
Adults 18-49	80,782	22,283	27.6	59.1	103
Adults 25-54	82,267	23,834	29.0	63.2	108
Men 18-34	12,764	2,643	20.7	7.0	77
Men 18-49	25,324	5,585	22.1	14.8	82
Men 25-54	25,173	5,766	22.9	15.3	86
Women 18-34	25,167	6,958	27.6	18.5	103
Women 18-49	55,458	16,699	30.1	44.3	113
Women 25-54	57,094	18,068	31.6	47.9	118
Occupation: : Professional and Related Occupation: s	20,830	6,473	31.1	17.2	116
Occupation: Management, Business and Financial Operations	12,575	3,766	29.9	10.0	112
Occupation: Sales and Office Occupation: s	23,516	6,814	29.0	18.1	108
Occupation: Natural Resources, Construction and Maintenance Occupation: s	5,457	1,117	20.5	3.0	77
Occupation: Other Employed	23,290	5,807	24.9	15.4	93
HHI150,000+	12,517	4,429	35.4	11.8	132
HHI$75,000-$149,999	34,466	10,622	30.8	28.2	115
HHI$60,000-$74,999	14,424	4,058	28.1	10.8	105
HHI$50,000-$59,999	11,273	3,353	29.7	8.9	111
HHI$40,000-$49,999	12,881	3,209	24.9	8.5	93
HHI$30,000-$39,999	14,667	3,621	24.7	9.6	92
HHI$20,000-$29,999	15,880	3,566	22.5	9.5	84
HHI<$20,000	24,885	4,835	19.4	12.8	73
Census Region: North East	26,299	8,161	31.0	21.6	116
Census Region: South	51,576	12,422	24.1	33.0	90
Census Region: Midwest	31,491	8,743	27.8	23.2	104

Fall 2008 Product
Household Products - Food products

Yogurt
Containers/Last 7 Days Heavy (4+) (Homemakers)
Base: Total Homemakers

Stub	Total '000	Proj '000	Pct Across	Pct Down	Index
Census Region: West	31,627	8,369	26.5	22.2	99
MediaMarkets: Top 5	29,022	8,311	28.6	22.0	107
MediaMarkets: Next 5	13,921	3,864	27.8	10.3	104
County Size: : A	57,179	16,378	28.6	43.4	107
County Size: B	42,317	11,235	26.6	29.8	99
County Size: C	21,396	5,347	25.0	14.2	93
County Size: D	20,102	4,735	23.6	12.6	88
Marital Status: Never Married	33,055	6,513	19.7	17.3	74
Marital Status: Now Married	71,417	22,876	32.0	60.7	120
Marital Status: Engaged	6,850	1,608	23.5	4.3	88
Marital Status: Widowed/Divorced/Legally Separated	36,521	8,306	22.7	22.0	85
Child age: <12 months	5,849	1,913	32.7	5.1	122
Child age: 12-23 months	5,005	1,751	35.0	4.6	131
Child age: <2 years	10,569	3,514	33.2	9.3	124
Child age: <6 years	25,515	9,043	35.4	24.0	133
Child age: 2-5 years	19,676	7,145	36.3	19.0	136
Child age: 6-11 years	23,710	7,865	33.2	20.9	124
Child age: 12-17 years	24,722	8,106	32.8	21.5	123
Years At Present Address: <1 year	24,089	5,904	24.5	15.7	92
Years At Present Address: 1-4 Years	43,656	11,729	26.9	31.1	100
Years At Present Address: 5+ Years	73,190	20,054	27.4	53.2	102
Home: Owned	93,677	27,068	28.9	71.8	108
Home value: $500,000+ Dollars	11,275	3,910	34.7	10.4	130
Home value: $200,000-$499,999	36,302	11,225	30.9	29.8	116
Home value: $100,000-$199,999	27,245	7,719	28.3	20.5	106
Home value: $50,000-$99,999	12,520	2,876	23.0	7.6	86
Home value: <$50,000	6,337	1,339	21.1	3.6	79
Race: White	110,029	30,662	27.9	81.3	104
Race: Black/African American	16,487	2,999	18.2	8.0	68
Race: American Indian or Alaska Native	* 1,228	278	22.7	0.7	85
Race: Asian	3,263	780	23.9	2.1	89
Race: Other	11,786	3,332	28.3	8.8	106
Race: White only	108,736	30,401	28.0	80.7	105
Race: Black/African American only	16,080	2,908	18.1	7.7	68
Race: Other Race: /Multiple Classifications	16,177	4,385	27.1	11.6	101
Spanish spoken in home (most often or other)	19,123	5,361	28.0	14.2	105

Fall 2008 Product
Household Products - Food products

Yogurt
Used in last 6 months Dannon Blended Yogurt (Homemakers)
Base: Total Homemakers

Stub	Total '000	Proj '000	Pct Across	Pct Down	Index
Total	140,993	7,155	5.1	100.0	100
Educ: graduated college plus	38,550	1,947	5.0	27.2	100
Educ: attended college	38,336	2,001	5.2	28.0	103
Educ: graduated high school	43,853	2,219	5.1	31.0	100
Educ: did not graduate HS	20,254	989	4.9	13.8	96
Educ: post graduate	12,277	629	5.1	8.8	101
Educ: no college	64,107	3,207	5.0	44.8	99
Age 18-24	12,397	772	6.2	10.8	123
Age 25-34	25,534	1,346	5.3	18.8	104
Age 35-44	27,948	1,505	5.4	21.0	106
Age 45-54	28,785	1,687	5.9	23.6	115
Age 55-64	21,545	900	4.2	12.6	82
Age 65+	24,784	946	3.8	13.2	75
Adults 18-34	37,931	2,117	5.6	29.6	110
Adults 18-49	80,782	4,571	5.7	63.9	111
Adults 25-54	82,267	4,537	5.5	63.4	109
Men 18-34	12,764	552	4.3	7.7	85
Men 18-49	25,324	1,176	4.6	16.4	91
Men 25-54	25,173	1,146	4.6	16.0	90
Women 18-34	25,167	1,566	6.2	21.9	123
Women 18-49	55,458	3,395	6.1	47.4	121
Women 25-54	57,094	3,391	5.9	47.4	117
Occupation: : Professional and Related Occupation: s	20,830	1,104	5.3	15.4	104
Occupation: Management, Business and Financial Operations	12,575	535	4.3	7.5	84
Occupation: Sales and Office Occupation: s	23,516	1,343	5.7	18.8	113
Occupation: Natural Resources, Construction and Maintenance Occupation: s *	5,457	161	3.0	2.3	58
Occupation: Other Employed	23,290	1,283	5.5	17.9	109
HHI150,000+	12,517	801	6.4	11.2	126
HHI$75,000-$149,999	34,466	1,439	4.2	20.1	82
HHI$60,000-$74,999	14,424	926	6.4	12.9	127
HHI$50,000-$59,999	11,273	558	4.9	7.8	98
HHI$40,000-$49,999	12,881	626	4.9	8.8	96
HHI$30,000-$39,999	14,667	651	4.4	9.1	87
HHI$20,000-$29,999	15,880	911	5.7	12.7	113
HHI<$20,000	24,885	1,243	5.0	17.4	98
Census Region: North East	26,299	1,282	4.9	17.9	96
Census Region: South	51,576	2,388	4.6	33.4	91
Census Region: Midwest	31,491	1,954	6.2	27.3	122

Fall 2008 Product
Household Products - Food products

Yogurt
Used in last 6 months Dannon Blended Yogurt (Homemakers)
Base: Total Homemakers

Stub		Total '000	Proj '000	Pct Across	Pct Down	Index
Census Region: West		31,627	1,531	4.8	21.4	95
MediaMarkets: Top 5		29,022	1,625	5.6	22.7	110
MediaMarkets: Next 5		13,921	717	5.1	10.0	101
County Size: : A		57,179	3,116	5.5	43.6	107
County Size: B		42,317	2,295	5.4	32.1	107
County Size: C		21,396	952	4.4	13.3	88
County Size: D		20,102	792	3.9	11.1	78
Marital Status: Never Married		33,055	1,836	5.6	25.7	109
Marital Status: Now Married		71,417	3,554	5.0	49.7	98
Marital Status: Engaged	*	6,850	431	6.3	6.0	124
Marital Status: Widowed/Divorced/Legally Separated		36,521	1,765	4.8	24.7	95
Child age: <12 months	*	5,849	310	5.3	4.3	104
Child age: 12-23 months	*	5,005	404	8.1	5.6	159
Child age: <2 years		10,569	630	6.0	8.8	117
Child age: <6 years		25,515	1,702	6.7	23.8	131
Child age: 2-5 years		19,676	1,340	6.8	18.7	134
Child age: 6-11 years		23,710	1,484	6.3	20.7	123
Child age: 12-17 years		24,722	1,741	7.0	24.3	139
Years At Present Address: <1 year		24,089	1,274	5.3	17.8	104
Years At Present Address: 1-4 Years		43,656	2,224	5.1	31.1	100
Years At Present Address: 5+ Years		73,190	3,657	5.0	51.1	98
Home: Owned		93,677	4,767	5.1	66.6	100
Home value: $500,000+ Dollars		11,275	541	4.8	7.6	95
Home value: $200,000-$499,999		36,302	1,950	5.4	27.3	106
Home value: $100,000-$199,999		27,245	1,324	4.9	18.5	96
Home value: $50,000-$99,999		12,520	566	4.5	7.9	89
Home value: <$50,000	*	6,337	386	6.1	5.4	120
Race: White		110,029	5,012	4.6	70.0	90
Race: Black/African American		16,487	1,178	7.1	16.5	141
Race: American Indian or Alaska Native	*	1,228	131	10.6	1.8	210
Race: Asian	*	3,263	211	6.5	2.9	127
Race: Other		11,786	738	6.3	10.3	123
Race: White only		108,736	4,926	4.5	68.8	89
Race: Black/African American only		16,080	1,160	7.2	16.2	142
Race: Other Race: /Multiple Classifications		16,177	1,069	6.6	14.9	130
Spanish spoken in home (most often or other)		19,123	1,282	6.7	17.9	132

Fall 2008 Product
Household Products - Food products

Yogurt
Used in last 6 months Dannon Light & Fit (Homemakers)
Base: Total Homemakers

Stub	Total '000	Proj '000	Pct Across	Pct Down	Index
Total	140,993	7,214	5.1	100.0	100
Educ: graduated college plus	38,550	2,605	6.8	36.1	132
Educ: attended college	38,336	2,124	5.5	29.4	108
Educ: graduated high school	43,853	1,876	4.3	26.0	84
Educ: did not graduate HS *	20,254	609	3.0	8.4	59
Educ: post graduate	12,277	803	6.5	11.1	128
Educ: no college	64,107	2,485	3.9	34.4	76
Age 18-24	12,397	833	6.7	11.5	131
Age 25-34	25,534	1,096	4.3	15.2	84
Age 35-44	27,948	1,316	4.7	18.2	92
Age 45-54	28,785	1,560	5.4	21.6	106
Age 55-64	21,545	1,263	5.9	17.5	115
Age 65+	24,784	1,146	4.6	15.9	90
Adults 18-34	37,931	1,928	5.1	26.7	99
Adults 18-49	80,782	4,053	5.0	56.2	98
Adults 25-54	82,267	3,972	4.8	55.1	94
Men 18-34	12,764	520	4.1	7.2	80
Men 18-49	25,324	953	3.8	13.2	74
Men 25-54	25,173	821	3.3	11.4	64
Women 18-34	25,167	1,408	5.6	19.5	109
Women 18-49	55,458	3,101	5.6	43.0	109
Women 25-54	57,094	3,151	5.5	43.7	108
Occupation: : Professional and Related Occupation: s	20,830	1,427	6.9	19.8	134
Occupation: Management, Business and Financial Operations	12,575	833	6.6	11.5	129
Occupation: Sales and Office Occupation: s	23,516	1,192	5.1	16.5	99
Occupation: Natural Resources, Construction and Maintenance Occupation: s *	5,457	232	4.3	3.2	83
Occupation: Other Employed	23,290	1,122	4.8	15.5	94
HHI150,000+	12,517	972	7.8	13.5	152
HHI$75,000-$149,999	34,466	2,408	7.0	33.4	137
HHI$60,000-$74,999	14,424	848	5.9	11.8	115
HHI$50,000-$59,999	11,273	601	5.3	8.3	104
HHI$40,000-$49,999	12,881	503	3.9	7.0	76
HHI$30,000-$39,999	14,667	497	3.4	6.9	66
HHI$20,000-$29,999	15,880	653	4.1	9.0	80
HHI<$20,000	24,885	733	2.9	10.2	58
Census Region: North East	26,299	2,130	8.1	29.5	158
Census Region: South	51,576	1,903	3.7	26.4	72
Census Region: Midwest	31,491	1,871	5.9	25.9	116

Fall 2008 Product
Household Products - Food products

Yogurt
Used in last 6 months Dannon Light & Fit (Homemakers)
Base: Total Homemakers

Stub		Total '000	Proj '000	Pct Across	Pct Down	Index
Census Region: West		31,627	1,309	4.1	18.2	81
MediaMarkets: Top 5		29,022	1,711	5.9	23.7	115
MediaMarkets: Next 5		13,921	886	6.4	12.3	124
County Size: : A		57,179	3,363	5.9	46.6	115
County Size: B		42,317	2,009	4.7	27.9	93
County Size: C		21,396	1,152	5.4	16.0	105
County Size: D		20,102	690	3.4	9.6	67
Marital Status: Never Married		33,055	1,576	4.8	21.9	93
Marital Status: Now Married		71,417	4,176	5.8	57.9	114
Marital Status: Engaged	*	6,850	323	4.7	4.5	92
Marital Status: Widowed/Divorced/Legally Separated		36,521	1,461	4.0	20.3	78
Child age: <12 months	*	5,849	237	4.1	3.3	79
Child age: 12-23 months	*	5,005	280	5.6	3.9	109
Child age: <2 years	*	10,569	518	4.9	7.2	96
Child age: <6 years		25,515	1,169	4.6	16.2	90
Child age: 2-5 years		19,676	781	4.0	10.8	78
Child age: 6-11 years		23,710	1,062	4.5	14.7	88
Child age: 12-17 years		24,722	1,061	4.3	14.7	84
Years At Present Address: <1 year		24,089	1,281	5.3	17.8	104
Years At Present Address: 1-4 Years		43,656	1,896	4.3	26.3	85
Years At Present Address: 5+ Years		73,190	4,036	5.5	56.0	108
Home: Owned		93,677	5,264	5.6	73.0	110
Home value: $500,000+ Dollars		11,275	914	8.1	12.7	159
Home value: $200,000-$499,999		36,302	2,338	6.4	32.4	126
Home value: $100,000-$199,999		27,245	1,449	5.3	20.1	104
Home value: $50,000-$99,999	*	12,520	400	3.2	5.5	62
Home value: <$50,000	*	6,337	162	2.6	2.3	50
Race: White		110,029	6,308	5.7	87.5	112
Race: Black/African American		16,487	362	2.2	5.0	43
Race: American Indian or Alaska Native	*	1,228	24	1.9	0.3	38
Race: Asian	*	3,263	153	4.7	2.1	91
Race: Other	*	11,786	417	3.5	5.8	69
Race: White only		108,736	6,261	5.8	86.8	113
Race: Black/African American only		16,080	354	2.2	4.9	43
Race: Other Race: /Multiple Classifications		16,177	598	3.7	8.3	72
Spanish spoken in home (most often or other)		19,123	789	4.1	10.9	81

Fall 2008 Product
Household Products - Food products

Yogurt
Used in last 6 months Dannon Fruit on the Bottom (Homemakers)
Base: Total Homemakers

Stub		Total '000	Proj '000	Pct Across	Pct Down	Index
Total		140,993	6,785	4.8	100.0	100
Educ: graduated college plus		38,550	1,897	4.9	28.0	102
Educ: attended college		38,336	1,920	5.0	28.3	104
Educ: graduated high school		43,853	2,318	5.3	34.2	110
Educ: did not graduate HS		20,254	650	3.2	9.6	67
Educ: post graduate		12,277	654	5.3	9.6	111
Educ: no college		64,107	2,968	4.6	43.7	96
Age 18-24	*	12,397	342	2.8	5.0	57
Age 25-34		25,534	1,056	4.1	15.6	86
Age 35-44		27,948	1,363	4.9	20.1	101
Age 45-54		28,785	1,673	5.8	24.7	121
Age 55-64		21,545	1,166	5.4	17.2	112
Age 65+		24,784	1,184	4.8	17.5	99
Adults 18-34		37,931	1,398	3.7	20.6	77
Adults 18-49		80,782	3,622	4.5	53.4	93
Adults 25-54		82,267	4,092	5.0	60.3	103
Men 18-34		12,764	498	3.9	7.3	81
Men 18-49		25,324	943	3.7	13.9	77
Men 25-54		25,173	989	3.9	14.6	82
Women 18-34		25,167	900	3.6	13.3	74
Women 18-49		55,458	2,679	4.8	39.5	100
Women 25-54		57,094	3,103	5.4	45.7	113
Occupation: : Professional and Related Occupation: s		20,830	998	4.8	14.7	100
Occupation: Management, Business and Financial Operations		12,575	627	5.0	9.2	104
Occupation: Sales and Office Occupation: s		23,516	1,165	5.0	17.2	103
Occupation: Natural Resources, Construction and Maintenance Occupation: s	*	5,457	160	2.9	2.4	61
Occupation: Other Employed		23,290	1,010	4.3	14.9	90
HHI150,000+		12,517	703	5.6	10.4	117
HHI$75,000-$149,999		34,466	1,455	4.2	21.4	88
HHI$60,000-$74,999		14,424	774	5.4	11.4	112
HHI$50,000-$59,999		11,273	626	5.6	9.2	115
HHI$40,000-$49,999		12,881	538	4.2	7.9	87
HHI$30,000-$39,999		14,667	721	4.9	10.6	102
HHI$20,000-$29,999		15,880	880	5.5	13.0	115
HHI<$20,000		24,885	1,087	4.4	16.0	91
Census Region: North East		26,299	2,002	7.6	29.5	158
Census Region: South		51,576	2,041	4.0	30.1	82
Census Region: Midwest		31,491	1,846	5.9	27.2	122

Fall 2008 Product
Household Products - Food products

Yogurt
Used in last 6 months Dannon Fruit on the Bottom (Homemakers)
Base: Total Homemakers

Stub		Total '000	Proj '000	Pct Across	Pct Down	Index
Census Region: West		31,627	896	2.8	13.2	59
MediaMarkets: Top 5		29,022	1,913	6.6	28.2	137
MediaMarkets: Next 5		13,921	714	5.1	10.5	107
County Size: : A		57,179	3,305	5.8	48.7	120
County Size: B		42,317	1,691	4.0	24.9	83
County Size: C		21,396	1,030	4.8	15.2	100
County Size: D	*	20,102	759	3.8	11.2	78
Marital Status: Never Married		33,055	1,419	4.3	20.9	89
Marital Status: Now Married		71,417	3,666	5.1	54.0	107
Marital Status: Engaged	*	6,850	137	2.0	2.0	42
Marital Status: Widowed/Divorced/Legally Separated		36,521	1,700	4.7	25.1	97
Child age: <12 months	*	5,849	214	3.7	3.2	76
Child age: 12-23 months	*	5,005	154	3.1	2.3	64
Child age: <2 years	*	10,569	368	3.5	5.4	72
Child age: <6 years		25,515	1,211	4.7	17.8	99
Child age: 2-5 years		19,676	945	4.8	13.9	100
Child age: 6-11 years		23,710	1,162	4.9	17.1	102
Child age: 12-17 years		24,722	1,326	5.4	19.5	111
Years At Present Address: <1 year		24,089	1,015	4.2	15.0	88
Years At Present Address: 1-4 Years		43,656	1,886	4.3	27.8	90
Years At Present Address: 5+ Years		73,190	3,884	5.3	57.3	110
Home: Owned		93,677	4,647	5.0	68.5	103
Home value: $500,000+ Dollars		11,275	582	5.2	8.6	107
Home value: $200,000-$499,999		36,302	1,628	4.5	24.0	93
Home value: $100,000-$199,999		27,245	1,316	4.8	19.4	100
Home value: $50,000-$99,999		12,520	745	6.0	11.0	124
Home value: <$50,000	*	6,337	376	5.9	5.5	123
Race: White		110,029	5,273	4.8	77.7	100
Race: Black/African American		16,487	910	5.5	13.4	115
Race: American Indian or Alaska Native	*	1,228	37	3.0	0.5	62
Race: Asian	*	3,263	188	5.8	2.8	120
Race: Other		11,786	480	4.1	7.1	85
Race: White only		108,736	5,206	4.8	76.7	99
Race: Black/African American only		16,080	872	5.4	12.8	113
Race: Other Race: /Multiple Classifications		16,177	707	4.4	10.4	91
Spanish spoken in home (most often or other)		19,123	831	4.3	12.2	90

Spring 2008 Product Summary

DAIRY: YOGURT
BASE: TOTAL PRIN. SHOP.(137,436,000)

	ALL			SHARE OF USERS	SHARE OF VOLUME	VOLUME/ USERS INDEX
	'000	%	UNWGT			
Total Used in Last 6 Months	72773	53.0	9186			
Forms:						
With Fruit - premixed	42359	30.8	5006			
With Fruit - not premixed	10130	7.4	1349			
Other Flavor	14459	10.5	1820			
Plain (Unflavored)	8953	6.5	1269			
Types:						
Organic	12331	9.0	1625			
Non-organic	40392	29.4	4951			
Kinds:						
Low Fat	32584	23.7	4096			
Non Fat/Fat Free	13313	9.7	1721			
Regular (Not Low Fat/Non Fat/Fat Free)	24061	17.5	2817			
Brands:						
Breyers Fruit On the Bottom	6772	4.9	789	5.0	3.7	74
Breyers Light	3232	2.4	376	2.4	1.5	63
Breyers Smooth 'n Creamy	2372	1.7	251	1.8	1.0	56
Colombo Blended	776	.6	123	.6	.5	83
Colombo Light	1185	.9	174	.9	.8	89
Dannon Blended Yogurt	8677	6.3	1017	6.4	5.4	84
Dannon Danimals	3485	2.5	354	2.6	2.2	85
Dannon Danimals Drinkables	2557	1.9	284	1.9	1.2	63
Dannon Fat Free Plain	2146	1.6	303	1.6	1.0	63
Dannon Fruit on the Bottom	7267	5.3	953	5.4	5.9	109
Dannon La Cr*me	2600	1.9	325	1.9	1.1	58
Dannon Light 'n Fit	8434	6.1	1097	6.2	7.4	119
Dannon Light 'n Fit Smoothie	1984	1.4	242	1.5	1.0	67
Dannon Plain	2494	1.8	341	1.8	.9	50
Dannon Sprinkl'ins	976	.7	107	.7	.4	57
Horizon Organic Nonfat	1698	1.2	200	1.3	.9	69
La Yogurt	2634	1.9	333	1.9	2.4	126
Light 'n Lively	2257	1.6	261	1.7	1.3	76
Mountain High	1505	1.1	164	1.1	.4	36
Stonyfield Farm	3749	2.7	582	2.8	2.3	82
Trix	2838	2.1	305	2.1	2.1	100
Yoplait Custard Style	4557	3.3	516	3.4	2.6	76
Yoplait Go-Gurt	5486	4.0	564	4.1	4.4	107
Yoplait Light	13785	10.0	1668	10.2	13.6	133
Yoplait Nouriche	659	.5	74	.5	.4	80
Yoplait Original	13525	9.8	1555	10.0	12.9	129
Yoplait Whips!	5945	4.3	717	4.4	3.9	89
Store's Own Brand	13035	9.5	1616	9.6	10.3	107
Other	8702	6.3	1216	6.4	8.6	134

Containers/Last 7 Days

Literature Review

It is no use to keep private information which you can't show off.
— Mark Twain

Introduction.

F.Y.I.

There is a great deal of secondary information that is available to both the entrepreneur and the student.

Most of this information you will find on the Internet or in the library. Find it, write it, and use it as the base of information before you start your research. There is no sense in hunting down information that already exists.

Marketing and Sales Management magazine produces an annual report called the *Marketing and Sales Management's Survey of Buying Power.* It is a good place to start. You might also try the Government Printing Office (GPO).

But the source of the most information will be on the Internet. If your brand is Midas, I feel confident you will find the usage of salt by state governments.

If your brand is Hershey, learn about what chocolate does physiologically. You can probably find the benefits of comfort food without too much problem.

More:

There are lots of places to find good information on how to write a strong literature review. You might try:

1. UNC has a pretty good review on their website.
   http://www.unc.edu/depts/wcweb/handouts/literature_review.html
2. Wikipedia has some good information:
   http://en.wikipedia.org/wiki/Literature_review

Research

Somewhere, something incredible is waiting to be known.
—Carl Sagan, American Astronomer

*Research is to see what everybody else has seen, and
to think what nobody else has thought.*
—Albert Szent-Gyorgyi, Hungarian Biochemist

Introduction.

Finding Out What You Don't Know.

The purpose for the Research section of your marketing planning document is to outline the information you've learned that will contribute to marketing the Brand. The world is full of facts. You need to accurately identify the ones that will help you market your brand more effectively.

In the Situation Analysis you learned what you know. Now you are smart enough to figure out what you don't know.

Research will give you that information. Usually this is information you've gathered just prior to the writing of the marketing document.

Changing Technology.

Technology is advancing so quickly in the marketing and advertising disciplines that the availability of resources and information is increasing at an incredible rate.

For example, the whole idea of tracking sales from specific advertising through single-source data was judged to be prohibitive only a few years ago. This technology has changed our thinking from "we can't do that" to "we can't do that, yet."

Computers are part of the reason for that change. Computers are not just a better way to prepare documents and presentations, they have become a method of acquiring information.

For that reason, this book, and your planning document, should be considered works-in-process—because the technology and available resources are advancing quickly and because the learning is continual and never-ending. Professionals, however, rarely define it this way. There are due dates and deadlines. As Apple founder Steve Jobs said, "Real artists ship." At some point, decisions must be made.

Two Research Sections:

There are two sections in the Marketing Plan that pertain to research— Base and Evaluation.

1. **Base:**

    This first research that you will do can be considered the base study. You will gather information from respondents to answer the issues for which you don't currently have an answer.

    That is the research for which this chapter exists. The result is a base of knowledge you will use to write the marketing document or plan.

2. **Evaluation:**

    The second research section falls under the label "Evaluation." This is an outline of the research you intend to do during the coming year as part of the plan. It will also include an evaluation of that plan, which will be revealed later (See Chapter Ten).

    The Evaluation portion of the plan will help us determine methods to improve the plan for the following year.

    The second research section could also be considered wave one of an ongoing tracking study with the research in this chapter as the baseline study.

So, the Base is what we know, and Evaluation is what we want to find out as we go—part of the process of getting smarter and marketing more effectively.

Our Primary Concern—Message Development.

This first research is primarily concerned with what will be communicated to current and potential buyers and users of the Brand.

We tend, therefore, to think of this as creative research—that is, research about what we will communicate. Certainly you may get information that will lead to executable ideas for below-the-line marketing ideas or even media ideas, but the primary reason for this research will be to determine what we will communicate to the user base.

This is a key issue. In reality, this research relates to the strategic positioning of the entire Brand as evidenced throughout the marketing plan.

Know Your Customer.

Advertising works when you know your customer.

Many people can and do bear testimony to this fact.

The better we know who will buy, recommend, or use the Brand, the better directed the advertising can be.

Three Pieces of Information.

We need to know three pieces of information in order to write advertising strategy. These three things are:

1. **The Target Audience:**

   Who is going to buy the Brand? Whether it's a product or service, this is the first piece of information needed for the marketing plan—who is the target audience?

2. **Factors That Motivate Purchase Behavior:**

   The second category of information needed is—what are the criteria the target audience use to make a purchase decision?

3. **Unique Characteristics of the Brand:**

   The third is—what are the unique characteristics of the Brand or business, i.e., the point-of-difference? Rosser Reeves called it USP.

   When these questions have been answered, the writing of the marketing plan can begin.

   We'll take the time to understand these three important points because this is what we are looking for in the research. After we analyze what we're looking for, we'll discuss how to find it.

Target Audience.
Who Will Be Interested in the Brand?

The first question, then, addresses who is going to be interested in the Brand. These people are called your Target Audience. They are the group to whom the advertising is written.

They can be buyers, users, or influencers of those who buy or use the Brand (or those you want to buy the brand). So, for example, if you were selling peanut butter, to be consumed by children, your target would include the mothers who purchase the product. Now it's easy to understand why Jif Peanut Butter's message is "Choosy Moms Choose Jif."

Demographics.

This Target Audience, or target group, is usually described in terms of the physical population characteristics (demographics) of gender and age. For example, a judgment might be made to advertise to women 18 to 49. Public relations people refer to this group as a "public."

These basic demographics can be expanded to include income, education, geographic dispersion (where they live), professional status, home ownership, race, family size, etc. But, additional secondary and primary research will most likely be needed to acquire this kind of information.

There are syndicated services, such as MRI, that can provide some general research on users (see Note A at the end of Chapter One). Their usefulness depends on the type of product or service for which the plan is being written. They do not provide information that covers all businesses.

Psychographics.

Every brand has to make a decision if it is worth the time and money to psychologically describe the potential customer.

The psychological or lifestyle and personal characteristics (psychographics) of your target audience can also be valuable.

This is often described as lifestyle information. VALS II is the most well-known supplier of this information.

This type of psychographic information is harder to acquire, and can be very expensive. However, it can be valuable to the creative product.

For example, when marketing a performing arts center, the motivations for buying tickets to see the "Nutcracker Suite" may have little to do with the quality of the performance.

Parents, or just as likely grandparents, buy tickets for children to see the "Nutcracker" for the holiday season because they want to share the experience of visiting the theatre with the child.

Consequently, it is more important to market the performance to "Belongers," with an emotional appeal than it is to address the factors that motivate purchase behavior (see subsection below).

In addition, there are multiple psychological dimensions. A person may be in one type of psychological mindset when pursuing leisure activities and quite another when purchasing office products. Even though the same person may purchase life insurance and candy bars, the psychological mindset is quite different.

Usage.
Occasionally, a manufacturer will find it useful to classify the target group by how they use the product. For example, the way kids use a cookie like Oreos is quite different from the way Grandma and Grandpa enjoy an old-fashioned oatmeal cookie like Archway.

Heavy Users.

Many good advertising agencies and marketers find that interviewing heavy users can be an especially fruitful method of gaining information.

After all, these people use the Brand more than the average user. They know more about it and know why they like it.

They understand its advantages and, even though they like it, they may also understand how the Brand could be improved.

They are able to articulate precisely (and often at some length) why they buy the Brand (these are the factors that motivate purchase behavior), and they can tell you which factors are most important to them. This may not be the whole answer, but it will certainly be a good start.

An account planner in Singapore told me one time that people will often give you hints, but they will never give you the answer. That you have to figure out for yourselves.

Good account planning often begins with heavy users, either one-on-one interviews or observation, ethnography.

Mini-saga.
A mini-saga can be a great way to help you understand who these people are. There is a note at the end of Chapter Seven that will give you a little more detail about a mini-saga.

Factors That Motivate Purchase Behavior.
Motivation and Rank Order.

The next issue addresses the factors that motivate purchase behavior. This information is defined first as the isolation of those parameters or factors the target group uses to decide between brands or companies in a given category; and second, the rank order of those criteria used by the target group for brand selection.

These can be different for subgroups within the target audience.

For example, the children who eat peanut butter and the mothers who buy it.

This is the challenge of Integrated Marketing Communications (IMC). There can be so many different target groups for each product (with different factors motivating purchase behavior) that different research may be required for each target audience. Another example might be Apple Computers. High-end graphic designers have very different concerns from parents picking out a computer for a young student.

Example: Yogurt.

If we consider the yogurt example in the situation analysis, the factors a young woman between the ages of 18 and 34 uses to decide first, whether she will buy yogurt, and second, the criteria she uses to decide which brand of yogurt to buy, are quite different than the criteria a 60-year-old woman might use.

Both women are likely to be interested in good taste, but the younger woman probably wants low calories, while the older woman is also very interested in the calcium content.

So a campaign directed at younger women will address weight loss. The simple strategy might be:

To convince: Women 18-34
To use: Dannon Yogurt
Instead of: Private label brands
Because: Dannon tastes great, yet has fewer calories

The campaign to the older women might use a simple strategy like:

To convince:	Women 55+
To use:	Dannon Yogurt
Instead of:	Private label brands
Because:	Dannon is an easy way to get your daily requirement of calcium.

Be sure to see Chapter Seven for more detail on writing a creative brief. This simple strategy is part of the creative platform or brief.

Formal research may be necessary in order to isolate these factors, but simple observation can get you started.

Example: Office Supplies.

Here's an example of those motivating factors in the office supply business. Business people buy yellow pads from one retailer because that retailer makes sales calls to determine what its customers need, delivers the supplies, and then follows up after delivery with a call to assure customer satisfaction.

This is service. Their customers, and consequently their target audience, are those perfectly willing to pay a few cents extra for a yellow pad because it's cheaper than sending an hourly employee to a discount place to buy what the office needs. They know they can count on the people at the office supply store to take care of their needs.

At the other end of the spectrum is an office or a small home-based business with tight controls on costs. To this target audience, it's important to save a few cents on every yellow pad and every box of pencils.

Service versus price is one consideration, but there can be many more nuances in the decision-making process.

One office supply company may stock Write Bros. pens instead of BIC. Another may be closer to the buyer's office. Another may send a catalog. Another may have a website and convenient online ordering.

Clearly, businesses buy office supplies from one store because that store has what they need, but there is probably more to the decision than availability.

In this case, there are four potential factors that motivate purchase behavior in the office supplies business. They are:

- price,
- service,
- availability, and
- convenience.

Target customers may judge price to be the most important factor, while convenience will outweigh the price factor for others.

Rank Order—The Importance of What is Most Important.
In the main, consumers simply consider the factors that are important to them in rank order. This assumes that some considerations are more important than others. Even with emotional, non-rational decisions, there is still rank order. Some things are more important than others.

It's the challenge of the interviewer, likely the account planner, to find a way to provide this weight or importance consideration to the team—then you will know the rank order.

Knowledge of how target groups rank the factors they use to make decisions is mandatory for the development of strategic direction.

In order to be successful, the marketing plan (and advertising) must address the purchase criteria consumers use to buy the Brand. And that marketing plan and advertising ought to give more consideration to the factor or parameter at the top of the list.

There are a variety of ways to get this information.

Additional Examples.
Another example is the pork sausage business. People who eat pork sausage make their purchase decisions based on leanness and taste. Nothing else matters very much. (Of course, cost is a consideration in virtually every purchase decision, but a strategy based on cost will likely attract customers who will not be loyal in the long run. Most price brands are unadvertised.)

When Hunt first started selling their tomato "Catsup," the Brand was sold for a few cents less than Heinz "Ketchup."

The advertising for Hunt's Catsup, however, only featured quality and taste. Hunt wanted customers to look for and buy Hunt's for the quality, then they would be pleasantly surprised at the low price.

Back to the pork sausage. People simply do not care if the sausage was made yesterday or last week.

Certainly, if it was made too long ago, people will not buy it. But freshness is usually assumed to be acceptable. Here, freshness is not an important factor when it comes to purchase motivation.

It only makes sense to address those factors in the marketing plan, and the resulting advertising, with which the target group is concerned.

There is a little interest in whether the package has a sell-by date, when it was processed, the delivery method, whether the whole hog was used or if it is just trimmings sausage. Mostly, people want to know if it tastes good and is relatively lean.

Effective advertising will probably tell potential users that the sausage is good, lean sausage that tastes good. The Bob Evans Farms Sausage advertising shown on the next two pages does just that.

The headlines in these print ads address the factors the target group uses to make up their minds which brand of pork sausage they will buy. This is not subtle advertising.

A Simple but Important Point.
The point is simple.

The more precise the listing and rank ordering of the reasons the target group uses for purchase selection, the more powerful the advertising.

This is the single most important piece of information needed to market the Brand or business.

It is the backbone of the marketing plan, and as we have seen, it just may be the headline in the advertising.

It is the responsibility of the account planner to determine this information. The account planner's obligation is to learn everything there is to know about current and potential users of the Brand, including the criteria used to make decisions in the marketplace.

"IF YOU'RE NOT BUYING BOB EVANS SAUSAGE, YOU MIGHT BE GETTING JUST LEFTOVERS."

Some sausage makers don't put the best cuts of pork into their sausage like we do at Bob Evans Farms.

They take the hams, and sell them as ham. They take the loins, and sell them as pork chops. Then they make sausage with what's left over – the pork trimmings.

Well at Bob Evans Farms, we don't settle for just leftovers. In fact, we include all the choice fresh hams and tenderloins in every pound of sausage we make.

That's why Bob Evans Sausage is tastier than a lot of other sausage. And why it cooks up plump and tender every time.

So try Bob Evans Farms Sausage. It's so meaty and delicious, you'll never have leftovers again.

Bob Evans FARMS®

WE DO IT RIGHT. OR WE DON'T DO IT.™

This advertisement was prepared by: **THE MARSCHALK COMPANY, INC.**

"SOME COMPANIES LIMIT THE MEAT IN THEIR SAUSAGE. WE LIMIT THE FAT."

There's a good reason why Bob Evans Farms Sausage won't cook away in your frying pan like some other sausage does.

You see, at Bob Evans Farms, we limit the amount of fat in every ounce of sausage we make. So there's just enough to bring out the farm fresh taste.

That's why Bob Evans Sausage always cooks up so tender and delicious. Not greasy. And why it won't shrink to nothing in your frying pan.

And while some companies don't put the best cuts of pork in their sausage, we include all the choice fresh hams and tenderloins. Not just the trimmings.

So try Bob Evans Sausage. Because while we always limit the fat in our sausage, there's no limit on the taste.

Bob Evans
FARMS®
WE DO IT RIGHT. OR WE DON'T DO IT.®

Consumer Journey:

This is the process involved in deciding to get, shopping for, choosing, and using a product. A consumer journey can help you to understand the process someone who buys, recommends, or prefers your brand will go through. Your understanding of the journey will help you and your team understand how people identify and use the criteria consumers use for purchase motivation. A consumer journey is similar to "A Day in the Life of my Audience," but works harder to understand their motivation than to simply track process.

Unique Characteristics of the Brand.

The Importance of Differentiation.

This last issue is the Brand's point-of-difference.

In order to understand what differentiates the Brand or business in the minds of customers, there must be a solid understanding of the competition.

If the office supply store is, in reality, no store at all but a delivery service run from a small room and a warehouse, then your point-of-difference has to be service. Convenience, if it exists, would relate to the online or phone-based shopping experience.

If you have chosen to differentiate pork sausage by positioning it as the Brand with little waste because it is lean, then the Brand had better be able to deliver on that claim.

Ideally, your point-of-difference is also a motivating factor for making a purchase decision.

In the example of the office supply retailer, you don't want good delivery to set you apart from your competition if your customers judge a large selection of brands to be the primary reason for store selection and judge delivery to be of minor importance.

The USP.

Rosser Reeves, the Ted Bates advertising legend who developed the USP (Unique Selling Proposition), related the story of a couple of guys who came into his office one day to convince him to handle their advertising. They sold chocolate for a living.

He asked if there was something unusual or different about their particular chocolate candy. They said no.

He probed a little, and finally they mentioned that their chocolate had a little candy coating.

He, of course, wanted to know what that did. One said that it prevented the chocolate from melting in your hands.

Rosser Reeves recognized immediately that this was a unique selling proposition; a method of differentiating this candy in the marketplace. M&Ms has used the line ever since.

Most often, the unique characteristics of the Brand work in concert with the factors that motivate purchase behavior. However, sometimes a brand is so unusual that the strategy is simply to communicate that it's different.

V-8 juice is a natural illustration of this point. The product was invented to differentiate the tomato juice category. It is said to be a window within a category.

Maps.

I feel confident that you have read about perceptual maps. They can be a good way to help you understand where consumers place your brand, when compared to competitors in the category. A simple perceptual map might plot price on one axis and quality on the other.

Most of us would judge BMW to be a good quality car, but we would also recognize that it also has a high price. On the other hand, we might also

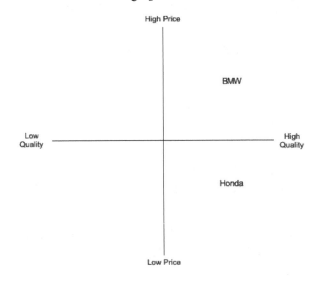

judge Honda to be a high quality car, but with a lower price. With some additional thought, we could plot Ford, Saab, Chevrolet, Dodge, Volvo, Buick, GMC, Citroen, Fiat, Isuzu, Volkswagen, Toyota, Nissan, Jaguar, Yugo, Mercedes, Kia, and many others on our perceptual map.

However, we could also create a map of usage behavior, future growth, styling, fuel economy, or any number of things. We could create a map based on criteria for purchase behavior.

It would be a boon to understanding the pork sausage consumer if we could plot taste versus leanness. This map might help us to understand how well our brand delivers on the criteria consumers use to make a purchase decision. In this case, Bob Evans would hope to be in the Lean & Tasty quadrant.

There is no way to know the quality or make up of sausage from a butcher shop, but it is likely that the butcher uses whatever meat is left over from making pork chops or tenderloin or bacon. The store brand will be made to the specification specified by the retailer. The judgements here are not intended to show superiority for Bob Evans or any other brand, but are used as an illustration that a map can be made with any parameter.

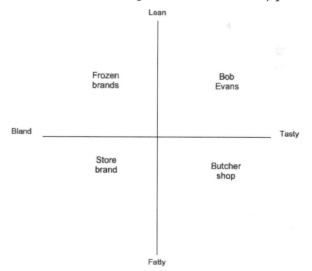

Different categories have different characteristics. Winston Churchill observed that we should never observe the making of sausage or legislation. On the other hand, watching someone make a banana split can be enjoyable.

Preparing the Research Plan.
Initial Information and Hypothesis.

If these three pieces of information are complete, your hypothesis for setting strategy should be clear. Or, at least, your initial hypothesis.

Quite often, the knowledge of what isn't known is needed before it can be determined what is needed. For example, you may need to know the percentage of office supply purchasers who consider service important and what price differential they will pay for good service.

If the information is incomplete or not substantiated, you'll need to conduct the research necessary to completely and as accurately as possible answer the three categories of information—target audience, factors that motivate purchase behavior, and unique characteristics of your brand. You must know these things before you will be able to write strategy.

If the advertising always addresses these three points in its strategic direction, the Brand will be more likely to have advertising that will effectively position the Brand in the marketplace. It's not guaranteed, but it is certainly more likely.

Write down your target audience, factors that motivate purchase behavior, and unique characteristics of it.

Do it before you conduct your research to determine how much you know. Write it in the Worksheet space.

Worksheet for Strategy.

Target Audience: _____

_____

Factors That Motivate Purchase Behavior: _____

_____

Unique Characteristics of the Brand: _____

_____

The research plan's reason for being is to answer these three issues.

Questionnaire Design.

The next step is to design a questionnaire that will allow you to acquire the information you need. See Note B at the end of this chapter for more information on writing a questionnaire.

Here Is How to Prepare the Research Plan Itself.

A. Objectives:

What We Want to Do.

The objectives of the research are synonymous with objectives in general. They tell us what we want to do.

> **For example:**
>
> *To gather information relating to how consumers make purchase decisions in the yogurt category.*
>
> *To isolate those characteristics of the Brand that are judged to be the most compelling when switching brands.*
>
> Research objectives can also be used to simply reinforce the overall marketing objectives:
>
> *To gain information that will aid the Brand to achieve the marketing objective.*
>
> These objectives are less specific, and as a result, less desirable.
>
> The more specific the research objectives can be, the easier it will be to implement the research and learn what you need to know.

B. Strategies:

Definitions.

Research Strategy defines how you will acquire the information. That means specifically the kind of research you'll need to fulfill the objective—but not how it's constructed (that is Method).

Talk to Your Target.

In order to determine how consumers make purchase decisions in the yogurt category, it might be necessary to first talk with them in a focused discussion group environment (these are also known as group sessions or "focus groups"), but the same basic information can be gained in one-on-one interviews.

Both of these methods are qualitative in nature.

> *To gain initial input via two focused group sessions among key purchasing agents of yogurt.*

or...

> *To gain initial information through one-on-one interviews with the*

Target Audience. This information will be used to provide background knowledge for a quantitative study.

In situations where little historical research is available, a good way to begin is to get a solid grasp of the way consumers think about the Brand and the category in some type of qualitative research, then substantiate your hypotheses through quantitative research.

The key to good qualitative research is the people to whom you talk.

Group Sessions vs. One-on-One.

Small businesses and college students in Campaigns classes will probably find group sessions too expensive. This is not necessarily a bad thing.

If you want to find out how women think about yogurt, hang out in the dairy aisle of the grocery store.

When someone picks up a package of Dannon Fruit-on-the-Bottom Yogurt, ask why. They might be taken aback, but you'll get the information you want. After you've talked to eight or ten people you'll start to get an idea of the criteria motivating purchase behavior in the yogurt category.

Be sure to talk to people who buy Yoplait and store brands, so you start to develop a complete understanding of the category. It's virtually certain the information you glean in this research will not be as sacrosanct as that from a focused group session. It will, however, be less expensive.

Quantitative and Qualitative.

The quantitative research will include questions to allow you to understand the factors motivating purchase behavior, usage patterns, and attitudes of both the category and the Brand, and their respective advertising, along with a host of other information.

The qualitative research will give you positive reinforcement that what you intend to do is correct. It's a way to gain additional insight into problems without total knowledge of the questions that should be asked.

It's a method of gaining consumer input into the problem or question facing the Brand. This may include understanding the target audience, the factors that motivate purchase behavior, and the unique characteristics of the Brand. The results of the qualitative research most often should then be put into a quantitative study—often, some type of survey.

This quantitative research will be the primary information gathering vehicle and will probably provide the basis or rationale for the marketing strategic direction.

C. Method:
How, Where, When, How Many.

Research people often talk about "methodology." That is incorrect. It should just be method. We are not studying different methods, which is what the "ology" means when tacked onto the end of the word method.

The method will be described in this section. It will outline how, where, when, sample size, and any unusual conditions.

Most often, this will be fairly straightforward. Method is the "nuts and bolts" of doing it.

It's important to point out anything that's not normally accepted. For example, a typical Method section might read:

The research was conducted using face-to-face interviews with respondents who were found using the intercept technique in shopping malls and business districts.

The research was conducted during the first two weekends in October.

A total of 532 interviews were completed. The research was verified using a random sample of respondents from the telephone book, using a table of random numbers to first determine the page number and a second table of random numbers to identify the phone number and find the respondent. Fifty interviews were conducted in this fashion in order to verify the intercepts.

This allows the reader to make a judgment concerning the validity of the study.

D. Summary of Findings:
Show the Most Significant Learning First.

The results of the research are shown here. The information should be rank ordered to show the most significant learning first.

Quite often, these findings are numbered with the most important of the findings or results being number one. Each finding should be a few sentences in length so it is clear to the reader what was learned.

The answers to the questions should be tabulated. That is the price of entry, but it is important that you go beyond a basic tabulation of the questions. Findings should exhibit key learning. If you were doing a survey on computer usage and one of the questions related to how respondents use their computers, the tabulations could show that 47% of respondents use their computers for personal usage. A bigger finding might be:

> Over half of all respondents use personal computers at home for business.

Inexperienced researchers are often guilty of not recognizing the key findings. They overlook something that may appear obvious to them, but has not been substantiated in the past.

Additional Information.
The questionnaire should be attached as an exhibit or an appendix, usually with the number of responses filled in the blank spaces.

This exhibit is to be used only if the reader (management) wants more information. The most important information is shown here in the written portion of the document. (See Note B for more information.)

For more information, please also read:

1. Lisa Fortini-Campbell. *Hitting the Sweet Spot*. (Chicago: The Copy Workshop, 1991).
   Chapters 10, 11, and 12 will prove useful to you as you write the research segment of this planning document.
2. Al Ries and Jack Trout. *Positioning: The Battle for Your Mind*. (New York: McGraw-Hill, 1986).
   The first nine chapters relate to this discussion on research.
3. Jon Steel. *Truth, Lies & Advertising: The Art of Account Planning*. (AdWeek Books, 1998).
4. Jack B. Haskins and Alice Kendrick. *Successful Advertising*

Research Methods. (Chicago: NTC Business Books, 1993). This book may be hard to find, but has useful information.

5. Hart Weichselbaum, ed. *Readings in Account Planning.* (Chicago: The Copy Workshop, 2008), 119.
Section III, Tools, may be useful. Each chapter covers an important aspect of research.

6. Jeffrey Durgee. *Creative Insight, The Researcher's Art: Finding Hidden Needs for New Products and New Brand Positionings.* (Chicago: The Copy Workshop, 2005).
This advanced research book can be particularly useful if responses and motivations are deeper and more complex.

7. Don E. Schultz and Beth E. Barnes. *Strategic Advertising Campaigns.* 5th ed. (McGraw-Hill, 1999).
Chapter Four relates to this chapter on research.

Interviewing

First you have to learn to think like a consumer.
—Lisa Fortini-Campbell

Introduction.

The Benefit to You.

Asking questions directly of potential users or buyers of your Brand is a luxury most professionals ignore or cannot afford. If you choose to do interviewing yourself, you will benefit greatly from the experience.

You will learn more than if you simply read the summary of the results from research someone else conducted. And you will gain new respect for those people who are hired to do the interviewing.

Finally, you will generate useful results for your campaign—insights that will become the foundation of your marketing strategic direction.

Marketing directors for many small businesses have told me that their primary method of market research is to talk to customers.

The MarCom director for a key telecommunications company told me that she often goes into a store and just talks to customers standing in line. The PR director for a major Southwest art museum often spends time in the lobby just talking to people who have come to view the art. The list could go on… presidents of banks, etc. McDonald's sends their management to Hamburger U so they not only learn operations, but also develop the ability to talk to employees and customers.

Interviewing is an integral part of the research process. It is vitally important that you do it well.

The Importance of Good Interviewing.

Poor interviewing can destroy all the careful work that has been done up to this point.

Care was taken to make judgments concerning the factors that motivate purchase behavior among a difficult target group, and that judgment was used to write a questionnaire. You pre-tested the questionnaire and found it to be solid, and it seemed to get the information you wanted from the research.

Gaining Insight.

This is the time to gain significant insight into your target audience. To do that you can't just stop some passerby and ask him or her to complete a questionnaire. Interview them. Look them in the eye. Ask questions that are not on the questionnaire. Use some judgment as you are working your way through the questions.

If a respondent gives you a reason why they buy that Brand, probe to learn more. Ask them if there are any other reasons. Then ask it again. Keep asking until the respondent has no more answers. Then go to the next question—ask why. Learn to be a two-year old. Ask why over and over again.

Keep probing until you have a total understanding of what each person uses to make up his or her mind about the category and the Brand.

Be Thorough.

You must interview the respondents thoroughly to get the information. Go beyond what is on the questionnaire. Learn. Put yourself in their place and ask questions until you understand how they think.

Probe.

When the interviewers fail to probe sufficiently, or are careless in stratifying the sample, or are lazy and skip questions when it's difficult to get the information—the quality of the research goes down.

Control.

Never let your respondents fill out the questionnaires by themselves unsupervised. If you let them do it while unsupervised, you will dramatically decrease the utility of the information.

Do the interviewing yourself. You should also experience what it's like to fill out your own questionnaire.

Advice for Student Groups.

Everyone Should Do Some Interviewing.

If you are a student group, make certain that every member of your group completes some interviewing. You will learn as much from looking people in the eye and reading their body language as you will from what they say.

Be sure to write notes on the back of each questionnaire about that interview. Then type out a few paragraphs (or pages if you want) about what you learned from the respondents at the end of each interviewing session. These notes and information will help you learn to think like the consumer.

Advice for Entrepreneurs.

Don't Just Sell—Learn.

If you're an entrepreneur, you can learn a great deal by talking with your customers—or potential customers.

Learn from them. Don't just try to sell to them. Try to get to know them, and understand how your product or service fits into their lives.

Harry was a client of mine many years ago. He once told me that focus groups were a lazy man's way to get information.

He told me this as we were trying to introduce Ortega's line of Taco products. He explained that if we would just stop by the grocery store on our way home from work every day and talk with people who were buying or were about to buy Mexican food, we would learn a great deal. I did just that.

The women I talked with might have thought I was a little strange, but after a short period we knew a great deal about why people bought tacos, who they were, how they were a bit different from other consumers, as well as virtually anything else we wanted to know.

This same concept can work for you.

Get Out of Your Office.

Get out of your office and away from your side of the desk or the counter. Try to really get to know the people who just might make your business prosper.

And, if you sell a food product for a living, "learn to hang out in grocery stores." Thanks, Harry.

The Questionnaire

*If I'd asked my customers what they wanted,
they would have said a faster horse.*
—Henry Ford

How to Get the Most Out of Yours.

The Face-to-Face Advantage.

As an entrepreneur or a student in an Advertising Campaigns class, you have the luxury of being able to conduct your interviewing face-to-face.

You may not judge this to be that much of a benefit, but there's a great advantage in being able to see your respondents' faces. You'll learn as much from what you see as you will from what they say.

Once your business grows, you'll start hiring more people to work for you. After you graduate, the market researchers do most of the work—you'll only see reports. It's not as good.

You'll have to rely on the numbers to tell you what people think. That's okay, and you should learn to understand what the numbers tell you, but you learn something different when you look into peoples' faces.

Learn to read body language. Pay attention to what they're saying between the questions. Learn to understand what they're *not* saying.

What you learn from the way people talk is quite often just as important as what they say.

All this listening and watching will help you understand the users, both current and potential, of the category and Brand.

The One-Page Advantage.

The questionnaire itself should be short and to the point.

Get the questionnaire onto one piece of paper.

Get it on one side of that piece of paper, if you can, even if you have to go to legal size.

Each time you write a question, ask yourself, "What will I do with this information?" If you don't know the answer, there's a good chance you should cut the question.

Direct Questions. Direct Answers.

Don't be afraid to ask what criteria people use to make a decision in the category. If it's clear and obvious, you've learned something. If it's not clear and obvious, you've still learned something.

The single mistake most often made by students is that they don't learn the most important reason why people choose a brand. They try to ask the question in a convoluted way that doesn't get the information.

Don't be reluctant to just ask the question in a straightforward manner. "How do you decide which brand you'll buy in this category?"

Do-It-Yourself.

The next mistake most often made is that students want to have respondents fill out the questionnaire by themselves. Wrong. Wrong. Wrong. And wrong. In that order. Never allow respondents to do that.

Sometimes there is no choice, but as the previous note indicated, this can often dramatically decrease the utility of the information you collect.

Imagine every possible way a question can be answered and then decide if you will get the information you want from that question. Then…

Pre-Test.

Be sure to pre-test your questionnaire.

Go to six or eight respondents and administer the questionnaire. Make sure it flows well. Make sure you are getting the answers you need. Ask the Right People.

Finally, when you actually start interviewing people, make sure they are members of the target group or the user base.

One semester I taught advertising campaigns, and Nutri-System, the weight-loss centers, was the client.

Students were not getting the kind of answers that seemed correct.

I finally discovered they were interviewing other students—skinny ones, at that. The research was a waste because those people didn't understand what it's like to want to lose weight.

Have Some Fun.

I would expect every entrepreneur and every member of a student team to interview at least fifty members of the user base.

This will take more than an hour or two, so I hope you make it fun.

I've found that business people who truly like their customers tend to do better and enjoy their jobs more.

I've also found that students who enjoy their work get better grades.

Store checks

What you show is more important than what you say.
— David Ogilvy

If it isn't in the store, it is hard for consumers to find it.

So go to the supermarket and find out what brands are available. I created the exhibit at the end of this section by going to supermarkets and looking for pasta brands. I chose Barilla as an example for this book.

You should do the same. If your brand is sold at retail, this is an easy way to see who the competitors are. You should record both facings and price.

If you are an advertising student and you are interviewing for a job on General Mills at DDB in Chicago, you might want to go to a supermarket in advance of the interview and do some store checks. If you walk into the interview with a chart similar to the one that follows, with information on cake mixes, you will have separated yourself from the other fifteen people who want the same job. And, it is just not that difficult.

If you are working on a brand, store checks are one of the easiest ways to learn about the brand. For a start, you might want to talk to the person stocking the shelves.

I was once doing store checks in Baltimore for ground turkey. I'd just come from suburban stores where ground turkey was prevalent. Then I went into a city supermarket geared to upscale young professionals. I was astounded. There was not only ground turkey in the regular refrigerated meat cases, there was also a six foot refrigerated case in front. It was full of ground turkey.

I found the man stocking the meat cases and asked him if this was a week's supply. He laughed and told me he would fill it again before the end of the day. He told me quite a bit about the kind of people who bought ground turkey.

Lisa Fortini-Campbell would have called him a "consumer detective."

Store checks are a great way to get started.

Barilla Store Checks

Pasta:

	Oklahoma			Dallas		Wichita	
	Albertsons	WalMart	Target	Kroger	Tom Thumb	Homeland	Dillions
Classic collection							
– Angel Hair	1 1.19	2 .86	1 .87	1 1.19	2 1.49	1 1.32	1 1.35
– Farfalle	2 1.19	3 .86	3 .87	4 1.19	3 1.49	1 1.32	3 1.35
– Fettuccine	1 1.19	2 .86	1 .87	1 1.19	1 1.49	1 1.32	1 1.35
– Gemelli	--	--	--	--	--	--	--
– Linguine	1 1.19	1 .86	1 .86	1 1.19	3 1.49	2 1.32	4 1.35
– Mostaccioli	2 1.19	--	2 .87	--	4 1.49	1 1.32	2 1.35
– Penne	2 1.19	2 .86	4 .87	6 1.19	3 1.49	2 1.32	2 1.35
– Rigatoni	2 1.19	--	1 .87	3 1.19	3 1.49	--	--
– Mezzi Rigatoni	--	--	--	--	--	--	--
– Spaghetti, one lb	1 1.19	3 .86	1 .87	1 1.19	2 1.49	--	1 1.35
– two lb	--	--	--	--	2 2.19	--	--
– Thick Spaghetti	--	1 .86	--	--	--	--	--
– Thin Spaghetti	1 1.19	2 .86	--	1 1.19	2 1.49	1 1.32	3 1.35
– Ziti	--	--	--	--	--	--	--
Mini Classics							
– Elbows, one lb	--	3 .86	2 .87	--	4 1.49	--	--
– two lb	--	2 1.50	2 1.52	--	--	--	--
– Fiori	--	--	2 .87	--	4 1.49	--	--
– Medium shells	2 1.59	3 .86	3 .87	--	3 1.49	--	--
– Mini Penne	1 1.19	3 .86	2 .87	--	3 1.49	--	--
– Pipette	--	--	2 .87	--	--	--	--
– Tubini	--	--	--	--	--	--	--
Salad Classics							
– Large shells	2 1.19	3 .86	3 .87	3 1.19	3 1.49	2 1.32	3 1.35
– Rotini	--	--	--	--	--	--	--
– Tri-color Fiori	1 1.19	2 .86	2 .87	--	4 1.49	2 1.32	2 1.35
– Tri-color Rotini	--	--	--	--	--	--	--
Soup collection:							
– Ditalini	--	--	--	--	--	--	--
– Orzo	--	--	2 .87	--	2 1.49	--	--
– Pastina	--	--	--	--	--	--	--

Barilla Page 2	Oklahoma			Dallas		Wichita	
	Albertsons	WalMart	Target	Kroger	Tom Thumb	Homeland	Dillons
Speciality collection:							
– Bucatini Rigati	–	–	2 .87	–	4 1.49	–	–
– Campanelle	–	–	–	–	–	–	–
– Cellentani	–	–	–	–	–	–	–
– Castellane	–	–	–	–	–	–	–
– Fettuccine Rigate	–	–	–	1 1.19	–	–	–
– Linguine Fini	–	–	–	–	–	–	1 1.35
– Rigati	–	–	–	–	–	–	–
– Spaghetti Rigati	1 1.19	1 .86	1 .87	–	1 1.49	–	–
Baking Collection:							
– Jumbo Shells	–	1 .98	3 .99	1 1.19	1 1.69	–	–
– Lasagne Oven-Ready	1 1.59	1 1.04	3 .99	–	2 1.69	2 1.79	1 1.65
– Manicotti	–	2 .98	4 .99	–	1 1.69	–	1 1.65
– Lasagne	1 1.59	2 1.01	2 .99	2 1.59	1 1.69	–	–
Sauces:							
Traditional red sauces							
– Garden Vegetable	–	–	–	2 2.69	–	–	–
– Green & Black Olive Sauce	–	–	–	3 2.69	–	–	–
– Italian Baking Sauce	–	–	–	–	–	–	–
– Italian Cheese Sauce	–	–	–	–	–	–	–
– Marinara Sauce	–	4 1.88	–	3 2.69	4 2.99	–	3 2.89
– Mushroom & Garlic Sauce	–	4 1.88	–	4 2.69	4 2.99	–	3 2.89
– Roasted Garlic & Onion Sau	–	–	–	–	–	–	3 2.89
– Spicy Pepper Sauce	–	–	–	3 2.69	–	–	–
– Sweet Pepper & Garlic Sau	–	–	–	2 2.69	–	–	–
– Tomato & Basil Sauce	–	4 1.88	–	–	4 2.99	–	–
Restaurant creations sauces							
– Suga Alla Genovese	–	–	–	–	–	–	–
– Suga alla Napoletana	–	–	–	–	–	–	–
– Sugo alla Romana	–	–	–	–	–	–	–
Filled Pasta:							
Tortelloni							
– Cheese & Garlic	–	–	2 2.99	–	–	–	–
– Porcini Mushroom	–	–	–	–	–	–	–

Barilla
Page 3

	Oklahoma			Dallas		Wichita	
	Albertsons	WalMart	Target	Kroger	Tom Thumb	Homeland	Dillons
Filled Pasta (cont): Tortelloni							
– Ricotta & Spinach							
• 8 ounce	--	2 2.58	2 2.99	2 3.39	2 3.39	--	2 3.69
• 13 ounce	--	2 2.58	--	--	--	--	--
Tortellini							
– Cheese & Spinach							
• 8 ounce	--	--		2 3.39	2 3.39	--	2 3.69
• 13 ounce	--	--	2 3.99	--	--	--	--
– Three Cheese Tortellini							
• 8 ounce	--	2 2.58	2 2.99	--	--	--	--
• 13 ounce	--	2 3.48	2 3.99	--	--	--	--
Barilla Plus:							
Traditional							
– Penne	--	3 1.42	2 1.69	1 1.99	4 1.99	--	2 1.99
– Rotini	--	3 1.42	2 1.69	1 1.99	4 1.99	--	2 1.99
– Elbows	--	3 1.42	2 1.69	1 1.99	4 1.99	--	3 1.99
– Spaghetti	1 1.99	1 1.42	1 1.69	1 1.99	2 1.99	--	--
– Thin Spaghetti	1 1.99	1 1.42	1 1.69	1 1.99	2 1.99	--	2 1.99
– Angel Hair	--	1 1.42	1 1.69	1 1.99	2 1.99	--	1 1.99

Competitors:

Oklahoma: Albertson's: American Beauty, Our Best, DeCecco, Coppula, Healthy Harvest (Ronzoni), Skinner, Albertson's, Anna
Walmart: DaVinci, Skinner, Country Pasta, Ronzoni, Heartland, American Beauty, Giulia, Great Value, Q&Q
Target: Skinner, American Beauty, Archer Farms (organic), Hodgson Mill, Ronzoni, Marekt Pantry

Texas: Kroger: Skinner, Kroger, DaVinci, Ravarino & Freschi, Healthy Harvest (Ronzoni), DreamFields, Hodgson Mill, F.M.V.
Whole Foods: Ronzoni, DeCecco, DeBoles, Vita Spert, Quinod, Hodgson Mill, Montebello, Rao's, DaVinci, Edwardo's
Tom Thumb: Safeway, Skinner, Ravarino & Freschi, Organics, Ronzoni, DeBoles, DreamFields

Kansas: Dillon's: Price Selection, Hodgson Mill, Healthy Harvest (Ronzoni), FMV, Martha Gooch, Kroger, American Beauty, Golden Grain, Dreamfields
Homeland: DaVinci, American Beauty, Healthy Harvest (Ronzoni), Best Choice, Hodgson Mill, Always Save, Heartland, Martha Gooch

Jim Avery
November 2009

Problems & Opportunities

If you want the rainbow, you gotta put up with the rain.
—Dolly Parton

Introduction.

A Result of Knowledge Gained...

This section of the marketing document is a summation of the problems and the opportunities. These will come out of the knowledge gained from the Situation Analysis and from the research that has been conducted.

Problems and Opportunities should be written to give direction to the marketing objectives.

An Example.

When my son was born, my sister called to ask if I knew the objective for raising children. I said I had not really thought about it, but she pointed out that there are some significant problems with raising children.

In the beginning you have to do everything for them. After that, they are messy, noisy, and generally out of control. She pointed out that, as a business person, I understood Odiorne's *Management by Objectives,* and that clearly raising children would be easier to accomplish if I had a solid grasp of the objectives.

Finally, she explained that the objective in the first two years is to teach them to walk and talk, and then for the next sixteen years the objective is to teach them to sit down and shut up.

This objective could never have been established if an understanding of the problem had not been determined in advance. My sister could not have come up with this objective if she had not, in her own way, first completed the Situation Analysis, completed the Research, and then defined the Problems and Opportunities.

Understanding Problems.

Problems are derived from situations of weakness and the inverse—competitive strengths.

It is insufficient to tell the reader of the planning document that sales are weak and, therefore, there is an opportunity for advertising.

You need to dig deeper, because, in a very real sense, marketing and marketing communications are about solving problems. But, before you can solve them, you have to learn what they are. We'll say this more than once: don't solve the wrong problem.

And now you are beginning to understand why there may be a great deal of research completed in order to determine precisely what the problems are.

Examples: Duds and Suds.
When Milk Duds did their research, according to Ries & Trout, they found a significant problem in the candy bar category was that candy bars did not last very long. This certainly was not true of Milk Duds. They found a category problem that the Brand could easily address.

The opportunity related to this problem was to take advantage of the desire for longer-lasting candy by advertising the fact that Milk Duds last a long time. In fact, it is impossible to eat Milk Duds quickly.

In the early 1970s, Ivory had been losing sales for a long time. To simply say the problem was that Ivory was losing sales is not only sophomoric, it really doesn't get to the heart of the problem.

Determining that Ivory washes quite well in soft water but rinses poorly in hard water identifies at least one of the problems. But it's not the only problem.

Another problem, which might not have appeared to be a problem until examined, was that Ivory was perceived as either a complexion soap or a soap for babies. The volume opportunity is not with babies'-bottoms positioning.

The volume opportunity is in the shower—not only because people use more soap in the shower, but because the water is continually beating down on the bar of soap melting it away.

In each case, identifying a meaningful problem offers the beginnings of a strategic direction.

Identifying Opportunities.
Once the problem has been identified, then the opportunities and possibilities can be thought through.

Opportunity: Ivory Soap.

The account person who wrote the recommendation to show Ivory Bar Soap in the shower in their advertising deserves a raise. This is where the volume opportunity is in the bar soap business.

For years, Ivory was showing ladies' faces and babies' bottoms. But some account-type recognized a significant opportunity for Ivory, probably through a detailed business analysis, to determine how the category was used.

A Common Mistake.

The most common error people make at this stage is writing problems and opportunities that can be solved by the advertising creative strategy they want to recommend.

This is kind of like telling Dad you want to borrow the car so you can run an errand for him at the hardware store while you are really trying to impress your friends. Your dad may let you get away with it. The marketplace will not.

This kind of problem description is usually not well thought out and only serves to illustrate what the writers really wanted to do before they did any homework. Again, you may get away with it in the short term. But in the long term, you will be found out.

You need to work to determine the real problems in the category or with the Brand. Then you need to write them in such a way that the reader understands that you really know the business. Then you will need to really solve the problem.

This section of your Marketing Plan is one that can be used to convince the reader/client that you have invested considerable work in it and that you really do know what is going on and what will work.

Getting to the Heart of the Issue.

Writing the problems and their matching opportunities is, at best, difficult. It requires a mind that wants to get to the heart of the issue.

The "Onion Theory" of problem-solving requires us to peel back all the layers of useless information. To do this and to identify what will really push the business ahead is an incredible challenge.

Doing it successfully is at the heart of a successful marketing plan.

As a friend observes, "many things are true." Throughout this book, you will see us work to identify things that will make a difference.

Your business analysis must include analyses of shipments and sales, media spending, competitive strategy, promotion dollars, promotion events, public opinion, attitudes, awareness, usage behavior, and on and on and on. And, as noted, many things are true.

The purpose for this is to remind you that, at first you need to recognize all the external factors that might normally be glossed over.

Then you have to identify the factors that are truly meaningful.

For example: Ivory sells more in soft water areas, Midas sells better in areas that use salt on the highways, and pork sausage does not sell well in predominantly Jewish neighborhoods.

Each is a meaningful problem related to the brand or product category.

All these things must come out of your Situation Analysis and your study of the category through secondary and then primary research.

Archway Cookies sold better to grandmas and grandpas than to moms and dads. More bath oil is sold for therapeutic reasons than for hygienic reasons. People don't want credit cards for credit; convenience is the primary reason to get plastic for your wallet.

You need to translate the information into problems and opportunities that are real and can be implemented.

An A-1 Example.

The problem with A-1 Steak Sauce was not one of taste. The problem was simply that people could not remember to put it on the table.

Almost every household had a bottle… somewhere. Usually, it was in the cupboard—not easily seen.

In this case, a key problem was simple—get the bottle out where people would see it on a regular basis, and they will be more likely to use it. And, eventually, they'll have to buy another bottle.

What was the related opportunity? Write the word "Refrigerate" on the package. That put the bottle where it was more easily seen and accessible, probably on the door of the refrigerator, and everyone in the family saw it on a regular basis.

Sales went up—what a surprise.

The Problems and Opportunities segment of the marketing plan for A-1 probably looked something like this:

> *Problem: In-home inventory is strong; home usage is sporadic.*

> *Opportunity: Motivate current users to use more A-1 Steak Sauce by finding a way for the user to have visual contact with the bottle immediately prior to key usage times.*

The problem and related opportunity became a lead or advance statement for the marketing objectives—which include advertising, promotion, public relations, and merchandising objectives.

Additional Examples.

The marketing pro who convinced the American Dental Association to agree to the copy on the side of P&G's Crest toothpaste package really understood what would motivate consumers in the toothpaste category.

> *Problem: Since dentists rarely endorse specific brands, concerned consumers have little basis for brand selection.*

> *Opportunity: A form of fluoride that can be used in toothpaste and has been proven to reduce cavities in children.*

> *Opportunity: Secure an endorsement, however qualified, from the American Dental Association (ADA).*

The fluoride formula used by Crest was indeed proven to be helpful in building up stronger tooth enamel, which was thus more resistant to decay. The ADA was willing to acknowledge this.

By the way, one of the key people on that project was John Smale, who went on to become chairman of P&G.

It pays to solve problems.

Competitive Response.

It is important that problems go beyond simply being set-ups for what you want to do in the advertising.

You should also try to think about what your competition will do when you isolate, analyze, and finally solve a significant marketing problem.

Instead of solving the problem, you could end up getting your teeth kicked in.

Anticipating Response.

When Hunt did all that research to find out what the significant problems were in the prepared tomato sauce (ketchup) business, what do you think they discovered?

Right, the stuff doesn't come out of the bottle fast enough—especially when it is a new bottle.

So, some good marketing professional at Hunt-Wesson decided the best thing to do was to make bottles with bigger openings.

> *Problem: Consumers prefer a thick product, but this thickness makes it difficult to remove the product from the bottle.*

> *Opportunity: Increase the size of the bottle's opening so the sauce will come out faster.*

Hunt's Catsup soon had wide mouth bottles, and their advertising showed how quickly it came out and how convenient it was.

Within a few weeks, Heinz had contracted for the use of the Carly Simon song "Anticipation" and used it as the audio track in television advertising that showed people sitting around waiting for the great taste of Heinz.

They communicated the thought that you could not have good taste if it came out of the bottle too fast. This is just one of those things you have to put up with in life. If you want great-tasting ketchup, you are just going to have to wait for it.

When was the last time you saw a wide mouth ketchup bottle?

Now Heinz has a squeeze bottle. This addressed the problem in a new way.

Preferred Format.

When it comes to format, I favor having at least one (maybe more) opportunity for each problem.

I find it helps to list them as separate events rather than as many opportunities that will aid us to solve a plethora of problems.

Another Way. S.W.O.T.

Another way to address problems and opportunities is to conduct a S.W.O.T. analysis. This stands for Strengths, Weaknesses, Opportunities, and Threats.

A S.W.O.T. analysis for Ivory Bar soap might look like this:

Strengths: Mild. Real soap, not petro-chemical, works well in soft water. Inexpensive.

Weaknesses: Rinses poorly in hard water. Old fashioned image.

Opportunities: Hand soap volume is in the shower.

Threats: Competitive brands are already established in the shower and do not "melt" as quickly.

In general, Weaknesses and Threats will be two types of problems.

Weaknesses will refer to deficiencies with the brand or in the category.

Threats will most often be external—a strong competitor or an overall threat to the category. For example, increased concern over obesity and salt consumption can be viewed as a threat across multiple categories.

S.W.O.T. Analysis

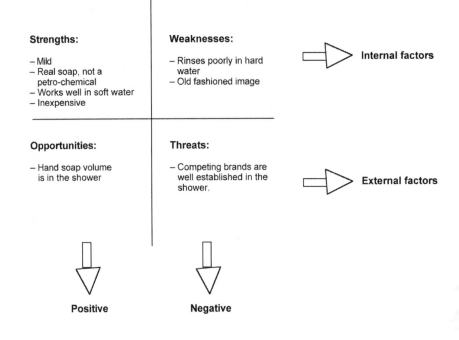

There is a similar relationship with Strengths and Opportunities.

Strengths will tend to be about positives that already exist—either with the brand or the category.

Opportunities will usually demand you at least imply some action.

The S.W.O.T. analysis can give a more complete understanding of the situation.

A Few Words to the Wise.

As we said, "many things are true." It is also true that the world is full of problems and opportunities. If we look hard enough, we can find more weaknesses than can ever be strengthened, more threats—both real and imagined—than can ever be met, and opportunities that, while tantalizing, will depend upon things not possible in the near term. The discovery of an anti-gravity device would most certainly reduce the weight of an automobile and improve mileage dramatically.

There is nothing wrong with a thorough examination of possibilities. However, identifying the most important and most actionable of those possibilities will be key to the success of your marketing plan.

Don't solve the wrong problem.

For more information, please also read:

1. Al Ries and Jack Trout. *Positioning: The Battle for Your Mind.* (New York: McGraw-Hill, 1986).
   Reread this timeless classic for a clear understanding of what you hope to do with this segment of the plan.

2. Scott Cooper and Roman Hiebing. *How to Write a Successful Marketing Plan.* (Lincolnwood, IL: NTC Business Books, 1999). Chapter Three discusses this topic.

3. George S. Odiorne. *Management Decisions by Objectives.* (Englewood Cliffs, NJ: Prentice-Hall, 1969).
   Odiorne's discussion on the purpose for setting objectives will help you write the Problems and Opportunities segment.

Marketing Objective

Objectives are not fate; they are direction.
—Peter Drucker

Introduction.

A Marketing Objective Is Most Often a Sales Number.

A marketing objective is quantifiable. Most of the time, that means it is a sales number. Sometimes it doesn't have to be just a sales number, it could also be a quantifiable objective that addresses awareness, usage, attitudes, etc. But these are not common. After all, real businesses depend on selling products or services.

That said, we must acknowledge that there are some cases when the marketing objective is not a number. However, in our view, this only happens when the people involved don't have the "chutzpah" to do what they know is right. To pick a number and live with it and try to achieve it throughout the year is a difficult taskmaster.

But the work will be better for it.

As Leo Burnett observed, "When you reach for the stars you may not quite get one, but you won't come up with a handful of mud either."

The marketing objective is most often a sales number.

It is a gauge against which progress will be measured.

If you were the Brand Manager on Johnson & Johnson Baby Shampoo, when they were running their adult campaign, you would have been seeing regular increases of 25% to 30% a year.

Sales increases such as this are not common for a mature brand like Johnson & Johnson Baby Shampoo, but they'd recently started to run a campaign that told consumers to try it on their own hair, instead of just using it on their baby's hair.

After all, if it was mild enough for a baby, it certainly wouldn't hurt an adult's hair, either. So, establishing a marketing objective that required sales increases of 25% was reasonable. In fact, it may have been too easy to get the objective.

Fulfilling the objective with very little effort is sometimes called "skating." It is a business situation where you can move ahead without working hard. Do not be seduced. Make the most of every opportunity. Don't be delusional in making your projections, but do be intelligently aggressive.

The purpose for this segment of the marketing planning document is to determine the volume commitment for next year.

This will require the combined talents of an economist, a marketing sage, and a prophet. But, assuming your crystal ball is out for repairs, we will track you through the process.

A. Number:

A Marketing Objective Should Be Measurable.
Remember, the marketing objective is a number.

This is because there must be a method by which you can determine if you have achieved that objective at the end of the year.

If not, then a change in strategy may be in order for the following year.

"SMAC"
Procter & Gamble uses the an acronym SMAC to describe objectives. They should be Specific, Measurable, Achievable, and Compatible (with everything else going on with the Brand at that time).

Examples of good marketing objectives might be:

- To ship 329,500 units in Fiscal Year 2011.
- To increase share of market by +1.9%, from 8.2% to 10.1%.
- To increase top-of-mind awareness by +10%, from 73% to 83%, as evidenced by the 2010 tracking study.

Note that the market share number will have a volume goal that can be extrapolated, and that top-of-mind awareness will most usually correlate with brand preference and sales.

In other words, each contains—or implies—a number.

B. Rationale:

Defend Your Objective.

This segment of the marketing plan is used to defend your quantifiable objectives. These number objectives should be substantiated with more numbers in the Rationale section.

The goal is to make the numbers go beyond believable to the point where the reader believes that you really do have a crystal ball.

For example, in the case of J&J Baby Shampoo, to substantiate an increase in sales of +28% the rationale could include the following: Sales History, Attitudinal Changes, and Marketing Effort.

1. **Sales History:**
    If sales have exceeded +20% for the past three years, show the specific numbers and outline why there has been such a dramatic increase in the past three years.

2. **Attitudinal Changes:**
    Show the numbers indicating that more consumers now think the Brand is good for their own hair.

3. **Marketing Effort:**
    If there is a significant change in the marketing plan for this year, then it should be discussed here.

    For example, if the new strategy is rolling into another third of the country, if the strategy will finally be available for network television, or if a new flag has been prepared for the packaging, then there is a rationale that the increase in sales will be spread over a broader audience.

Defend Your Projections.

It is essential that numbers be used to defend your market projections.

Some students make the mistake of believing that if they write something down it will instantly become believable—just as if they read something in the newspaper, it must be true, because they read it in the newspaper. Wrong.

Your projections must be made believable. The best way to do that is to substantiate them with numbers.

As a classroom teacher, I have become such a fanatic about making sure that students support what they write, that a group of students bought me a rubber stamp with SUPPORT written in 36-point type.

I use it every semester. Thanks.

For more information, please also read:

1. Don E. Schultz and Beth E. Barnes. *Strategic Advertising Campaigns.* 5th ed. (McGraw-Hill, 1999).
   Chapters Four and Six relate to this chapter.

2. George S. Odiorne. *Management Decisions by Objectives.* (Englewood Cliffs, NJ: Prentice-Hall, 1969).
   Odiorne's discussion of objectives and their purpose in marketing will prove valuable to the entire planning document, but will be especially useful here.

3. David A. Aaker, Rajeeve Batra, and John G. Myers. *Advertising Management.* 5th ed. (Upper Saddle River, NJ: Prentice-Hall, 1996).

Marketing Flow Chart

A picture is worth a thousand words.
—Chinese Proverb

Introduction.

Now that you've established your objective, you know what needs to be accomplished during the coming year—or the planning period under consideration.

But the question keeps coming up about what we are really doing here. A flow chart can help.

Understanding the Process.

Putting It in Perspective.

A schematic flow chart may aid you in understanding the process and putting it in perspective.

Page 122 of this text shows an example of a marketing flow chart.

It diagrams the process you will go through in order to market a product or to fulfill a marketing plan.

The "Marketing Molecule."

As I was making the original of this schematic, I had a secretary who was certain it had something to do with chemistry. She insisted on calling it the "Marketing Molecule"—I still use that name.

The marketing flow chart you see here is one that was made for a new food product, so it includes the actual development of the product.

Your flow chart will probably be different.

Decision Points.

The schematic diagram shows the decision-making points, the sources of information needed to make those decisions, and the actions that need to be taken.

You will notice that the flow chart is like a recipe—it calls for specific things to take place at specific points in time.

For Example:

You can tell that pricing decisions need to be made before a budget can be established for the media plan.

You need to establish a creative strategy before you can write advertising copy.

You need to determine how the category is viewed before you can set marketplace positioning for the Brand.

Some Decisions Have Been Made.

In many cases, some of these decisions have already been made. Issues like pricing and distribution are most often taken on by the client, not the advertising agency.

While it is true that a great advertising agency does everything it can to get into every aspect of their clients' businesses, being involved in something like pricing is not common. Don't shy away from these, but they aren't the first issues for advertising people to tackle.

The Importance of Margins.

A good, solid business analysis may reveal a category where margins have eroded to the point where generating a little more margin may allow a significant increase in the advertising.

This will lead to an increase in the share of voice for the Brand. This may increase preference and volume. It is also testable.

On the other hand, you may find a category where the margins are high, leaving a niche large enough to drive a powerful price Brand.

The point—make that molecule fit what you want it to do.

Make Your Own Flow Chart.

The Process the Marketing Document Will Describe.

Study the chart. It will help you understand the process the marketing document will describe.

You may want to make your own marketing flow chart—one that meets the needs of the Brand you are about to market.

Some Approaches.

This schematic was done in a drawing program.

There are also scheduling programs that can help you add another level of organization to this critical process.

You may want to start with chalk and a blackboard or pencil and paper.

If you have a wall or bulletin board, yarn and some 3" x 5" cards or large Post-It® notes, they can help you develop a marketing molecule of your own.

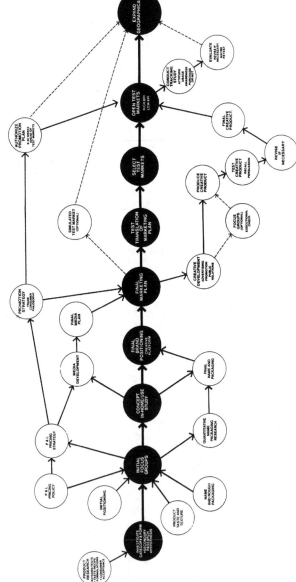

Budget

The budget is the power to choose.
—John F. Kennedy

Trust, but verify.
—Ronald Reagan

Introduction.
Purpose of the Budget Segment.
The purpose for this part of the planning document is two-fold:

1. To provide substantiation for the quantity of money that will be spent during the coming year
2. To outline where the money will be spent

Format Variations.
Some plan outlines call for the Budget to be in the Situation Analysis or in the Marketing Strategy. However, in our view, we will give more importance to the elements within the budget by placing the budget in its own section or chapter.

This makes it easier for the reader to find the budget segment and to understand how and why marketing monies will be allocated.

Occasionally, a marketing plan will have the budget at the end of the plan near evaluation, but here in Chapter Five between the Marketing Objective and the Marketing Strategy seems ideal.

We know what we want to do in the objective, and the budget provides the resources for how we will do it as outlined in the strategy.

Be Prepared to Defend Your Budget.
The budget should be defended in as many ways as possible.

If you're developing a substantiation for the budget in a case study for an Advertising Campaigns class or for a contest like the American Advertising Federation's NSAC, one point of substantiation might be as simple as the fact that the budget was provided in the case. You might find substantiation through your secondary research. But that is just not good enough.

For example, the budget may be a client directive. Clients are often smart, but not always. Ian Batey (author of *Asian Branding*) cites a few mistakes made by smart clients:

- In 1927, H.M. Warner of Warner Brothers said: "Who the hell wants to hear actors talk?"
- In 1943, Thomas Watson, Chairman of IBM, said: "I think there is a world market for maybe five computers."
- In 1962, Decca Records rejected the Beatles, proclaiming: "We don't like their sound, and guitar music is on the way out."
- In 1977, Ken Olson, president, chairman, and founder of Digital Equipment Corp., observed, "There is no reason why anyone would want a computer in their home."
- In 1981, Bill Gates, said: "640K ought to be enough for anybody."

Clearly, relying totally on clients is not a good idea. Though, they are the client, and it is their money. Our point, you need to substantiate the budget. When you are spending money—yours or someone else's—this is always a good idea.

You must be as certain that the quantity of dollars recommended to the client is as correct as is possible.

This is easier said than done. We will suggest a method to support what you are recommending. One other way to be certain that the quantity of dollars is right is through testing (see Chapter Eleven for more detail).

At a major packaged goods company like General Mills or P&G, preparing for a budget meeting is a rite of passage for young advertising people. At most companies, successfully defending your budget will be a critical factor in your success or failure.

Rights, Responsibilities, and Risks.
Key client management has the right to know how and why you developed the number you did. They will want to know the support for what you want to spend.

They have a right to expect a reasonable rate of return on their investment, and you have the responsibility to present a sound, logical plan on why this budget will deliver on that return.

In an advertising class or an AAF/NSAC contest, the penalty is a bad grade or losing at the regional level.

In the real world, the penalty is much more severe.

Getting It Right.

First, you need to generate the numbers so you can use good judgment to determine the right budget. Then, you have to defend those numbers.

Normally, if you can convince a client or boss that your rationale for the initial numbers is correct, they'll buy the whole line of thinking.

The real test, of course, comes when you actually spend the money.

The Need for Test Markets.

Since most clients make the mistake of underspending, it is usually a good idea to recommend a test market to measure the impact of increasing advertising weight by 50% or so.

This should be done in one or two markets—representing at least 1% of the U.S. population.

More detail on this testing can be found in Chapter 11, Test Marketing.

It is likely that we will not have the results of that test market when this section is being written, yet we still have to substantiate the budget.

In addition, one must consider competitive response. Others are also looking at your test market. If what you are about to do could be easily replicated, be prepared to implement quickly if results are good.

Still, if possible, it is better to test dramatic changes in spending or strategy before implementing system wide.

The Straight Line Method.

For a brand that has been around for a few years, the straight line method is the most common. It is easy to understand for those who have not worked with forecasting before.

Quite simply, you project two numbers and then multiply them.

First, project the number of units you believe the brand will sell during the period under consideration—probably next year.

Then, project the advertising to sales ratio (A to S ratio) or the case rate, if it is a packaged goods brand.

Next, multiply the projected number of cases to be sold (as defined by the marketing objective) by the advertising to sales ratio or case rate.

Here's How to Do It, Step-by-Step:
First, Project Units Sold:

To project the number of units you expect the Brand to sell during the year under consideration, you need to have a record of sales for the past three to five years.

One clear way to make the projection is to plot the information on graph paper, with one axis showing sales and the other axis representing time.

Then you can plot sales over time, and it is a simple matter to see where you think sales will go.

We will assume that you have created an outstanding marketing plan for this brand, while a lukewarm or mediocre plan may have been used in the past.

This would indicate that it is likely you will surpass a straight line method of sales projection. On the other hand, if competitive efforts are intense, it will take outstanding effort merely to hold share.

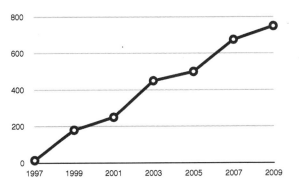

Unit Sales Over Time

It is clear that sales are not exactly in a straight line. Though, the trend is steadily upward.

In 1997 sales were only 15 units while in 1999, 180 units were sold.

In 2001—250 units, in 2005—500 units.

On this basis, we should assume that sales in 2009 would be 750 units because we can show a straight line to project sales in the future.

If we feel that the Plan we are recommending is significantly better than anything that has been used in the past, we might be able to substantiate

775 units or even 800 units to be sold in 2010—and so on. If the competition is strong, category growth is slow, or the Brand's share of voice is relatively small, these factors might make the task a bit tougher. Still, management will expect solid progress.

Determine the Advertising to Sales Ratio:

History and Inertia.

The A to S Ratio will likely remain unchanged.

If the brand spent 5.25% on advertising last year, and the same percentage in the year before that, you will have a hard time defending an Advertising to Sales Ratio of anything other than 5.25%.

The same is true for packaged goods products. If the Brand has been spending $1.00 a case on advertising each of the past five years, it is pretty likely that it will spend $1.00 on advertising for each case sold next year.

If the rate has been changing in recent years, plot the rates on graph paper showing time on one axis and advertising as a percent of sales (or case rate) on the other axis.

After you have a visual representation of the rates over time, you will be able to project the following year.

This may be as simple as continuing a straight line into the future (as we did for the volume projection), but more likely it will require clustering or judgment to forecast the following year's rate.

New Products.

If it is a new product, the forecasting will be a little more difficult.

It may be that you will have to find information that has been written by professionals and published.

For example, when the AAF case study was Saturn, there were a variety of articles published in *Automotive Week, AdWeek,* and *Advertising Age* that addressed volume expectations for Saturn.

Allocate Elements of the Budget.

The Great Allocation Debate.

There has been very little written on the subject of how much to allocate to advertising and how much for promotion or public relations.

For example, when Bud Frankel, of the sales promotion agency Frankel & Co., wrote his book on sales promotion, he spent many pages pointing out how and why dollars allocated to sales promotion will yield great and immediate sales.

Al Ries talks about the benefits of public relations in *The Fall of Advertising and the Rise of PR*, a book he wrote with his daughter Laura.

On the other hand, a book written by David Ogilvy, of the ad agency Ogilvy & Mather, maintained that advertising would not only yield greater sales in the long run, but that the use of sales promotion was generally in poor taste—kind of like being a bait fisherman in the movie *A River Runs Through It* (See the quote at the beginning of Chapter Nine).

All three of these books were written by authors with a vested interest in the allocation of marketing dollars. Proponents of Internet and interactive opportunities, as well as all those who have written books on how direct is the only answer, will surely lend their voices—and books—to the debate.

Strategy, on many levels, is about choice. Once you establish the budget, your allocation of dollars is the next critical task.

As you review the chapters on media planning, public relations, and sales promotion, you will gain additional understanding of what these tools are intended to do.

Quantity and Category.
The marketing budget must break out the quantity of money that will be needed for advertising and for sales promotion. A dollar amount will be needed for each of the following. Some marketing activities, such as events and sponsorships, may kind of slide around or show up in multiple areas. Some promotions receive advertising support. Direct marketing is in the process of migrating to the Internet. These categories are just a basic outline of what's involved in budget allocation. You will have to determine the final categories and allocations. That said, here is a useful list of expense categories.

1. **Advertising**
   a. Media
   b. Production

2. Sales Promotion
   a. Event
   b. Production

3. Public Relations
   a. Legislative action
   b. Publicity
   c. Sponsorships
   d. Production

4. Direct Marketing
   a. Mail
   b. Telemarketing
   c. Miscellaneous Media
   d. Production

5. Event Marketing
   a. Event
   b. Production

6. Miscellaneous...

Of course, agency fees need to be added in.

The Debate Continues...

For years, the key issue has been: how much do you give to advertising and how much to sales promotion. There's no right answer that works in every case.

And with a growing variety of new marketing communication vehicles and programs, things have become even more complicated. Still, you have to decide.

If you're working on a Brand that's used advertising and sales promotion in the past, look at what's been used and what's been successful.

And, of course, we all have informed opinions. Generally, I think too much is spent on sales promotion. By giving your customers, whether they're current or potential, additional value, you're training them to buy only when value is increased through some kind of an incentive.

Think about it. If you're a student at a university, how often do you go to Pizza Hut when you've got a coupon versus how often you go to a competitor when there's a coupon? Or how often do you go to Pizza Hut when you don't have a coupon?

My editor has his own informed opinion. He believes that marketing is too focused on recruiting new customers and not enough on building the "installed base." So he would take marketing dollars and walk up to every current Pizza Hut customer and give them a card that said, "Thank you for being our customer. Bring this card and a friend and we'll pay for half of your pizza." Now it will be time for you to make your decisions.

Most packaged goods companies allocate about half of their budget to sales promotion with the remainder going to advertising.

If you need people to act immediately, you may need to give them a better value, but the cost of motivation may be quite high.

If you can wait a little longer, the cost is lower, and if the decision is made based on the brand rather than the incentive, they'll probably end up being more loyal customers.

Adding the Details.
Clearly, there will be detail given in each element of the marketing plan for each of these entries.

For example, your Media Budget will have specific numbers for each medium, and it will be outlined by quarter, half, and total year. (See Chapter Eight for more detail on what a media budget will entail.) But that doesn't go here. This is to give an idea of how much you will allocate to each medium. Do not reveal media strategy in the budget segment of your plan.

The Production Budget for each element should contain information for print or commercial production, including: talent, prints, shipping, printing, photography, editing, etc. This will be included in the creative segment of the document.

These don't have to be complete working estimates, but the writer of the marketing document should recognize the need for the various elements of the budget and provide a budget number that includes all the required monies.

You must make good decisions and good choices. Easier said than done.

For more information, please also read:

1. Don E. Schultz and Beth E. Barnes. *Strategic Advertising Campaigns.* 5th ed. (McGraw-Hill, 1999).
   Chapters Four and Eight relate to this chapter.

2. Jack Z. Sissors and Roger Baron. *Advertising Media Planning.* 6th ed. (Chicago: NTC Business Books, 2002).
   Chapter Sixteen will provide more insight into the budgeting process as outlined in this chapter.

3. David A. Aaker, Rajeeve Batra, and John G. Myers. *Advertising Management.* 5th ed. (Upper Saddle River, NJ: Prentice-Hall, 1996).
   Chapter Sixteen provides some additional information that will supplement Schultz's discussion of budget setting.

4. John Phillip Jones. *How Much is Enough?/When Ads Work.* (Lexington Books, 1992/1995).
   In these two books, this respected professor, a former JWT/London advertising executive, addresses, among other things, the relative performance of advertising and sales promotion.

5. Al Ries and Laura Ries. *The Fall of Advertising and the Rise of PR.* (Collins Business Books, 2002).

Marketing Strategy

Return on ideas.
—Written on the wall at Draft/FCB in Hong Kong

All these players have all the strategies.
The bottom line is that you just have to play a better game.
—Venus Williams on Wimbledon

Introduction.

How You Intend to Achieve the Objective.

The marketing strategy is how you intend to achieve, or deliver, the marketing objective. This section is dedicated to marketing strategy.

Remember, the marketing objective is a number. The objective is what you want to do; a strategy is how you're going to do it.

So, marketing strategy is how the Brand will sell enough cases to finally deliver the objective, or "make your number."

Account Management.

Developing and then executing marketing strategy is the essence of an account manager's career. It is the same for someone in brand management on the client side. Both jobs involve developing and executing strategies.

Sometimes students and professionals in smaller markets have the idea that an account executive is the liaison with the client—that means they take work developed by other people at the agency and deliver it to the client. It is true that, in some agencies where client control of strategy is no longer shared, the job has, sad to say, been diminished. But this is not how it should be. Becoming a well-dressed messenger is neither the goal nor the account executive's reason for being. That's the job of guys on bicycles who risk their lives in midtown traffic.

Account people should be responsible for strategy development.

The account manager should be excited about this part of the plan.

Account Planning.

Account planners are somewhat different. They are primarily responsible for strategic development. Sometimes these people are called strategic planners. An account planner is half researcher and half account manager.

It's the account planner's responsibility to represent the consumer in any and all conversations concerning the development of marketing strategy. Lisa Fortini-Campbell's book, *Hitting the Sweet Spot,* is a great source of information on this subject.

It is the goal of the account planner to understand how the consumer uses and thinks about the product and then translate those insights in such a way as to inspire those developing creative messages.

When Goodby & Silverstein developed a campaign for Sega, the planners spent weeks playing video games with kids ten to fifteen years old.

They spent time in their homes, in basement recreation rooms, in video arcades, at shopping malls, and anywhere else these kids would talk in order to better understand the intersection between users and the Brand. The planner is looking for simple human truths, or consumer insights. Simple. Human. Truths.

The popular "Got Milk" campaign came from "deprivation" research. The agency asked consumers to go without milk for a week. The account planner then talked to these deprived milk users and developed deeper insight into the importance of milk to the average consumer.

The result was a "deprivation strategy" and breakthrough advertising.

If your group does not have an account planner, consider changing things around so that you can have someone whose job is account planning—understanding the consumer—as part of your team.

Second best is to make someone pull double duty in order to fill this position. If not, the job will fall squarely on the shoulders of the account manager, copywriter, and researcher.

The goal is to create a stronger marketing strategy—marketing strategy that will be strong enough to deliver the marketing objective.

The Five Ps.

The marketing strategy is many strategies. It should be divided into a section for each of the five Ps—promotion, product, price, place (distribution), and people.

The first of these will receive the most attention because it addresses the marketing plan. Promotion (with a capital "P") includes advertising, sales promotion, merchandising, public relations, and any other form of marketing communications appropriate for your particular needs ... both above- and below-the-line.

In most cases, for student work, the issues of product, price, place (distribution), and people can be handled briefly.

Entrepreneurs will labor for years on these elements.

Strategy as Objective.

A marketing strategy is, in its own way, a specific discipline objective. That means the precise language found in Chapter Seven for a creative objective will be found in this section as a marketing strategy. For example, the marketing strategy might be:

To establish Simplicity Patterns as the quick and easy way for the target audience to obtain the clothes they want.

Now, turn to the example in Note A following Chapter Seven and compare the creative objective that is listed there with this marketing strategy.

The Creative Objective is:

To establish Simplicity Patterns as the quick and easy way for the target audience to obtain the clothes they want.

You see precisely the same language is used in both cases.

The Marketing Strategy for Creative Is the Creative Objective.
There is a reason for this. Remember: an objective is what you want to do, and a strategy is how you will do it.

The marketing objective is a number. The marketing strategy is how you will fulfill that number.

But on the next level, the marketing strategy becomes the objective—what you want to accomplish in creative or media or any other specific marketing discipline. Take a look at the diagram below.

Then the creative strategy, which you will develop, will tell management how you plan to accomplish the creative objective. The creative strategy becomes a subset of marketing strategy—same with media. The creative strategy part of your marketing strategy becomes the creative objective.

One More Example.

This time, suppose that we have been asked to market Levi's Dockers. We may write our marketing strategy, under Promotion, as follows:

To deliver a target audience of men 35 and older with special attention given to those with higher income and education.

Turn this time to the objectives in Chapter Eight on Media, where you will find the objectives for a media plan (page 189).

Look at the first example. It uses exactly the same language as does this marketing strategy. The media strategy then becomes a subset of the marketing strategy, and, in turn, becomes the media objective.

This chart explains it clearly.

Here is how to prepare this segment of the Marketing Planning document.

A. Promotion:

This is Promotion with a capital "P." It is not to be confused with sales promotion.

At Least Two Segments—Probably More.

The promotion part of the marketing strategy will be divided into at least two major segments—Above and below the line or if you like advertising and all the other disciplines including sales promotion. In this era of increased costs and reduced efficiency it is more likely to have multiple segments.

We will discuss six here and give suggestions for more.

Here is a quick summary of these segments:

- **Advertising** is intended to work over the long run. Advertising provides an intangible, logical, or emotional reason to buy without the immediate discount or reward—other than the benefits offered by the brand itself.
- **Sales promotion** uses a tangible motivation to buy in the near future—a bribe if you will, though *incentive* is a more commonly used word.
- **Public relations** seeks to build positive relations with specific groups of people, most of whom will be stakeholders of the brand—employees, consumers, stockholders, legislators, etc.
- **Direct marketing** works to build a relationship with the consumer by communicating directly with him or her instead of going through a retailer. If you already have a customer base, and you have their names and addresses, or you have a very narrow target audience, some sort of direct-marketing program may be appropriate.
- **Viral marketing** involves getting your customers to recommend your brand. It can be word of mouth or even better, eWOM. Sometimes this is called C2C.
- **Event marketing** involves relationships with customers based on a specific event, usually sporting or cultural in nature. Students are often the target of this type of marketing, from Orientation Week and sporting events all the way to Spring Break.

- **Miscellaneous.** We will also cover a few other areas that may have application for a student project. They are: personal selling, packaging, merchandising, and promotional products.

"IMC," MarCom and More.

The "IMC" initials stand for "Integrated Marketing Communications." Ideally, IMC works best when all the elements of reaching the end consumer are pulled together in a synergistic process.

MarCom stands for Marketing Communications. Often, companies have MarCom departments and managers. Students with degrees in advertising not only look to advertising agencies for careers, but to MarCom departments of major advertisers.

MarCom is the same as IMC, except that IMC is more concerned with the integration part. Certainly any good MarCom manager will understand the importance of synergism, so you may find me referring to IMC as MarCom, or MarCom as IMC from time to time. You'll be able to figure it out. There can be a synergism that takes place when everything uses the same advertising campaign line, but integrated marketing communications is really more than that. It is marketing planning with the consumer as the central focus.

Account Planning/Personal Media Network.

Account Planning and other concepts such as the "personal media network" are broader concepts applied to advertising.

Consumer Insight/Brand Contact Points.

"Consumer insight" and "brand contact points" are similar concepts applied to IMC.

Both are really trying to get the consumer's perception and a more effective consumer connection into the work.

IMC is interested in getting a response, not to the advertising, but to the Brand. Advertising is just one of the channels. But, for most brands, it is the most important channel—and, quite often, one of the biggest parts, or very much the biggest part, of the marketing budget.

For this reason, the next part of our document will begin with advertising. Though, in some cases, for example a high-tech startup, public relations and interactive might more appropriately be the lead sections.

1. **Advertising:**

   This advertising portion of the plan will be subdivided into creative and media. Sometimes production can be the third category.

   Sometimes an overall advertising strategy statement is added before the specifics of a creative or media strategy are stated. We won't do that here because it seems to be a little redundant.

   a. **Creative:**

   The marketing strategy that addresses creative is an objective in the Creative segment of the planning document. It depends on the level in the plan as to where it is placed. The key consideration is how the advertising creative product will contribute to the fulfillment of the overall marketing objective. It is what you want the advertising creative product to accomplish.

   When you begin this statement with the words "To establish," whether it is at the Marketing Strategy or Creative Objective level, it is easier to understand the purpose of the statement. This will also force the thinking to be about what the Brand will become in the mind of the consumer as a result of the advertising.

   The complete marketing creative strategy should be as follows:

   To establish (the Brand name) as _____.

   Here is a specific example:

   To establish Simplicity Patterns as the quick and easy way for the Target Audience to obtain the clothes they want.

   Here is another example:

   To establish Nestle as having superior quality chocolate within the solid milk chocolate segment of the total candy line.

   Usually, there is only one marketing strategy written for the creative function, as there is usually only one creative objective.

   b. **Media:**

   The marketing strategies that address media are also media objectives and help fulfill the overall marketing objective. Again, these strategies state specifically what the media plan is intended to accomplish.

In media, however, it is not uncommon to have more than one objective, since media marketing strategies contain statements that address the target audience, geography, seasonality, continuity or flighting, creative constraints, and reach versus frequency.

The language used here will be identical to the language used in the objective section of the media portion of the plan.

Examples of a media marketing strategy are:

Target Audience:

To deliver advertising to women 18 to 34 primarily, with secondary importance given to men of the same age.

Geography:

To advertise throughout the United States with additional support in those areas with greatest sales potential.

Seasonality, target audience media habits, and other factors may also play a part. We will provide additional information and detail in Chapter Eight, Advertising Media.

Be sure to include a marketing strategy for media for each media objective used in Chapter Eight.

c. Production:

The marketing strategy that addresses production will explain how production helps achieve the marketing objectives.

Each separate advertising medium will require production. It is common to explain production in the section to which the production pertains: Production of advertising elements will go in the Creative segment, production of sales promotion materials will appropriately go in Sales Promotion.

Television production is obviously quite different from newspaper production. In both cases, you have an opportunity to spend more money to achieve more quality, or to have a little less quality for a little less money.

The Unattainable Triad: Price, Quality, Time.

The Law of the Unattainable Triad was developed for production people. The three elements are: price, quality, and time.

You can generally have two of the three at the cost of the third. That is, you can have it fast and in the best possible quality, but you will pay through the nose for it.

You get two of the three. It is impossible to have high quality, low prices, and fast turnaround time simultaneously.

A decision must be made which of these will impact generally in the plan.

After this advertising segment, we will discuss the Below-the-line disciplines.

2. **Sales Promotion:**

Sales promotion is an attempt by the marketer to stimulate behavior in the marketplace The primary approach is to influence behavior by changing the perception of the basic value (or price) of the product by either reducing cost or increasing what the consumer receives. Or both.

Value to the consumer (or the trade) increases either way.

This can be through direct decreased cost, as is done with a cents-off coupon, or more indirectly by providing more product for the same price, as is done with a "bonus pack" (i.e., 16 oz. for the price of 12 oz., often in a package that shows the extra size graphically). These things cost money—either in the extras being offered or in the cost to the bottom line of the cents-off reduction. Think about it. You have the cost of the cents-off coupon *and* the reduced income. Hopefully, you can make it up on volume.

Sales Promotion is usually considered more expensive than advertising. Sales increases that are solely a function of temporary price reductions are very expensive to the Brand—particularly if they do not convert a user.

Sales promotion can be considered successful if the consumer is converted to become a loyal user.

Two Segments: Consumer and Trade.

In planning, sales promotion can also be broken into two segments—consumer and trade.

If the plan shows synergism between these two promotion strategies, then an overall marketing strategy addressing sales promotion should be listed first. This will set the stage for the specific strategy that addresses consumer and trade promotion. If this takes places, we are said to be thinking in an integrated fashion.

a. Consumer Promotion:

Coupons, rebates, bonus packs, sweepstakes, and contests are some of the commonly used sales promotion events.

The marketing strategy statement written in this part of the marketing plan should be an overall statement that indicates how consumer sales promotion will contribute to achieving the marketing objective.

Individual events should be listed in Section Nine. (See Chapter Nine, Below-the-line, for more detail.)

Consumer promotion can be used:

- to build trial;
- to "load" the consumer (build in-home inventory);
- to reinforce current usage; or
- to be competitive.

b. Trade Promotion:

The marketing strategy statement for trade promotion addresses how trade promotion will augment the marketing objective.

The most common trade promotion events in packaged goods are display allowances and advertising allowances.

3. Public Relations:

When public relations is built into the marketing plan, its strategy generally goes here in the planning document.

Most public relations is divided into two major segments, marketing public relations (MPR) and corporate public relations (CPR).

Corporate public relations has to do with employee relations, stockholder and investor relations, legislative action, and crisis management. If you work on Tylenol and someone tampers with your capsules, that is crisis management—not marketing.

There are other needs and functions of public relations, but those are beyond the scope of this book.

Marketing public relations is the segment that is valuable in the marketing plan. Key elements of MPR are: press releases, press conferences, new product announcements, media relations, and consumer relations.

There are two key target groups for MPR: the media and the consumer. Public relations professionals refer to these target audiences as "publics."

Again, the marketing strategy for public relations will be identical to the objective in the public relations part of the document.

An example of a public relations objective is (See Chapter Nine):

> *To enhance public opinion of Nuprin as a quality source for sporting pain relief.*

For the milk "Mustache" campaign, the advertising and public relations objectives were exactly the same:

> *To reposition milk as a contemporary adult beverage.*

...or more likely,

> *To establish milk as a contemporary adult beverage*

In many areas of marketing, particularly with high-tech and business–to–business, public relations are an important factor in the overall marketing operation.

4. **Direct Marketing:**

The goal of direct marketing is to convince the customer to order directly from the marketer. In the case of Bowflex, this is the manufacturer, while in the case of Land's End, it is a direct retailer (or direct merchant).

a. **Direct Response Media:**

Direct marketing can include direct mail, such as the Land's End catalogue, and direct response advertising on television or in radio, magazines, or newspapers. The Internet has made some aspects of direct marketing much easier and much less costly. However, it remains just as difficult to find the right customers and reach them with an effective message.

Relationship Marketing.

A related form of direct marketing is relationship marketing or CRM (Consumer Relationship Marketing).

Once someone becomes a customer, CRM focuses on enhancing the lifetime value (LTV) of that customer.

Sometimes this involves selling more goods and services. Other times it involves merely building the relationship in whatever way is appropriate for the brand and category.

b. Telemarketing:

Telemarketing also has two segments.

Inbound telemarketing goes from the consumer inbound to the advertiser. Usually, the customer calls to place an order or ask a question. Land's End makes sure that everything they publish has their 800 number on it. This allows customers to call with an order from the catalogue or to call and ask the attendant to look up the number from the shirt ordered six months ago.

Inbound telemarketing may be part of direct response marketing or relationship marketing—usually both.

Outbound telemarketing goes from company to consumer. Many companies rely on the telephone as a sales tool.

A telemarketing strategy might be:

To reach the target audience at least once in each six-month period.

5. Event Marketing:

Event marketing (and sponsorship) is to consumers what media relations is to the media. Some consider event marketing a type of sales promotion. PR professionals consider it a function of public relations ... back to the turf wars.

Since it is different than most other forms, it is broken out into a different segment. There are consumer events and trade events.

a. Consumer Events:

If you have a student target, which is quite common in NSAC competitions, you may well have some sort of event marketing as part of your marketing plan.

You may also have advertising that supports the event and public relations that publicize the event.

Event marketing can be a sports-related, such as Sprint sponsoring a NASCAR race or Reebok sponsoring an Olympic team. Golf and tennis are attractive to marketers who wish to build their brand's reputation with an upscale target audience.

British Petroleum sometimes sponsors art exhibits or symphonies, and Phillip Morris supported cultural events. This is also event marketing. (Tobacco marketers were active participants in events, as more and more limits were placed on where they could put their marketing dollars.)

b. Trade Events:

Trade shows can be very important events. But this time, the target audience is the trade, not the consumer. The National Restaurant Show or the Sporting Goods Show at McCormick Place in Chicago are significant trade show events.

E3 is a key event for the electronics industry.

Smaller groups with specialized suppliers, such as the Direct Marketing Association, will also have events that are critical for bringing key groups in specialized industries together.

Some of these events, such as MacWorld, attract both the consumer and the trade.

6. Miscellaneous:

Marketing strategy often addresses other elements than those listed above. The decision is a function of the objectives and budget available to the brand. As you can see, there is wide range of marketing tools available and a wide range of possible marketing decisions and priorities. Here are three more, generating great interest

Viral, Social, WoM.

These three aspects of marketing are receiving increased attention. For viral marketing, the goal is to increase consumer engagement with the brand. On-line social marketing got the attention of marketers when the population of Facebook users went past

200 million. Word of mouth, at 78% is the most trusted form of advertising. Initiative in Hong Kong claims that "online WoM @ 61%" is right behind.

While there are many options, we have one name for it—the "marketing mix." The marketing mix chosen can also address other aspects of marketing, such as personal selling, packaging, merchandising, games, and promotional products.

a. Personal Selling

Requires someone to make sales calls that go directly to customers. For large packaged goods companies there is often a sales department whose job it is to check the grocery shelves, make recommendations to retail buyers, and establish and maintain good relations with "the trade." Some companies have "driver/salesmen" who will make sales calls as they deliver product.

b. Packaging

Can be a key element in the marketing mix. Sometimes, it can be the key communication vehicle for a brand. (Have you ever read all that copy on the back of a Bisquick package? The information includes: recipes, nutrition, fat content, ingredients, a Web address, and an 800 number. The package can be a key marketing communications tool.)

c. Merchandising

Takes place at the store level. In fact, it's the promoting of the advertising or sales promotion of the Brand at the trade level.

Merchandising is a term most often used for retail or generic clients. Occasionally, companies will call it merchandising when they have to sell the advertising or sales promotion to their own sales force or to the trade.

When the California Washington Oregon Pear Bureau puts up point-of-purchase advertising over the Anjou pears in a Kroger store in Cincinnati, they refer to this activity as merchandising.

According to the American Marketing Association, merchandising is *"The planning involved in marketing the right merchandise or service at the right place, at the right time, in the right quantities, and at the right price."*

d. Games

Have become incredibly popular marketing tools. There can be product placement in games. VW Polo (not sold in the US), for example, has a free iPhone/iPod Touch application with a driving game. It is not a complicated game, but it is an easy way to increase touch points.

e. Promotional Products

Can range from that pen you picked up at the bank, and a good percentage of the T-shirts in your free T-shirt collection, to more expensive items adorned with logos and other messages.

The Promotional Products Association's advertising theme is "Advertising that remains to be seen." And that is exactly what it is. It can be a very strong advertising or marketing tool.

Nonetheless, it is not uncommon for a marketing planning document to have no reference to merchandising or public relations.

The most common elements of Promotion (TTL) are Advertising and Sales Promotion. They should almost always be addressed in the Marketing Strategy section of your Planning Document. Public relations can also play an important role for new brands and, effectively done, can be a valuable supplement to virtually and brand's efforts.

B. Product:

In most marketing plans, the product segment of the marketing strategy will be short. It might simply be:

There will be no change in the product.

Product Improvements and New Products.

If, however, there is a product improvement, or if the marketing plan is for a new product introduction, this part of the strategy will explain how this new product will contribute to achieving the marketing objective.

Example: Bisquick.

Let's say you're working on Bisquick for General Mills, and new research shows that Jiffy is both equal to and perceived to be equal in quality to Bisquick. General Mills may seek a product improvement.

The strategy might be:

To provide product superiority over all competition as evidenced by consumer reaction.

This would require that the product not just be superior in a test-kitchen environment, but would be an improvement consumers would notice in their own kitchens.

This is just one example of how Bisquick might strengthen its total marketing mix in the product area.

This product improvement might work in concert with an increase in ad spending, a new sales promotion plan, or even a change in price.

The Need to Define New Products.
Generally, a new product introduction will require more definition, including how the brand will address consumer demand in terms of how this product will fulfill consumers' criteria for making purchase decisions, and how it will be unique in the marketplace.

C. Pricing:

When there is a small amount of inflation, this segment will usually be short. A statement indicating no change in price is all that is needed.

The brand will maintain current pricing.

The strategy statement might also be short if the price needs to be increased only to cover a modest increase in production cost.

Only when the price will change dramatically up or down as a change of intent—how pricing will impact on demand—will this part of the plan be more than a sentence or two.

In that case, this section should address why the change will contribute to the fulfillment of the marketing objective.

D. Distribution (Place):

Again, this part might be short if there is no change in how the product is distributed. It should show how the distribution plan contributes to the volume opportunity expressed in the marketing objective.

This is true whether the plan dictates the use of company salespeople to sell the brand to wholesalers who warehouse and sell the brand to retailers who store the brand and sell it to the end user, or if it is a multi-level distribution system such as Amway or Nu-Skin.

The marketing strategy addressing distribution needs to communicate how this distribution system helps complete the marketing objective.

Areas of Opportunity.

Make certain all possible areas of opportunity are explored and found.

Example: Nestle.

Nestle discovered that they could significantly increase volume when they sought distribution in video stores. They learned that each video store produced about the same volume as a convenience store.

They also learned they could double the volume of an average grocery store by placing a rack with chocolate bars in the dairy case.

Since retailers did not like the idea of multiple locations for candy bars in the supermarket, this tested distribution idea was only recommended for limited-time sales promotions events.

E. People:

A Relatively New Idea.

The inclusion of a "people" segment in the marketing strategy is a relatively new idea. It makes a great deal of sense because most successful new products are based on what consumers want.

Think about it. The entire marketing plan is based on consumer wants and needs. And the business itself cannot succeed without the ongoing approval of people who buy the brand.

A "Consumer First" Focus.

A major thrust of IMC planning is working from a "Consumer First" focus. This is the primary focus of the account planner—as we discussed earlier. The "People" segment helps bring this emphasis to the fore.

The intent of this segment of the marketing strategy is to describe, in detail, who will buy, use, or influence buyers or users of the Brand. This will take a detailed analysis.

Target Audience Analysis.

Target Audience Analysis will identify the target audience and explain why it will buy enough of the brand to meet the marketing objective.

The Target Audience should be described in terms of demographics, psychographics, and any other information, including a mini-saga or consumer wants and needs, that will impact the volume of the Brand.

The value of the account planner is easily recognized when writing this important section.

The Target Trade.

Another part of the people segment may be the trade. When you allocate more trade promotion dollars than consumer promotion dollars, you are making a decision that the people who buy the brand as middlemen are more important to the success of the brand than are the end users.

F. Rationale:

Defend Your Decisions.

Everything that has been written in the marketing strategy section must be defended. There should be quantifiable substantiation for each and every strategy.

The substantiation should show that the marketing strategy will provide the Brand with the impetus to achieve the marketing objective.

The specific execution of the marketing strategy will be listed or clarified within the specific disciplines of the planning document.

Example.

There will be a defense for why the marketing strategy for advertising creative will contribute to fulfilling the volume specified in the marketing objective.

It should be stated in a clear and quantifiable fashion in this portion of the document.

How that marketing strategy is put into action via a copy platform or creative brief will be found in the seventh section of the plan (Chapter Seven, Advertising Creative), as will the substantiation, support, rationale, or defense for that segment of the plan.

Where to Find Support.

This information can come from secondary resource materials such as:

- Mediamark Research, Inc. (MRI)
- Simmons Market Research Bureau (SMRB)
- Leading National Advertisers (LNA)
- SRI International (VALS II)

(See Notes A and B in Chapter One for a more complete list.) This can also come from the primary research discussed in Chapter Two.

One other thing:

This chapter could have been organized by:

1. Business-to-consumer (B2C)
2. Business-to-business (B2B)
3. Consumer-to-consumer (C2C)

Each of these has a unique and distinct configuration. And, of course, a new product or start-up will be much different than a mature brand. The important thing is to make it clear and complete, to make it make sense in the category or segment in which you're competing.

For more information, please also read:

1. Don E. Schultz and Beth E. Barnes. *Strategic Advertising Campaigns.* 5th ed. (McGraw-Hill, 1999).
   Chapters Nine provides an overview of strategy development.

2. Al Ries and Jack Trout. *Positioning: The Battle for Your Mind.* (New York: McGraw-Hill, 1986).
   The first nine chapters set the stage for strategy development.

3. Al Ries and Jack Trout. *Marketing Warfare.* (New York: McGraw-Hill, 1986).
   Chapters Six through Ten will help with strategy development.

4. Bendinger, Altman, Avery, et al. *Advertising & the Business of Brands.* (Chicago: The Copy Workshop, 2009)
   Chapters Seven and Eight of this introductory book provide useful overviews of Marketing Services and Strategy Development.

5. Scott Cooper and Roman Hiebing. *How to Write a Successful Marketing Plan.* (Lincolnwood, IL: NTC Business Books, 1997).
   An excellent and comprehensive book, primarily written for Marketing Directors.

6. Don E. Schultz and Stanley Tannenbaum. *Essentials of Advertising Strategy.* (Lincolnwood, IL: NTC Business Books, 1991).
   Chapters Five and Six are useful.

MarCom & Idea-Driven IMC

*"The real voyage of discovery consists not in seeking
new landscapes, but in having new eyes."*
—Marcel Proust

Introduction.

Creativity and Creation.

Howard Gossage, the 1960s San Francisco firehouse adman, started his discussion about creativity this way...

> *"Creativity is quite different from creation, which happened a long time ago. One seventeenth century educator, the Reverend John Lightfoot, even fixed the exact moment. He said, 'Heaven and Earth, center and circumference, were made in the same instant of time ... the twenty-sixth of October, 4004 B.C. at nine o'clock in the morning.' At 9:30 the account executives came in and started talking about creativity."*

This is exactly what has happened to "IMC."

IMC = Better MarCom

MarCom, short for marketing communications, has been around for years, particularly with marketers who used a relatively high proportion of public relations.

Integrated Marketing Communications (IMC) is a relatively new idea, but it's simply a better way to implement MarCom.

The premise was to make all elements of the marketing communications package work together, particularly with marketers who used a relatively high proportion of advertising and sales promotion and a growing range of MarCom programs.

It's kind of a synergistic thing.

Somebody said, let's make sure all elements of our marketing communications are integrated ... and IMC was born.

Much of marketing is about budgets. So, in the haste to expand and learn how integration works, it's not surprising that it has become the bailiwick of the business and numbers people, who want to minimize risk and maximize returns on investment.

But in reality, at the key to effective IMC for the biggest brands, is creativity—an integrated creative concept.

Example: Apple.
"Think Different" helped integrate Apple Computer's communications across a wide range of disciplines.

It communicated. It differentiated. And it integrated.

With a strong understanding of the power of integrated design, Apple continues to market effectively in an integrated way across an increasingly wide range of products.

Example: Nike.
"Just do it" has a similar effect. It allows Nike to speak to a wide range of athletes, with very dissimilar "factors that motivate purchase behavior." Yet it all hangs together.

Again, this unified voice manages to project an integrated brand image even as it ranges across a growing spectrum of products and sports activities.

Example: Walmart/Target.
Now let's contrast two large retailers, each with a wide range of offerings. They each manage to speak with a unique and consistent voice. Walmart focuses on low price with a larger value benefit for those who shop. Target offers more of a high-style feel and then pays it off with low price.

And, of course, McDonald's is another excellent example. None of these marketers is too big to lose their consistency—so, clearly, no smaller marketer has an excuse.

Getting Started.

First you have to allow your thinking to be integrated. You can think about which shirt, pants, and shoes you will wear, how they will look together, and how you will feel. So, if you can dress yourself, you are on your way to learning to thinking about how things integrate.

Example: Ford.

Ford spent $10 million in advertising on the same day, they also sent a press release to virtually every newspaper, radio, and television station in the country.

Then they communicated this to their dealer network and told them this is the first time there has every been a "global road block."

The two-minute commercial featured all seven Ford nameplates on 38 networks. This was a new idea. This had both consumer and trade, as well as advertising and public relations, components.

This is an example of thinking integrated.

First, Get Their Attention.

Integration is about managing the connection to your target audience so that they receive a reinforcing message however they receive it and whatever you do to get their attention.

Here are a few reasons why this is even more important:

1. **Ratings are down:**
   Remember that television viewership has been steadily declining since the early eighties. At the same time cost per point has been going up. This has forced advertisers to think about new ways to reach their target group.

2. **There are more media vehicles:**
   There are now over ten thousand consumer magazines in this country alone. Each one of them seeks a specific target audience, some are broad and some are narrow.

   Some of the newer, smaller magazines would never had survived in the era of high television ratings.

There would have been no reason for advertisers to try to seek out smaller market segments.

You can now buy advertising on the front of shopping carts, on the back of public bathroom stalls, on the sides of downtown trash cans, on bus benches, and on virtually any kind of clothing. (It is a novelty to see a T-shirt without a silk-screened message.)

This growth in the number of media vehicles has dispersed the audience. This makes them more expensive to reach.

3. **The growth of cable:**
   Cable television is now available across all of America. This means there are more channels available, which means each channel has fewer people watching.

   This means the advertiser has to buy more networks or stations or programs then ever before.

   Ford bought 38 networks. Wow! It was not that long ago we only had four networks, and just a few years before that we only had three.

4. **People spend less time with traditional media:**
   With increased time spent on the computer as well as the increased use of Tivo and DVR, people spend less time with traditional TV and, for the most part, use other media vehicles less—such as magazines and newspapers. People are also more active than they have ever been. And we still do not yet know the impact of computers as replacement for television.

   That simply leaves less time to spend with consumer media vehicles.

   Marry this with the increased number of vehicles and you can quickly see why it is important for advertisers to work harder to reach the same number of people they did in the past.

5. **Sales promotion is expected:**
   More consumers buy when the Brand is on special. Midas has a sale on shock absorbers every spring. Many customers wait, even when their shocks are worn out, to take advantage of the sale.

   This is common. For many, coupon ads determine where they will enjoy dinner on Friday night.

Customers are less loyal. The battle to keep your customers from going over to the competition takes place every day.

6. **The quantity of marketing messages is increasing:**
Some studies indicate that the average American now sees 1,500 advertising messages a day—some say 3,000.

Viewers can only remember eight or ten of those, and often they remember the storyline rather than the advertiser.

So the marketplace is a highly competitive environment that forces every marketer, every advertiser, every MarCom manager to be more creative and demand more productivity for every marketing communications investment—because all these other factors are making each message less productive.

"More bang for the buck" will be more important in the coming years than it has ever been.

Advertisers have to find new ways to deliver the target group without breaking the bank.

Synergy-Synergy.
Little Caesar's ran television advertising to communicate Pizza-Pizza. Then they used newspaper inserts to back up Pizza-Pizza with coupons to increase the value-price relationship.

Then they back it up again with direct mail to recent buyers to reinforce usage.

Example: Nuprin.
Nuprin identified a hole in the analgesic market. Their identified niche positioning was to convince sports enthusiasts that Nuprin would relieve the pain incurred during sporting accidents.

Advertising ran that showed grand slalom and downhill racers taking big-time tumbles. It was not only humorous, but reinforced the sports pain relief positioning.

Sports personalities said of pain that they would "Nupe it."

Nuprin sponsored downhill races at major ski resorts and gave away yellow buttons that read "Nupe it."

They gave away prizes to spectators with "Nupe it" buttons. They gave a special trade displace allowance during the promotion to get yellow in-store "Nupe it" signs.

The media was involved with special viewing locations to report on the races with "Nupe it" signs.

This is a great example of integrated thinking.

All of these Nuprin elements worked together:

1. Advertising
    a. Television
    b. Newspaper
    c. Radio
    d. Signage
2. Sales promotion
    a. Consumer
        - contest
        - coupons
    b. Trade
        - display allowance for POP
3. Public relations
    a. Press releases
    b. Press relations
4. Merchandising

This is an idea that takes advantage of creativity. Everything works together in a synergistic fashion so it is integrated.

But before it could work together, there had to be an idea.

Someone had to do the work to find the hole in the competitive analgesic positioning. Someone had to have the idea for the sports positioning, and someone had to recognize the idea was viable.

Mark Goldstein, then director of marketing at Fallon in Minneapolis, noted: *"Integration isn't about charts and spreadsheets and datamining. Integration is about ideas... ideas big enough to unify a brand and motivate consumers and employees and Wall Street...."*

Big Ideas Make Everything Bigger.

Integrated Marketing Communication is a way to talk about advertising campaigns that are bigger than just advertising. Check out the Pedigree story at the TBWA website. Here are a few examples.

All of the marketing communication elements work with the advertising and become part of the entire campaign.

Advertising has always been about ideas—it's an idea business. And now those ideas have to drive the brand communication beyond advertising. And when the idea is right, everything works better.

The importance of those ideas will continue to grow as time goes on. As people watch less television and ratings decrease, as media options increase, and consumers become less loyal, advertisers will have to work harder to find ways to get their message in front of customers.

Print

And ideas have the power to unify a brand's messages across all forms of marketing communications.

A pop-up store in Times Square.

The Need for More Reach.

Michael Naples did a significant study in the early seventies and learned that advertisers need to increase frequency in order to have an impact on the viewers.

Outdoor in Central Park

157

His study, and one by MacDonald in England, taught us to think in terms of three-plus reach.

If those studies were done today, we might be thinking in terms of five-plus reach or six-plus reach. But most advertisers can't afford five-plus reach or even three-plus reach.

They can, however, use their creativity to find new ways to deliver that same target audience. And ideas have the power to drive the integration of the message.

Remember that the e-world is here. At the writing of this chapter,

- There are 250m facebook users
- 300m YouTube users
- 275m Skype users
- Wikipedia is in 250 languages
- There are 200 million bloggers
- There were 800,000 laptops lost last year in airports
- About ten trillion talk minutes are used on mobile phones
- Over 80% of online users have watched a video
- YouTube accounts for over half of all viewed video
- There are 12,000 hours of video loaded on YouTube everyday
- Three-quarters have read a blog
- Three-quarters of journalists rely on blogs for research
- Almost all teenagers have joined a social network
- Fifty-five percent have uploaded a photo

Oh, and by the way, the average teenager has over a hundred illegal tracks on their MP3 player. These people no longer have time to watch television. The ideas you create have to get their attention.

Advertising is an Idea Business. Go to the websites of any of the top multinational advertising agencies.

As it grows into new forms of brand communications, it's still ideas that connect with consumers that will make the difference.

The MarCom Matrix.

All of the MarCom channels should, each in their own way, be harnessed to effectively deliver that idea so that, cumulatively, the idea of your brand is delivered through multiple channels.

Naturally, budget and circumstance will force some prioritizing. Use your brain. Figure it out.

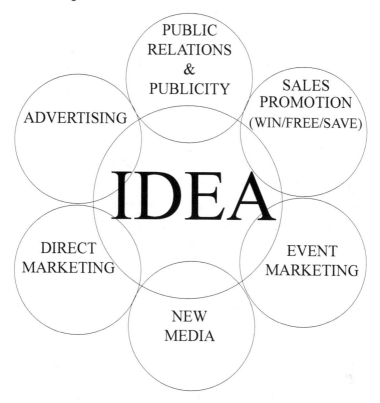

It's a noisy world. Clear, consistent messaging across all MarCom disciplines will help you be heard.

Advertising Creative

The essence of creative strategy is sacrifice.
— Bill Bernbach

Introduction.

The advertising creative product is most often the single element of the marketing plan that can provide the greatest impact on sales.

In a world where we work long and hard to gain a few more percentage points of efficiency, the difference between an effective and ineffective creative presentation can be significant.

For this reason, more time is spent on the development of advertising's creative product and more energy is consumed trying to make advertising stand out from all the other advertising that exists, than on any other element of marketing.

The Power of the Creative Message.

Never underestimate the power of the creative message.

When I was working on the introduction of Ortega Tacos, we had two potential messages.

The first described a taco and how to make and eat them. Our identified target audience was mostly uneducated about Mexican food.

The second simply told the target that Ortega Tacos are *"Fun to Make. Fun to Eat."* The target was the same.

The second commercial was many times more effective, memorable, and persuasive than the first. The strategy was essentially the same. The target was the same. But the creative staging of the message allowed more people to relate easily to tacos generically and to Ortega specifically.

Another example: the Nissan Altima was a disappointment in Japan, yet sales went through the roof in this country. The car books panned it early on, yet consumers loved it. Why?

Brilliant Advertising.
They took the Lexus positioning well-known in the U.S. and made it available for thirty thousand dollars less. The advertising made the difference.

What about Federal Express? How successful would they be without "When it absolutely positively has to be there overnight." Or even McDonald's without "You deserve a break today." One of my favorites is "Just do it."

These are examples of advertising that has made a significant difference in the success of a Brand in a highly competitive marketing environment.

A Definition of Creative Advertising.
My definition of creative advertising is advertising that is different from other advertising. Bruce Bendinger, who wrote *The Copy Workshop Workbook*, is concerned with "making a relevant connection in a noisy world." Fair enough.

Many advertising art directors and copywriters will not even consider an advertisement that is similar to other ads. There's a good reason for this. You need to be a bit different to get noticed. And, if you don't get noticed, how can you make that "relevant connection?"

Creative advertising is innovative and fresh. It is usually an application of something that is common in an uncommon way. And, somehow, it gets noticed.

The Importance of Creative Advertising.
There are three primary reasons why so much time is spent on the creative side of advertising:

1. **Sales Generator:**
   Advertising that is different attracts attention. In order to sell something to your target group, you must first have their attention. Then, and only then, will you be able to present an effective sales message.

   While the numbers vary depending on who you talk with, most advertising professionals agree that the average American sees thousands of advertising messages a day, but can only remember about nine.

Of those nine, the average person incorrectly remembers the brand name for about half, so only four or five advertising messages a day are really doing what they need to be doing.

Now this is tempered somewhat, because different people remember different messages, but the point remains that little advertising is really memorable.

There is a high probability that the ones that are remembered are the ones that are different in some way from common advertising. If it's different, many people would judge it to be creative.

However, advertising is not judged to be creative just because it is different; it must also address a business reason for being. This business reason is most often called strategy.

If the advertising communicates the points in the creative strategy it is said to be "on strategy."

Benton & Bowles (a predecessor of the now defunct DMB&B) used to say, "It isn't creative unless it sells." Now we all know that this isn't exactly true. Some very creative things might not sell, and some fairly uncreative messages, like "FREE," may sell very well.

But there is a higher probability of your advertising delivering that selling message effectively if it is "creative."

2. **Career Advancement:**
   Copywriters and art directors progress in their careers by winning awards. They win awards by being creative.

   At the same time, their messages must be on strategy in order to sell the advertising to their account management groups and to their clients. But their clear motivation is to win awards.

   In my view, one of the best award competitions is the "Effies." They measure sales effectiveness as well as creativity.

   Creative people gain prestige among their peers when they win awards. They also get raises based on winning awards. One midcareer copywriter in Los Angeles told me, "If I win a Belding it's worth a five thousand dollar raise." (A Belding is an award from the Los Angeles Advertising Club.)

Then again, quite simply, if your ad won an award, it got noticed. Usually, this is a good thing.

3. It Is Fun:

Clients spend more time with the advertising creative product because it is one of the best ways to increase sales. As one client noted, "It gives advertising dollars great elasticity."

Clients get raises and promotions based on increasing sales for their brands. This is the story they tell; however, part of that truth is that it is just a lot more fun to work on advertising than a promotion allowance for a grocery chain in Ft. Wayne.

While the actual creation of the advertising is the responsibility of the copy and art members of the group (called the creative people), the creative process is the heart of advertising and is probably the most fun you will have working in business—advertising or any other business, for that matter.

Jerry Della Femina said, "it is the most fun you can have with your clothes on."

Advertising is about ideas. The advertising campaign that DDB used for themselves for many years was *"Better ideas. Better results."*

Creative Development.

The Development Sequence.

It is important that you understand where creative development fits into the scheme of advertising development.

Some of this we've already covered, and in great detail, but we'll repeat it here so that you can recognize the chronology of the stages of creative development. In general, the process is as follows:

1. Understand Your Target Audience:

Know your audience. You need to know where they live, when they buy, demographics, psychographics, purchase cycle (how often they buy), and all the other information we discussed back in Chapter One when we discussed the Situation Analysis.

I have a new way to describe this. I call it a mini-saga. I will give a little more detail about it at the end of this chapter. The short version is write 50 words to describe one member of your target group.

2. **Understand Their Motivation:**
   Isolate the factors that motivate purchase behavior. Understand what is unique about your Brand. Find a uniqueness that is relevant to your target—one that connects with that motivation.

   The relationship between these two pieces of information will likely be the basis for your strategic direction.

3. **Differentiate Your Brand:**
   This differentiation can take place either strategically or executionally. Many of the unique brand icons developed by Leo Burnett (e.g. the Jolly Green Giant, the Marlboro Cowboy, and the Pillsbury Doughboy) connected with a generic category benefit. They differentiated executionally.

4. **Write a Creative Platform:**
   We will get to that in just a few paragraphs. Be patient.

5. **Concept Development:**
   Here is where you will develop your selling premise. Quite often this selling premise will contain a campaign line.

   Often that unique combination of motivating factors and brand uniqueness can be combined into a proposition. P&G often uses slogans that are propositions. Examples are:

   Dirt can't hide from intensified Tide.
   Choosy Moms Choose Jif.
   Bounty is the Quicker Picker-Upper.

   Bruce Bendinger presents this information in *The Copy Workshop Workbook.* He thinks you should look for the "Selling Idea," since many very creative ideas don't actually sell.

   As you spend more time in advertising, you will begin to recognize that we have created many accepted labels for stages of the process, strategies, concepts, ideas, selling ideas, propositions, and even the elements of the advertising itself. As a result, you may run across some of this with other labels.

6. **Advertising Execution:**
   This is the advertising itself. Tactics.

   In the case of traditional media, this will likely take the form of copy and layout for print advertising and storyboards and scripts for electronic media. For non-traditional media, it may take the form of a layout for a Facebook page or copy for Twitter. It could be photos you want posted to Flickr.

As computer sophistication and skills become more readily available, the finished quality of student work has become more polished. In fact, it has improved dramatically.

There is now even an entire magazine, *CMYK,* devoted to examples of outstanding student advertising. Find a copy and look at it.

Copy Platform. Creative Platform. Creative Brief.
The purpose for this segment of the planning document is to present what was once called "The Copy Platform" and which we will refer to as the "Creative Platform" or "Creative Brief."

Again, there are a variety of names and a variety of formats.

Y&R has a "Creative Work Plan." Saatchi & Saatchi call theirs an "Ideas Brief." Many call it simply, "Advertising Strategy" or "Communication Strategy."

Those who use Account Planners, which, these days, is almost everyone, often use "Creative Brief." This is a document that combines Strategy with other background materials to "brief" the creatives.

Note A: There is an example of a good, commonly used Creative Brief in Note A of this chapter. The remainder of this chapter will outline the purpose for each segment of the Creative Brief and how to write it.

A. Target Audience:
The Most Likely Candidate.
This is a description of who is the most likely candidate to be motivated to do something as a result of the advertising.

Most often, this description is stated in demographic terms, but psychographics and usage-related descriptions are also appropriate.

MRI or Simmons are good sources of information for the user-base, which can translate into the target audience referred to earlier. If psychographics are used, SRI International's VALS II can be used. This information will come from the Situation Analysis in Chapter One.

Marketing Strategy/People.

The language used in the People part of the Marketing Strategy should be represented here as you describe your Target Audience.

It need not be identical wording, but care should be taken to make certain that the same group of people is being addressed.

If you choose to describe the people who will use, buy, or influence buying behavior in a more extensive fashion, this is the place in your Marketing Plan to do so.

Be sure to include a mini-saga. This is covered in Note D.

B. Objective:
"To Establish…"

The Objective Statement indicates what it is that you want the advertising to do.

Usually this starts with the words *"To establish…."* I say usually because there are examples of when it does not start with "to establish…."

As you gain more experience, you can use other phrasing to start a creative objective, but it won't be as good. *"To establish…"* will start you off in the right direction, because it will force you to write what you want the advertising to accomplish.

Remember, this language should be exactly the same as the language found in the Marketing Strategy for Advertising Creative.

C. Strategy:
"To Convince…"

This is how you want the advertising specifically to accomplish the objective above. Again, there are many formats, but I prefer:

To convince: _____.

To buy: _____.

Instead of: _____.

Because: _____.

Of the many creative strategy formats that are in use by advertisers and advertising agencies, this one, developed by Wells Rich Greene in the eighties, is good because it forces the writer to address competition.

Virtually every brand sold in the world today must compete with something. As Procter & Gamble says, *"A copy strategy is a document which identifies the basis upon which we expect our customers to purchase our brand in preference to competition."*

People have to give up something to use our Brand. They are already full.

D. Insight:

Consumer insight is a simple human truth. Dave Weaver at TM, a leading Dallas agency, says it this way, "Simple. Human. Truth." The insight is a connection, sometimes called an intersection, between the brand and the people you want to use the brand—your target. See Note D at the end of this chapter for more detail.

The marketing world has gone crazy collecting insights. Mark Earls, in his book *Herd,* observes that we most often make decisions of what to do or what to buy based on what other people are doing and buying. This changes the dynamics of consumer insights.

Once you understand consumer insight, it often becomes quickly clear what the advertising should do.

E. Support:

A Reason to Believe...

Support is the reason to believe the strategy.

It can be either research that supports the strategy or an advertising "reason why."

In the case where a Brand's primary reason for purchase motivation is emotional, this segment will be a "reason why" the Brand should be purchased.

Some companies call this a "permission to believe."

The substantiation for this part of the Plan will most likely come from Section Two, Research (See Chapter 2). Specifically, it will be in answer to the questions asked in the primary research that address the criteria for purchase motivation.

In the case of Dannon Yogurt advertising to older women, the Brand might consider a Health Strategy. The Support might be:

One serving of Dannon Yogurt provides 25% of the daily recommended calcium requirement for adults.

Source Credibility.

Your Support should give the target group a reason to believe. A helpful concept for developing that support is Source Credibility.

The credibility of the advertising message is not just who is delivering the message—as in public relation's view of "source credibility"—but it may encompass why the consumer will believe the advertising.

Certs added "Retsin" to their candy. Retsin gave permission for the consumer to believe that Certs were "two mints in one." It didn't matter what Retsin really was; it was a "reason why" Certs could be both a candy mint and a breath mint.

As you examine the use of celebrities in advertising, you will notice that some are more credible than others. Those who succeed have found their own way of adding source credibility to the message.

Best of all, some advertisers have themselves become credible. NIKE, Apple, and Volvo have each created their own "source credibility."

Public Relations and Source Credibility.

This is another reason why public relations has become a part of more and more marketing programs. The source credibility of third-party mentions, such as a news feature, can make the advertising more credible.

Entertainment brands, such as movies and rock musicians, work very hard to combine PR with advertising in their marketing. Quotes from movie reviews and music critics can play a vital role.

F. Considerations:

This is the place where you would put other things that you would like to have built into the advertising, if space or time allowed.

Advertising is all about communicating one key point. If I throw six tennis balls at you at the same time, it is probable that you won't catch any. But if I send them one at a time, you can probably get them. The same is true with advertising. Try to communicate just one point ... the one that addresses the factors that motivate purchase behavior and that key Consumer Insight.

This section of the copy platform is where you add items two and three. That is, what is second most important, or third most important to consumers. The strategy, above, has the first, or single most important point.

This section could also include Mandatories. This section of the creative platform sometimes will include all the client dictates. Some companies and their advertising agencies refer to these as "Mandatories," which can also include legal requirements. Pharmaceuticals have so many legal restrictions, like providing a list of side effects, that it may be almost impossible to write a thirty-second television commercial. Most of the time these brands use sixties.

G. Tone:

The Way That You Say It.

This is the philosophy of your advertising in tone form.

It may be a statement or just a couple of words about the best way to speak to the Target Audience.

It can also be a complete "Brand Character Statement," which marketers like P&G use to describe the "enduring values" of the Brand.

However, the shorter format of a couple of words or so is preferable.

Advertising should get to the point. So should your Tone Statement.

H. Rationale:

Reinforce Your Recommendation.

This is the section where you explain the decision-making process, including the defense for what you have chosen to recommend.

Remember, there are no right or wrong answers in this market planning document. The only thing that matters is how well you have supported what you want to do.

In Chapter Two you conducted research to determine:

1. Who is the Target Audience?
2. What are the factors that motivate purchase behavior?
3. What are the unique characteristics of the Brand?

Cite that information here as substantiation that the Creative Platform you are recommending will build the business better than any other strategic direction.

The account planner's "Consumer First" focus can be tremendously helpful at this stage—framing the recommendation in terms of insights into the Target Audience.

Your Goal.

Your goal in writing this Rationale segment of the Creative Brief or Chapter Seven is to prove that the Creative Platform you are recommending is a clear delineation of the Creative Objective, which is the Marketing Strategy.

This Marketing Strategy will, in turn, allow the fulfillment of the Marketing Objectives. It's all connected.

The substantiation in this segment should be quantified whenever possible, and it should be conclusive.

Three Reasons.

When I was working on Procter & Gamble business at Compton (now Saatchi & Saatchi), my boss told me that there are always three reasons to do something, and three reasons why something is right.

He said that if you only have two reasons you don't have enough evidence to do what you are recommending, and if you have four—then three of them are more important than one of them, and the least important reason should be eliminated. (There is a psychological superstition about threes. You might as well use it to your benefit.)

There is a relationship that can be drawn between Factors That Motivate Purchase Behavior and the Unique Characteristics of the Brand.

This relationship forms the foundation of your Creative Strategy.

Example: Ivory.

Let's say, for example, you knew the following were all true:

1. More doctors recommend Ivory than any other cleaning bar.
2. Ivory is $99.^{44}$% pure—so obviously it is good for the baby's bath.
3. Ivory is inexpensive, so it is a good soap to keep by the back door when people come in from working outside.
4. Ivory is good in the bathtub because it floats (so when the kids are covered in dirt, you can still find the soap).
5. Ivory is good for washing dishes because it doesn't have any artificial creams or deodorants to get on the dishes.

6. Ivory is mild, so it is good as a woman's complexion soap.

You could sell Ivory Bar Soap with a strategy based on any of the reasons. You should select only one in order to keep the strategic direction tight.

Strategy development is the process of deciding on the one reason that will build the most volume (or occasionally the correct volume).

The one you should select is the one that consumers use as criteria to make up their minds as to which brand of bar soap they will buy—the Factor that Motivates Purchase Behavior.

Niche Marketing Factors.

There are some exceptions to this rule—the most notable of which is when you are involved in niche marketing.

You still need to base your strategy on what your Target Audience uses to make decisions in the category. But when you are trying to find a small hole in the marketplace, the numbers may not indicate your criteria base for the niche, or what Ries and Trout call a "créneau," as being a major concern to those people who will buy the Brand.

Example: Rover.

For example, the primary reason why people buy a four-wheel drive utility vehicle is to provide safety. They believe that they will be in a situation when they will be on slick roads or off the road where they will need additional traction.

This is not the selling premise for Rover's four-by-four.

Rover maintains the elitist niche for four-wheel drive vehicles, and does quite well within that niche. At more than twice the price of most American or Japanese-made four-wheel drives, they couldn't survive on the base premise of off-road or slick road safety.

Look for Visual Opportunities.

The Rationale segment of the Creative section can be a great place to use a visual device. Don't just say it. Show it.

Example: Levi's Stretch Jeans.

For example, during a project for Levi's stretch jeans we found that our target audience wanted jeans that were not really a fashion jean, but not a basic jean either.

They liked the idea of an American pair of jeans, but wanted to feel like it was a little European. But they didn't really want the expense of an imported product.

The strategy of deciding where the Brand would fit in the marketplace was starting to get complicated. We felt a visual representation would make things more clear.

A visual device, a simple graph, made it much easier to communicate the strategic direction, or positioning, for this new Brand from Levis. We used the following visual device:

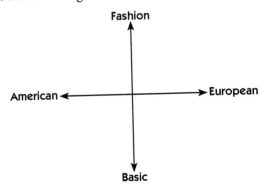

Occasionally there are windows of opportunity, or spectrums of consumer wants, that can be illustrated.

This is the place where you can use your imagination to communicate the strategy for defending this portion of the plan. Again, don't just say it. Show it.

H. Tactics:

Tactics = Creative Executions.
The tactics are the creative executions themselves.

While the actual advertising should not appear in the planning document, you may include a few items that are common to all the advertising.

If the intent is to have advertising that is based on humor, it may be appropriate to make that point here and tell why humor will have a greater impact on the sales of the Brand.

Then again, you may wish to make the point earlier in the Tone section of your Creative Strategy.

If there is something tactically different from what has been used before (a new look to the advertising, a new spokesperson, a new theme song) it should be communicated and defended here.

It goes here if the change is not strategic, but only tactical.

When Maytag changed from the old repairman to the younger one, this was a tactical change, not a strategic change.

For more information, please also read:

1. Bruce Bendinger. *The Copy Workshop Workbook.* 4th ed. (Chicago: The Copy Workshop, 2009).
   This book features additional help on developing Creative Strategy and a variety of Creative Strategy formats. Also use it for the creation of the advertising itself.

2. Award Books: *The One Show, Communication Arts* Magazine
   These are an excellent resource for looking at the best of current creative advertising.

3. *CMYK Magazine.* http://www.cmykmag.com.
   This magazine features some of the best student work from around the country. It will demonstrate the level of work being done by students like you.

4. John J. Kao. *Managing Creativity.* (Englewood Cliffs, NJ: Prentice Hall, 1991).
   Read the introduction for a clear understanding of creativity. Read the rest of the book to understand how to manage it.

5. Luke Sullivan. *Hey Whipple, Squeeze This: A Guide to Creating Great Ads.* 3rd ed. (New York: Adweek Books, 2008).
   This entertaining book offers advice on the kind of advertising creative directors look for.

6. Kenneth Roman and Jane Maas. *The New How to Advertise.* (New York: St. Martin's Press, 1992).
   Chapters One and Twelve will aid with this chapter. Chapters Two, Four, and Five will aid in developing creative.

7. Hanley Norins. *The Y&R Traveling Creative Workshop.* (Englewood Cliffs, NJ: Prentice Hall, 1990).

This book is out of print, but if you can find a copy, you'll have an invaluable resource on one of the best creative planning systems in the advertising industry.

8. Mark Earls. *Herd: How to Change Mass Behaviour by Harnessing Our True Nature.* (West Sussex: Wiley, 2007).

9. Daniel Pink. *A Whole New Mind: Why Right-Brainers Will Rule the Future.* (New York: Berkley Publishing Group, 2005). Another useful take on the creative process and the creativity in us all.

Creative Brief

Thanks to copy machines we no longer need copywriters.
What we need are idea writers.
—David Koch

Introduction.

A Clear Statement.

The creative brief (or copy platform) must be a clear statement that both defines the direction of what the advertising needs to accomplish and differentiates the Brand in the marketplace.

It should encompass the target audience, the Factors that Motivate Purchase Behavior, and the Unique Characteristics of the Brand.

Your creative direction will be clearly defined through the creative platform you propose, and it must show the strength of the Brand.

It should not be so tight that only one kind of advertising can be created. If it is too tight, the creative people will have no interest in working on the project.

If it is too loose, then there will be some probability that the advertising will not help sales. It will simply be interesting to people who see the advertising.

A Road Map.

The strategy should provide the basis for differentiation (Unique Characteristics of the Brand) and a road map for where the Brand is going in the future.

Once it has been completed and agreed to, it should not be changed often. Advertising developed on this strategy may be developed on a regular basis.

Pepsi used essentially the same "*Generation*" strategy for thirty years.

Creative work should not begin without formal agreement as to what the strategy is.

Strategic Options.

In the following example, notice that the Creative Platform is not based on a cost strategy, but seems to be based on an "ease" strategy.

If you sew your own clothing with Simplicity Patterns, you will be able to get the clothing you want much faster and more efficiently than if you look through all the department stores and boutiques.

This strategy is based on research and insight into the Target Audience.

I would have guessed that the primary reason for the category was money saving, but this strategy seems to indicate that I am wrong. Be careful to not use your own opinions. Make sure your strategy and action are based on consumer wants, needs, and demands—not just what you think.

As you pause to think about the strategy and the Target Audience, you will see there are other things going on here.

This Strategy reinforces the self-image of the Target Audience.

It doesn't say, "You can't afford to shop at stores, so you have to do it yourself." Rather, it says, "You're smart, you're capable, you can dress stylishly with Simplicity Patterns and have exactly what you want."

Furthermore, it helps differentiate the Brand by associating Simplicity with contemporary boutique fashion.

Simplicity could have also used a strategy based on quality or a strategy based on individuality. The basis is what the people who sew use as criteria for making selections of patterns—not our opinion. No other reason matters.

The format for this strategy part of the Creative Platform was developed by Wells Rich Greene.

Simplicity Patterns—Creative Brief.

Target Audience: Women 18 to 34 with a college education.

Objective: To establish Simplicity Patterns as the quick and easy way for the Target Audience to obtain the clothes they want.

Strategy:
To convince:	Target Audience (defined above)
To buy:	Simplicity Patterns
Instead of:	Shopping for clothing in boutiques and stores
Because:	Simplicity is the most efficient method of obtaining first-quality clothing with the right color and style.

Insight:
- Women are time-strapped with loved ones and careers.
- They like to maintain a personal look and identity.
- People want to have new clothing.

Support: Simplicity Patterns eliminates the difficulty of searching for the right clothing because the Target Audience can select the fabric and color and because the patterns are current, durable, and active.

Considerations:
1. Easy-to-follow instructions.
2. Can be made in a few hours.
3. Sewing reduces fitting frustrations.

Tone: Active, yet fashionable.

Ideas & Ideation

When you reach for the stars, you may not quite get one.
But you won't come up with a handful of mud, either.
—Leo Burnett

Introduction.

Did you know that Brainstorming was invented by someone in advertising? Alex Osborn, the "O" in BBDO, developed techniques that are still used today. That's just one of the areas we'll cover.

The Need for Team Creativity.

As you work together, you'll also need to have ideas together. In general, one person's idea will feed off another's. Then you'll have to make decisions as a group as to which is the best idea.

Together, you'll have to determine what the problem is, and then you'll have to think up the solution.

It's one of the toughest jobs in advertising and marketing. And it's one of the most enjoyable.

Three Topics.

In this section, we'll cover three things:

A. **The Ideation Process:**
   There are some surprisingly similar ways that different ideas are developed. We'll briefly summarize what we know about how people have ideas.

B. **Brainstorming:**
   There is a formalized technique, developed by Alex Osborn, that you can run in your own agency group.

C. **Team Creativity:**
   Finally, we'll give you a few more thoughts on ways your agency can develop the ideas you'll need for a winning campaign.

A. The Ideation Process:

James Webb Young, a well-known copywriter (he worked for JWT in Chicago), wrote a terrific little book called *A Technique for Producing Ideas*. He gave us the definition still used most in advertising: *"An idea is nothing more or less than a new combination of old elements."*

Here is the way most of us put ideas together. It has six stages:

1. **Preparation:**

   This is where you and the agency team collect input and "do your homework." During this preparation stage, you'll start by being logical, and the information will go into the left side of the brain (Verbal/Storage/Memory).

2. **Frustration:**

   While ideas may seem logical after the fact, getting those two previously unrelated things to combine isn't always a logical process. So, unless the answer is obvious, the result is often frustration.

   You and your group may be frustrated. You worked hard to get the information together—so where's the answer?

3. **Incubation:**

   Now the right side of your brain—the part of your brain that associates things and makes connections—goes to work. Individually, and as a group, you'll shuffle through the information—consciously or subconsciously. And you'll associate new and old information in new combinations.

   You may actually want to "sleep on it" as you mull it over. It's a natural process.

   This is a time for your group to have fun. Have a pizza together as you talk it over. Your brains will be working in the background.

4. **Illumination:**

   This is the moment when you have the insight. You make the connection you never made before.

   It's the "AHA" moment. The light bulb goes on as two previously unrelated elements connect.

   That said, don't always expect a blinding flash of light.

As Leo Burnett observed, *"The secret of all effective originality in advertising is not the creation of new and tricky words and pictures, but putting familiar words and pictures into new relationships."*

5. **Evaluation:**

This is difficult. Yet, we don't know any way to make it easier.

You have to decide whether or not your idea is a good idea.

Your agency may have lots of ideas, but how do you tell the good ones from the bad ones? How indeed.

One of the ways to do this is to go back to the Critical/Analytical Left Side of your brains. While you've been having ideas, it's usually best to be nonjudgmental. Now it's time to be a bit more tough-minded. See Chapter Ten for more detail.

It's one of the critical decisions you'll make as a team.

6. **Elaboration:**

Although this is not part of James Webb Young's original outline, I think it makes this more clear.

Finally, you have to work on those ideas. You have to flesh them out from the initial bones of your thinking.

You may find that when you combine two of the new ideas you've created, you'll have even more new ideas.

Keep working at it. Remember that the more you know, the more things you have to combine with other things to create one of the most interesting things in our business—an idea.

B. Brainstorming:

Alex Osborn invented brainstorming in the 1930s. His book, *Applied Imagination,* was a bestseller. It's an easy-to-understand system of ideation that you can run in your own agency group. Here's how it works.

Brainstorming Guidelines.

First, there are four guidelines. Then we'll cover the six stages:

1. **Suspend Judgement:**

No negative comments. No critics.

Evaluation and criticism are postponed until later.

During the sessions there are "no bad ideas." (Though, of course, we know that there are.) During the session, if you don't like something, keep it to yourself. Later, there will be a time to "thin the herd."

2. **"Free Wheel":**

Let go of traditional inhibitions like "saying something silly."

Wild ideas are encouraged.

It's easier to tone something down than think something up.

3. **Quantity not Quality:**

The object is to think up the most ideas possible.

Often, one idea will spark another. This is good.

4. **Cross-Fertilize:**

It's okay to work off of someone else's ideas. In fact, it's encouraged. Something you say may spark an idea in someone else. And vice versa. Don't worry about authorship.

Remember, an idea doesn't care who has it.

The Six Stages of Brainstorming.

To get started, you'll need a Leader, hopefully someone who can write clearly and quickly. You'll also need lots of large sheets of paper and a room where you can put the paper up on the wall.

Usually, you give people time to prepare, though you'll all know the topic. If you want to invite one or two clever friends, that's okay, too. Eight people is about the maximum.

Here's how it works:

1. **The Problem:**

The Leader states the problem. Discuss the problem.

Let people say what's on their mind related to the problem.

2. **"How To..."**

Next, restate the problem in a "how to" format.

This should be done in as many ways as possible.

These "How To" statements are written at the top of large sheets of paper and posted around the room, which will stimulate more thoughts and more restatements.

Everything is written down and displayed. (Now you see why you need a big room.)

3. **"How Many Ways..."**

   The group selects the first statement for the brainstorm.

   Now rewrite the statement in a "How many ways..." format.

   Everyone calls out solutions and writes them down. If the Leader starts to fall behind, write down your ideas and wait your turn. It's easy for a good group to get ahead of the person writing things down.

   As ideas dry up on the first restatement, move on to another. Ideas are numbered and built on. You can refer to a previous idea and build on it with a new idea. Do this until the group is through generating ideas. A bit of a "lull" will occur.

   As everyone takes a break, agree on which is the best "How To..." This is your Basic Restatement.

   Rewrite it clearly, and display it prominently.

4. **The Warmup—"Other Uses For..."**

   During this next stage, everyone steps away from the problem for five minutes or so.

   Participants throw out ideas related to "Other uses for..." anything... a paper clip, pizza crust, whatever. The purpose is to get everyone's mental muscles loosened up again.

5. **Brainstorm!**

   Read the Basic Restatement and call out for ideas.

   Sometimes these will relate to ideas that were already mentioned. Remention them and move on quickly.

   Write things down as quickly as possible.

   By this time, you may have drafted a second person to write things down. Or people may write down their own ideas.

   By now, everyone should be into it. Ideas are continually generated and built upon.

6. **The Wildest Idea:**

   When it seems like everyone's done, take the wildest idea generated and try to make it into something useful.

   You may want to do this with a few ideas.

Sometimes this can stimulate one more round of ideation.

After the Brainstorm.

Now is the time for an initial evaluation by the group. With Post-Its, stickers, or colored markers, members can go around the room and indicate their favorite ideas.

Then, one or two members of the team go away and write up all the ideas, putting the favorites in the first section and all of the others in a follow-up section.

In a day or two, it's time to meet again and evaluate the best ideas from the session.

C. Team Creativity:

Over time, you will have developed working relationships as a team. There is little we can do to help you manage all the complexities of a half-dozen human beings working together.

But we can give you useful advice about how and where to do it.

"The Brain Wall."

One of the powerful aspects of brainstorming is the visual display of many different ideas. This works because it stimulates new connections. And when we make new connections, we tend to have new ideas.

So, you should find a place where you can put a lot of things up on the wall. Agencies do this all the time, that's why they have lots of rooms with corkboard and pins.

"The War Room."

Some agencies also have rooms dedicated to thinking about certain important projects. When they do, this room is usually called "The War Room." Some agencies have more than one.

If possible, your agency should try to find a War Room of your own. If it's not possible to have a room dedicated to this, try to find a room you can use often and get ready to put stuff up and take it down on a regular basis. We also have some notes on that—Note C.

A Business of Ideas.

At an agency, ideas are everyone's job.

The more you learn to have ideas, recognize other good ideas, and work to make those ideas better, the better you'll do.

War Room

"I want to see the logic track for your ideas."
—Steve Forcione, President Y&R International

Introduction.

The war room has been a tool used by advertising agencies for at least a couple of decades. My online dictionary defines it as a room from which a business or political strategy is planned.

But it is not just a conference room in which the planning takes place. It's a room that contains everything that can possibly relate to your plan. Most of it is pinned or taped to the walls. It has to be a physical room—a virtual room won't work.

Up Against the Wall.
A big wall—or board—or piece of foam core that can display all of the information you've been generating is critical.

The key activity to this room is the systematic development of information the outcome of which is the brand strategy. Commonly, it would include the elements that lead to strategy:

1. The target audience
2. The criteria for purchase motivation
3. The unique characteristics of the brand

Therefore, it would have information from the situation analysis relating to the people that you want to reach with the advertising. The research segment of the plan will reveal the criteria these people use to (1) make decisions about whether they will buy the category and (2) make decisions concerning the choice of brand.

Example: Red Robin.

Let's say you are working on a plan for Red Robin Gourmet Burgers. First, you need to identify the user group. One market segment may be moms. You will tell who these people are demographically, psychographically and any other way you can. You will write a mini-saga to help understand them (see Note D).

If you choose an audience with a household income of $75,000 to $149,999 you might ask yourself what percent of the total United States makes that amount of money. If it is only 7.5%, you will have to decide if that is enough to run a business. Then again, if it is 30% of the zip codes where Red Robins are located, that is something else entirely.

You will also need to list the key criteria that this group uses to make decisions about whether they will go out to eat or eat at home. You will want to understand the decision-making process for what kind of restaurant... do they just want food or do they want something a little bit nice?

The choice between fast food and Red Robin may be significant. If we find that they will choose a casual dining restaurant, then we may be in the running, but we need to know the criteria for restaurant selection within that category. This is critical information.

Our current and potential customers may choose based on mood, price, variety, food quality, atmosphere, location, and any number of other things. We will want to know the rank order of these criteria.

Next, we want to know what is unique about Red Robin. Certainly, the variety of hamburgers and cocktails is quite positive. This is not a McDonald's. Each restaurant has a distinctive combination of posters and memorabilia on the walls. The tower of onion rings is a "signature dish" that can separate them from the crowd.

Key to this section is understanding how these unique characteristics relate to what consumers want and need in a casual dining environment.

War Room

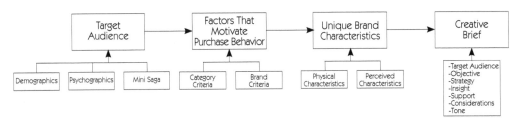

Finally, all this information has to run through your brain to develop a creative brief. Shahvez Afridi, director of planning at BBDO in Singapore, once told me that consumers only give you hints. They will never give you the answer. You have to figure that out on your own.

A Place for Everything.

That is the purpose for the war room. To provide a place somewhat removed from other distractions—a place where you can make certain that you have worked through all the information and have arrived at the best strategic alternative.

Print out the information from your computer. You might add pictures of the target group. Some use brightly colored string to link thoughts together. Get it up on a wall where you can see it all. Talk it through. Make sure you have considered everything.

At some point, you have to decide. Strategy is about choice.

If the respondents in your survey told you they make purchase decisions based on first price, and second taste; you still don't have to have a strategy based on either, and you still have not thought it through to the point of "uniqueness." There may be other differentiators discussed. You can have a freshness strategy, but you have to explain why freshness is superior to either price or taste.

You cannot simply choose to ignore the results of your research.

And you do have to decide.

Having a consistent place to make those decisions does improve the quality of those decisions. That's why you need a War Room.

Mini-saga

You can't teach height.
—Greg Taucher, DDB, on basketball

Introduction.

Tell a story. We all love stories. This story will be a short story about one member of your target audience, what Christie Abshire, a planner at Tracey-Locke in Dallas, calls her "peeps."

This short story will give some detail and help us to understand one member of the target audience.

It must be involving. It must have a beginning, a middle, and an end. It should show emotion in order to involve the creatives with the audience. Be sure to use all the insights you have.

Example:

Joey, third of five, left home at sixteen, travelled the country and wound up in Nottingham with a wife and kids. They do shifts, the kids play outside and ends never meet. Sometimes he'd give anything to walk away but he knows she's only got a year and she doesn't.[1]

We now know quite a bit about Joey as a result of this mini-saga. We know that he was a middle kid and left home quite young. We know that he and his wife don't have much money. They probably work in a factory and do shift work. Because the kids play outside, their home is probably small.

We know that Joey would like a better life, but he knows his wife only has a year to live and he will be the only continuity for the family. We know enough to appeal to him if we are selling mass consumption food or a program for him to improve his education or…

Your Turn.

Now it is your turn to write a mini-saga about one member of your target audience. It will help you to understand your "peeps." It may take a bit of practice, but when you are finished it will be a way for your creative team to understand and relate to the people you want to persuade to do something as a result of the advertising.

[1] A Life. by Jane Rosenberg, Brighton, UK. From *A Whole New Mind* by Daniel Pink. Berkley Publishing Group. New York. 2005.

Advertising Media

In simpler times, advertising people had two concerns: what to say and how to say it. Now the issue is where, when and how can advertising reach receptive prospects. Today's toughest question is how to find your customers at the most strategic time— that's why media is the new creative frontier.
—Keith Reinhard, Chairman, DDB

Introduction.

Efficiency. Effectiveness. Target Identification.
The advertising media planning process seeks to select those media that will deliver the Target Audience so as to allow the advertiser to place advertising in front of the most desirable group of people using the least resources.

Quite simply, the advertiser wants the most efficient and the most effective medium to reach the identified Target Audience.

Increasing Opportunities. Increasing Complexity.
The media plan continues to grow in complexity as the media opportunities have increased.

We have evolved from three television networks that could deliver a large audience at an efficient cost, to a complex world of strong local independents, "Superstations," unwired networks, cable TV, and other emerging broadcast systems such as cinema advertising, in order to deliver an increasingly fragmented audience.

And, this doesn't even count digital media.

It is, however, still one of the key areas of advertising that relies on numbers in its decision-making process. Furthermore, clients generally feel much more comfortable with media than they do with creative, because it is quantifiable.

Increasing CPMs and a general decrease in advertising effectiveness is a concern for most marketers.

The Media Planning Process.

As you write the media plan, try to visualize the key buyers and users of the Brand and those who influence the buyers and users of the Brand.

A great deal of the process is to identify who these people are and how they are different from other people—where they live and work, when they buy, how often they consume what they buy, and what is the best way to reach them.

The following is set up to be similar to what you will write in the media section of your marketing planning document. It covers objectives, strategies, rationale, tactics, and buying.

A. Objectives:

What Will You Accomplish?

The objectives of the media plan are intended to describe what the media plan will accomplish. This should be in the same language as the marketing media strategies, which in turn are intended to describe how the marketing objectives will be fulfilled.

Refer back to the marketing strategies you wrote in Chapter Six for the language to be used in the media objectives.

Though the plan may be lengthy, the objectives should be short and to the point. It is rare when media objectives will exceed one page.

Common objectives would include:

1. **Target Audience:**

The Target Audience is most often described demographically.

Gender and age are the most common demographic terms used. But additional characteristics can be added depending on the capability of the auditing service to provide ratings for a more detailed group, and the information you have to define your target audience.

If you have information that indicates you have a target audience of homemakers, it is likely that you will use daytime television.

If you know that your key consumer is a working woman, it is more likely that you will use a daypart that woman is likely to watch—early fringe, prime access, prime, late fringe, or late night. It is unlikely that a working woman will watch daytime television (except, of course, those who record a program and timeshift).

An example of the objective might be:

To deliver a target audience of men 35 and older, with special attention given to those with upper income and education.

2. **Geography:**
Geographically, the media objective identifies where the advertising should appear in order to fulfill the marketing objective.

Virtually every brand sold will have a geographic skew. It is easy to understand that more snow tires are sold in Michigan than in Arizona or that Florida is a good market for denture cleansers.

This geographic objective will identify how you give importance to those markets that will yield greater sales.

If the media plan is based on developing Brand potential, then the following example could be used:

To provide a base of advertising nationally, with additional advertising placed in areas with the greatest opportunity for sales as defined by a brand potential index. (See Note A.)

If the geographic allocation of media funds will be determined by a current brand development index, then the objective might be:

To provide a base of advertising nationally, with additional advertising placed in areas that have historically had the greatest sales.

3. **Seasonality:**
The seasonal objective of the media plan will identify when sales are expected to be the greatest.

Even in Michigan, more snow tires are sold in September than in April, and more canned tomato soup is sold in fall and winter than during the spring and summer.

This objective will provide the guide for what you want to do to take advantage of sales peaks throughout the year. The following might be considered for some brands:

To deliver advertising throughout the year in line with sales as evidenced by historical trends.

However, if you choose to allocate funds throughout the year based on the statistical smoothing method described in Note B, then the Seasonality objective for media might look like this:

To deliver advertising throughout the year in line with how advertising will lead sales.

4. **Continuity, Flighting:**
   This objective will address whether advertising is desirable in bursts or at a lower level on a continuity basis.

   An example of an objective for this section might be:

   To deliver advertising in a continuous fashion throughout the year.

   If it is clear that sales are skewed to one season, snow tires in Michigan or ice cream novelties anywhere in the U.S., then the objective should look more like this:

   To flight advertising delivery in line with past sales.

   This objective might also be appropriate if you choose the advertising seasonal smoothing method, which is explained in Note B of this chapter.

5. **Creative Constraints:**
   Occasionally, a product will need a specific medium in order to communicate the benefit.

   Generally speaking, food is better presented in a medium that allows the visual communication of appetite appeal.

   Music might be more effectively sold through a medium that offers good sound reproduction than one with good visuals—although unique album graphics and print media with a high concentration of iTunes buyers may yield other advantages. Be careful with this kind of objective.

   The intent of this objective is not to dictate the media, but to establish constraints that may exist.

   The other consideration for the media objectives based on creative constraints is when there is no quality advertising for the Brand in a given medium. (It seems the creative strategy cannot be translated into a good outdoor board for Crisco.) Then, the creative constraint might be a medium—outdoor.

An example of a media objective that addresses creative constraints for Bisquick might be:

To use media that allow for the visual representation of the appetite appeal of food prepared with Bisquick.

6. **Reach Versus Frequency:**
Finally, the media objectives should address whether the Brand will benefit from more reach or more frequency.

An example might be:

To maintain a four-week frequency of at least four, and to maximize reach within the budget.

B. Strategies:
Allocation.
Media strategies are statements of how media objectives will be fulfilled. Strategically, many advertisers have chosen to allocate media monies to:

1. Times of the year when sales are greatest
2. Markets that yield the greatest sales
3. Target Audiences that have proven that they buy the product

Some plans have become so exacting that a portion of the budget is spent in direct proportion to where and when each case is purchased.

For example, if a company expects to sell 10,000 cases a year and spends $1,000,000, then they are spending $100 in advertising for each case of product sold. If we estimate 200 cases will be sold in the Glendive DMA, then $20,000 will be budgeted for Glendive.

This philosophy can also work with the allocation of media impressions instead of dollars. Impression allocation is a little more accurate, but rewards each market for its sales potential (however that potential has been defined) with no regard for media cost.

This impression allocation method will therefore deliver the right number of GRPs to a given DMA, though its CPM may be totally out of line (San Francisco for example). It would under-deliver a DMA like New York (which is very efficient) compared to a dollar allocation method.

While somewhat less common, this same system can work in the seasonal allocation of media dollars. Some seasons are relatively more expensive.

Continuing with the example, if 15% of sales take place in June, then it is desirable to have 15% of our media weight influence sales in June—or slightly before. (See Note B at the end of this chapter for more detail.)

Seasonal Costs.

Historically, fourth quarter has been the most expensive. The Christmas season, along with the first weeks of a new television season, has been the most expensive within that quarter.

If we want to know if the more expensive weeks of the year are worth it, we simply develop an index to compare the difference in expected sales at that time with the premium to be paid for the advertising during the weeks under consideration.

This index could be used in conjunction with the impact of no advertising during a given period and advertising that would be greater than what the index would suggest.

Offensive Strategies.

Offensive strategies, wherein the advertiser chooses to allocate more funds to those areas where sales are poor and more funds to those months with less sales, are less common.

The idea seems great—a little more advertising in July and we can start to even out the seasonal sales curve. But there may be a strong reason why sales are poor in those particular times and places, and advertising dollars can't fix it. People just aren't going to buy more snow tires in Phoenix, and the market for hot chocolate is clearly limited in August.

However, virtually every new product must allocate its monies using an offensive strategy. Remember, you can only spend money once.

Once these issues are resolved, it's time to organize them into a media strategy.

The Media Strategy Format.

The media strategy format that follows may be shortened by combining some of the elements if the plan is not complicated. If it is very complicated, headings may be added.

1. **Media Mix and Types:**

   The strategy statement should simply identify if there will be a mix of media or not and identify which media will be used.

   If the plan will use both network and spot television, this is the same medium—not a mix.

   The statement might read:

   To use a media mix of television and outdoor.

   Or...

   To use magazines as the sole advertising medium.

2. **Media Format or Classes:**

   This is where the plan will identify the subgroups within each medium. The strategy statement will ascertain which dayparts will be used in television and whether it will be spot or network. The statement will identify which group(s) of magazines—national, men's, news, fashion, women's service, etc.—will be used.

   An example of the media format or classes strategy follows:

   To use newsweeklies and men's action magazines.

3. **Geographic Use of Media:**

   The specific method that will be used to determine which markets will receive advertising support and which will not, should be included in this strategy statement.

   Brand development indices are a good starting point for determining where marketing funds will be allocated.

   Markets should likely receive a proportionately higher allocation of available media resources based on BDI. (See Note A in this Chapter.)

   This would indicate a strategy like:

   To allocate media on a market-by-market basis, using brand development as the key parameter to determine individual market advertising weights.

   It is also possible to have a strategy wherein all markets are judged to be equal.

Strategically, the strategy might then be:

To allocate media evenly throughout the United States.

Which markets receive advertising is of major importance in the media plan.

Allocating that weight based on which markets can contribute to the greatest sales is consistent with the philosophy discussed at the beginning of this section.

4. Seasonal Use of Media:
The same is true of seasonal use of media as it is of geographic use. If the objective is to put more advertising in those months when sales have always been the best, then strategically the statement might read:

To advertise in key sales months with secondary emphasis given to lesser sales periods.

For more information see Note B on Seasonality.

5. Flighting versus Continuity:
The media strategy that addresses flighting and continuity must be consistent with all other media strategies by stating how the media plan will fulfill the media objectives, which in turn are stating how (as marketing strategies) the marketing objective will be satisfied.

Specifically, the strategy might be:

To use pulsing throughout the year with two-week flights and three-week hiatus periods.

This strategy could address the objective for continuity and flighting listed in the objectives section.

C. Rationale:

This is where the plan is to be defended. (Some media planners prefer to give the rationale for each segment after each strategy. That method is also sound for structure and understanding, but we will illustrate the rationale as a separate segment.)

The defense or substantiation for the plan should convince the reader that the media plan will contribute to the fulfillment of the marketing objective.

Comparison to Alternate Plans.

Very often, this requires a comparison of the recommended plan to another strong plan, particularly if the Brand has been using a significantly different plan than the one you are recommending.

For Example.

If the media plan uses a foundation of magazines with a little spot television for reinforcement to the low reading quintiles and to give additional geographic support to DMAs with strong brand potential indices, then an alternate plan might consider all television.

Network television could replace magazines for the national segment of the plan, with spot being unchanged. This alternate plan can be used to show the strength of the recommended plan.

Under no circumstances should this alternate plan be a "straw man" used solely to show substantiation for the recommended plan. It should be a real and substantive alternate.

This rationale, or defense, should be broken into two key parts:

1. **Support of Strategy:**
   This is the substantiation for how the media strategies of the plan will satisfy both the media objectives and the marketing objectives. If the media objectives are clear, then substantiation of those media objectives will be easier to communicate.

2. **Support of Delivery and Efficiency:**
   This part of the Rationale should seek to cite quantitative support for why the plan will fulfill both the media and marketing objectives.

   A very clean defense is to simply show that Plan A delivers, for example, +21% more GRPs than Plan B, or that Plan A delivers more GRPs to the low-reading quintiles—thereby, not under-delivering a major segment of the target audience.

D. Tactics:

The tactics segment of the media plan includes the specifics of how the plan will work, and what it will look like.

The following list is intended as a starting point to describe the media plan. Usually each of the following points are charts or tables of numbers with little or no explanation.

Each should be on a separate page.

1. **Media Vehicles:**
   This chart should be a simple list of the vehicles recommended by the plan, separated by medium.

2. **Reach, Frequency, and GRP Summary:**
   These numbers should be shown by quarter and total year. The following is a good setup for the chart that will be completed for this tactic. Fill in the numbers for the plan you are working on to see how it looks.

Exhibit A

ABC Brand
Reach, Frequency, and Gross Rating Point Summary

	1st Q		2nd Q		3rd Q		4th Q		FY '00	
	R/F	GRP	R/F	GRP	R/F	GRP	R/F	GRP	R/F	GRP
National:										
— Magazines										
— Network TV										
— Total National										
"A" Markets:										
— Spot TV										
—Total "A" Mkts										
"B" Markets:										
— Spot TV										
—Total "B" Mkts										

Please note that the reach, frequency, and gross rating points are not additive between "A" and "B" markets, because "A" market viewers will not see advertising that will appear in "B" markets.

3. **Cost Summary:**
   The Plan should also be shown by quarter and by total year. Some corporations will require that a specific split in the dollars be maintained from quarter to quarter or from first half to second half (i.e., no more than 60% of dollars may be spent in the first half, or no more than 40% of dollars in any one quarter).

This chart will allow the reader to ascertain compliance with corporate financial philosophy. (Columns, 1st half, and 2nd half, may be required additions.)

The following is a good setup for the chart that will be completed for this tactic. Fill in the numbers for the plan you are working on to see if the numbers are consistent with your intent.

Exhibit B

ABC Brand
Cost Summary ($M)*

	1st Q		2nd Q		3rd Q		4th Q		FY '00	
	$	%	$	%	$	%	$	%	$	%
National:										
— Magazines										
— Network TV										
— Total National										
"A" Markets:										
— Spot TV										
—Total "A" Mkts										
"B" Markets:										
— Spot TV										
—Total "B" Mkts										

*Percent of total budget by medium

The chart should show the percentage for each medium by time (i.e., 26% of magazine dollars are spent in the first quarter).

The percentage column under FY '00 should show the percent that each medium represents of the total budget.

Again, please take notice that the dollars are not additive between "A" and "B" markets, because "A" market viewers will not see television that is aired in "B" markets.

4. **Flow Chart:**

The flow chart is a visual representation of everything that will be in the media plan for a full year. It is one of the better ways to present an overview of the media effort to management—and to those less familiar with the details, such as franchisees of Midas or Taco Bell, for example.

A separate flow chart should be completed for every market that has a different media plan. If there are two groups of markets that will receive extra weight, then there will be three flow charts—one for the national plan, one for "A" markets (which will receive the highest level of local support) and one for "B" markets (which will also receive additional weight, but at a level below the "A" markets).

The Flow Chart Should Contain the Following Elements:
a. Media.
Show what media will be used, at what level, and when the advertising will appear (or be heard) via that medium.

Be sure to include specific vehicles and the size of the advertisement for newspapers and magazines (unless the list is long, then include it in a separate chart—see Tactic 1), day-parts and GRP levels for television, GRP levels, or showing for outdoor, and number of spots per week for radio.

If possible use a different color or pattern to designate each distinct element of the plan.

b. Seasonality.
A Seasonality index should be included at the top of the chart to indicate sales indices for each month of the year.

This allows the reader to quickly see when advertising will appear in relationship to the key sales months.

c. Budget.
The dollar budget for each medium should be included on the far right side of the chart.

This allows the reader to compare costs of the various elements of the plan easily.

d. Reach and Frequency.
These numbers should be calculated on a Target Audience basis and filled in at the bottom of the flow chart. This allows the reader to see instantly how well the plan delivers the Target

Audience, without thumbing back through the charts to find the total numbers.

Finally, the flow chart should contain the Brand name, a designation for the year, as well as the date when the plan was completed, and the planner's initials at the bottom of the page.

See the Flow Chart on page 208 for more detail.

5. **Sales to Advertising Comparison:**
The advertising to sales numbers should be shown in two ways:

- over history, and
- for this year's plan in comparison to sales in each DMA.

a. **History.**
This chart is used for substantiation of the budget.

It shows how advertising dollars, brand sales, and the resulting case rate have changed over time.

Exhibit C

ABC Brand
Advertising, Sales, Case Rate—Comparison
(Index versus year ago)

	Fiscal Year 2010		Fiscal Year 2009		Fiscal Year 2008	
	Dollars	(Index)	Dollars	(Index)	Dollars	(Index)
Advertising Budget	$9150.0M	(109)	$8425.2M	(112)	$7551.3M	(106)
Cases Sold	4596.1M	(109)	42166.6M	(112)	3764.8M	(106)
Case Rate	$ 1.99	(100)	$ 2.00	(100)	$ 2.01	(100)

Please note that, in this case, the budget needs no substantiation once the reader agrees to the marketing objective, because the case rate has been consistent over a three-year period.

Detailed substantiation would be necessary if the marketing plan author chose to change the case rate or the method for the allocation of funds for some reason. But, since the plan recommends continuity within the realm of what has been done in the past, the reader must agree after seeing the numbers.

b. **DMA by BPI:**
This chart is used for substantiation of the geographic allocation

of the media funds and should show the quantity of dollars in comparison to the brand potential index.

Exhibit D
ABC Brand
Advertising to Sales Potential Comparison

| | Media Allocation | | | |
	Dollars	(Index)	BPI	Ratio
Abilene-Sweetwater				
Albany, GA				
Alb-Schenectady-Troy				
Albuquerque				
Alexandria, LA				
Alexandria, MN				
Alpena				
Amarillo				
Anniston				
Ardmore-Ada				

The ratio column is a mathematical comparison of the media allocation index to the Brand potential index. It can be subtraction or division. It doesn't matter—the purpose is to allow the reader quick access to the information by showing the markets that are in line with one another and which markets are inconsistent.

The chart should be completed through all 210 DMAs.

6. **Competitive Media and Sales Review:**
This review will act as substantiation for both the media and the marketing of the plan. Remember, some of this information was developed for the Situation Analysis.

a. **Category Sales History.**
This chart may be used to defend the marketing objectives by showing history as support for future projections. It should show the brands to which growth is accruing over time.

This chart will make it easy for the reader to see which brands are growing, which are declining, and the vitality of the category.

ABC Brand
Category Sales History
(Index & Change versus year ago)

| | Fiscal Year 2010 | | | | Fiscal Year 2009 | | | |
	Sales	Index	Share	Change	Sales	Index	Share	Change
ABC Brand								
Brand D								
Brand E								
Brand F								
Brand G								
Brand H								
All Others								
Total								

b. Competitive Case Rates.

A case rate is the number of dollars an advertiser allocates to the advertising budget for each case sold.

The competitive media spending chart (see the Situation Analysis) can be combined with the sales chart (Exhibit "E") to make a category case rate chart in order to see how the Brand's spending rates compare with the category.

ABC Brand
Category Sales History
(Index & Change versus year ago)

| | Fiscal Year 2010 | | | Fiscal Year 2009 | | |
	Sales	Media	Case Rate	Sales	Media	Case Rate
ABC Brand						
Brand D						
Brand E						
Brand F						
Brand G						
Brand H						
All Others						
Total						

The Case Rate.

The case rate is a budgeting method similar to the percentage of sales method. A simple percent of sales method can be substituted for those brands and categories that do not use the case rate method. For example, a brand like Dial Soap may spend $1.50 a case in marketing, commonly divided between advertising and below-the-line. A brand like Chevrolet may spend $300 per car. Hillshire Farms may spend 4% of sales on advertising. Each method is a little different, but all get the brand to the same place.

7. **Target Group/User Analysis:**

    This segment will support the Target Audience selection made in the People part of the marketing strategy. This same Target Audience is used in the media objectives.

    The Target Audience should, at a minimum, be substantiated using the standard demographic parameters of gender, age, income, education, and professional status. When it is important, include other parameters provided by MRI or SMRB, or from primary or other secondary research that has been gleaned on behalf of the client.

    The chart that substantiates the demographics of the Target Audience of Viva Paper Towels might look like this:

Exhibit G

Viva Target Audience Demographics
Paper Towels Category
(Incidence of Usage, Index to Average)

	All Users		Heavy Users		Light Users		Viva		Bounty	
	Incd	Indx	Incd	Indx	Incd	Indx	Incd	Indx	Incd	Indx
Age:										
25–34	84.7	100	34.0	95	12.6	98	13.7	93	38.9	95
35–44	85.0	100	40.5	112	10.0	77	15.8	107	42.1	102
45–54	87.6	104	38.8	108	10.4	81	15.1	103	42.4	103
55–64	85.5	101	38.9	108	10.9	84	18.5	126	44.8	109
65+	84.4	100	32.4	90	20.2	157	14.9	101	43.8	107
Income:										
$60M +	89.5	106	44.0	122	8.3	64	20.3	138	49.0	119
$50–60M	86.6	102	43.1	120	8.7	67	17.6	119	46.9	114
$40–50M	86.6	102	41.2	114	8.8	68	16.8	114	44.0	107

Source: SMRB

Note that in the portion of the chart addressing age, enough age breaks are included to substantiate our Target Audience age of 35 to 64. It is easy to see that usage of Viva Paper Towels is significantly lower under age 35 and over age 64. This chart will make it easy for the reader to see this difference quickly. Additionally, this age target will put Viva in a good position to attract heavy users, not light users.

In this case, the income portion of the chart need not continue past the $40,000 break because it is a straight line continuum. It may be sufficient to simply target Viva as "upper income."

The same type of information should be continued in this chart for education and professional status. Simmons does not break out gender for the paper towel category, so it is not included here.

Be sure to read the county size information because it can help identify if the Target Audience is located in city or rural areas. This would impact the geography allocation part of the media plan.

It is likely that psychographic parameters should also be included. Most often actual research will be unaffordable to determine which psychographic groups will be interested in the Brand—and often quite difficult to match it up with media usage, unless the connection is quite behavior specific. For example, ferret owners and *Modern Ferret* magazine, or those in the advertising industry who will tend to read *AdWeek* and *Advertising Age*.

After studying the characteristics of the groups, it is likely that some conclusions can be drawn based on other information you have available for users of the Brand.

8. **Detail on Planned Medium:**
   A decision grid should be developed for the primary medium that is planned.

   Note A in Chapter 8 gives some detail on decision grids and how this discipline can be used to make a decision concerning which markets (DMAs) are appropriate for the Brand to buy extra advertising.

   That same decision grid discipline can be used to determine which vehicles to include in the plan within an already established medium.

If magazines have already been established as the primary medium for Tree Top Apple Juice, vehicles in rank order of value could be established by using parameters like CPM, cost, and reach against the Target Audience (W 25–34), against the category (apple juice) users, and against orange juice users.

Other parameters that could be considered might be editorial content, number of days reading time, or number of children in the household. The list of other information to consider is virtually endless.

The chart used to determine the values of the parameters might look like this:

Exhibit H

Tree Top Apple Juice
Vehicle Selection Parameters
(Raw Numbers)

	Efficiency		Reach			
	CPM	Cost	W 25-34	Categ. Users	O.J.	Circulation
Magazines:						
Better H & G	$ 12.09	$ 119.0 M	17.7	20.6	20.0	8,143.0 M
Cosmopolitan	14.33	53.2	13.2	8.2	8.0	2,760.0
Country Living	17.42	43.7	5.6	6.6	5.1	1,833.8
Family Circle	10.80	76.1	16.7	19.0	18.6	5,922.5
Gourmet	19.34	24.6	2.2	2.0	2.0	806.3
McCall's	11.77	69.2	17.0	15.5	14.5	5,142.5
Redbook	12.61	65.9	17.8	11.6	26.2	3,950.5
Seventeen	13.85	35.2	2.5	3.5	3.1	1,752.3
Woman's Day	10.96	73.1	14.3	16.9	16.4	5,571.6
Working Mother	24.52	30.5	3.0	2.7	2.5	905.4

Source: SMRB, SRDS

The magazines considered in the grid should meet some basic constraints—over 800,000 circulation, minimum brand reach, high incidence of usage, etc. The reasons must be able to be substantiated.

Turning Numbers Into Values.

The next chart will turn these numbers into values.

The first step is to determine which of these parameters is the most important and to give them values which add to 100.

The decision grid chart would then look like this:

Exhibit I

Tree Top Apple Juice
Vehicle Selection Decision Grid
(Calculated Values)

	Efficiency		Reach				
	CPM	Cost	W 25-34	Cat. Use	O.J.	Circ.	Total
Values	35.0	5.0	20.0	15.0	10.0	5.0	100.0
Better H & G	31.3	1.0	19.9	15.0	7.6	5.0	79.8
Cosmopolitan	26.4	2.3	14.8	6.0	3.1	1.7	54.3
Country Living	21.7	2.8	6.3	4.8	1.9	1.3	38.8
Family Circle	35.0	1.6	18.8	13.8	7.1	3.6	79.9
Gourmet	19.5	5.0	2.5	1.5	7.6	0.5	36.6
McCall's	32.1	1.8	19.1	11.3	5.3	3.2	72.8
Redbook	30.0	1.9	20.0	8.4	10.0	2.4	72.7
Seventeen	27.3	3.5	2.8	2.5	1.2	1.1	38.4
Woman's Day	34.5	1.7	16.1	12.3	6.3	3.4	74.3
Working Mother	15.4	4.0	3.4	2.0	1.0	0.6	26.4

Source: SMRB, SRDS

The magazines that are the best choices for Tree Top, based on the decision-making criteria established, are *Better Homes & Gardens* and *Family Circle* with *Woman's Day* a little farther down the list. *McCall's* and *Redbook* would also be good choices.

Every chart in the marketing plan should have the initials of the person who prepared the chart, the date of the preparation, and the source of the material. It will surprise you how often this information is useful.

Additional Charts.

It is likely that additional charts may be required to fully describe the media plan.

For example, it may be that a chart comparing plan "A" to plan "B" on a quarterly GRP basis will make the convincing argument for the second part of the Rationale. That chart should be developed and included in this Tactics segment.

This is the fun part of the project—finding new ways to present the information and new ways to substantiate the plan.

Too many people use the time allotted to simply complete the project and have no time to have fun with it. That's sad. A lot of work has been done—now take some time to play with some of your ideas. Not only will you learn more, you'll probably end up with a better media plan.

E. Buying:

The last segment of the media plan contains the instructions for the buying group. These instructions should contain two parts.

1. **Constraints:**

   List those items that are to be restricted from the media buying. An example here might be that the client prefers to avoid television programming that is controversial in nature.

2. **Rationale:**

   This is where the defense or reasoning for the buying direction is provided.

The part of the plan allocated to buying may be extensive, but it also may be as short as a paragraph in length.

For more information, please also read:

1. Marian Azzaro. *Strategic Media Decisions*. 2nd ed. (Chicago: The Copy Workshop, 2008).
   Chapters Nine provides an overview of strategy development.

2. Jack Z. Sissors and Roger Baron. *Advertising Media Planning*. 6th ed. (Chicago: NTC Business Books, 2002).
   The first nine chapters set the stage for strategy development.

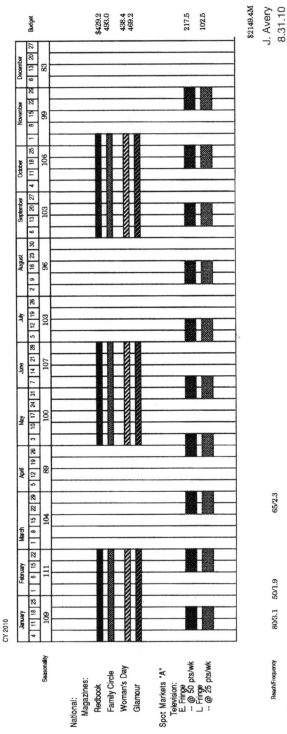

Flow Chart
ABC Brand

Geographic Allocation of Media Dollars

"Fish where the fish are biting."
—Unknown

This discussion will help you to determine how to allocate media dollars across a large number of markets.

Allocate Based on Sales Potential.

This geographic allocation of resources should be based on sales potential. Clearly the first step is to determine sales potential.

The Geography part of the Situation Analysis was used to determine those areas that have had the greatest history of sales as evidenced by BDI. This Note A will show how to transform the BDI (Brand Development Index) into a BPI (Brand Potential Index).

We will seek to project the Brand's sales potential in every district, region, state, or DMA in the country.

If a BDI is not available as the base, then this process will be more difficult, but a projection of sales by DMA can still be made.

If a BDI is available, it is the first step—because BDI is a measure of the history of the Brand's success, adjusted for population.

It is likely that this history will be repeated if nothing new has been implemented. Most often, however, the next step is to adjust the BDI by factors other than sales that may impact on those sales in the coming year.

Selecting Parameters.

There is no specific number of parameters that should be used to adjust the BDI, but I usually recommend that students seek seven or more parameters. The selection of these parameters should be based on what will contribute to the sales of the Brand. *Your goal is to think of what influences the Brand's sales.*

It may be the incidence of the target group by DMA, but it could also be some outside characteristic.

Examples.
Ivory Bar Soap, for example, works better in soft water than it does in hard water. A measure of water hardness by DMA would help you to understand Ivory's sales potential. Mufflers wear out faster in states that use salt to control ice and snow. Highway department information that tells where and how much salt is used might be used to project future sales for Midas Mufflers.

If the usage of the Brand is tied to some other product or category (butterscotch topping is probably tied to the sale of ice cream) then the sales of that category could be used to project sales of the Brand. If you look, you will be surprised at the number of outside influences there are—hamburgers and ketchup, syrup and pancake mix, bar soap and water softener, fish and lemons, etc.

You will soon begin to see that the writing of a marketing plan contains many of the same elements found in sleuthing. Be a good detective.

Incidence of Current Users.
Another parameter to consider is the incidence of current users (or target audience) on a DMA basis.

The U.S. Census can provide the information, or check *Sales and Marketing's Survey of Buying Power.*

MRI or SMRB can provide some information, but the information is only available on a regional basis. While that is better than no information at all, it is not very sensitive when we are trying to allocate resources on a market-by-market basis.

Work to find the information on a DMA basis. It is possible to gain this information on the incidence of age and gender, income, education, etc., on a DMA basis.

If you are certain that you have isolated the best possible target audience, then allocating more funds to where these people exist should produce better geographical sales.

If, for example, you know that people who earn more than $60,000 a year have a higher propensity to buy your Brand, then you might factor that information into the decision-making process.

Do not, however, use the absolute number of people in an DMA who earn $60,000 a year or more. Use instead the percent of people in the DMA who earn this amount.

The absolute number will give too much importance to the physical size of the DMA. While that may be important, make sure you can control the importance of all parameters by making them comparative to all others, and by having a reason for doing so.

Calculating the BPI.
BPI stands for Brand Potential Index. This helps us understand where to hunt for new customers.

Let's assume we are seeking to increase awareness of Midas automotive shops among young professional women. The first step is to calculate BDI by DMA. Next, information needs to be found that we judge will impact the sales in each DMA during the period of time for which the plan is written. All this information can then be put on one chart or table.

The BPI is calculated by simple mathematical weighting to determine the BPI. The chart itself could look like the one that follows.

Exhibit A

Midas Muffler and Brake Shops
Brand Potential Index FY '10

	BDI	HWY Salt	%US Pop	Incidence of the Target Group			
				W 18–34	$40M+	Coll. Ed.	BPI
Abilene-Sweet							
Albany, GA							
Alb-Schen-Troy							
Albuquerque							
Alexandria, LA							
Alexandria, MN							
Alpena							
Amarillo							
Anniston							
Ardmore-Ada							

Sales Potential Rationale.

The Media segment of the planning document should contain an overview of markets with greatest sales potential. This would be found in the strategy segment, under geography, and the substantiation for why those markets have the greatest sales potential under the rationale heading.

That substantiation is a defense of the parameters shown on the chart chosen to adjust BDI in the decision grid.

It is a simple task to point out why a greater incidence of women 25 to 34 in a given DMA will impact on sales (if that is the target audience).

But take care to avoid just defining the parameter; justify why that parameter will impact on future sales.

After all, if the reader agrees with your choice of parameters and the weighting, then they must agree with your conclusions.

Offense or Defense.

The decision to develop a defensive or offensive strategy will be saved for the strategy segment of your document, but you may well find this a difficult decision.

Most packaged goods manufacturers choose a defensive strategy because there is a history of success and they seek to reduce risk. Areas where business is strong usually represent additional genuine potential. It is likely that there are historic and geographic reasons why the brand is preferred in this area.

Business has inertia. Remember, inertia means things at rest will tend to stay at rest and things in motion will tend to keep moving.

Areas where business is strong will tend to respond well. Areas where business is weak tend to remain that way.

Tide will probably sell more detergent next year in Denver simply because, historically, Tide has sold more detergent in Denver every year for the past twenty years.

On the other hand, the low BDI areas have an appeal.

Sometimes we feel that all they need is a little more advertising pressure to make these markets into real opportunity areas. Clearly, they yield less than their fair share of the marketplace, and it may be that a small adjustment in the plan will put a low BDI market more in line with what it should yield. You may be right. As they say, "Hey, it could happen."

However, you should also remember that every dollar you allocate to a low BDI area is a dollar you may not spend in a proven high BDI area.

A company like Boingo relies on business travelers for the backbone of its business. With only two outlets in Ada, Oklahoma, it is likely the BDI is low. It is not likely they will allocate funds to Ada in order to build BDI because this will require they take money away from markets that have a much higher incidence of business travelers and more outlets.

This is the reason for a Brand Potential Index.

Search for New Ways to Look at Things.
Part of the fun and the useful learning that comes from working on the media portion of the plan is finding new ways to accomplish what you want and new ways of defending that plan.

Sometimes it is appropriate to make up new formulas.

For example, a BDI or BPI is commonly referred to geographically, but an index that is similar to BDI or BPI could be developed to show history or sales potential by demographics or Seasonality.

These are useful, but less common, so you will need to find a new name for them, like Demographic Development Index or Seasonality Development Index.

Remember, one of your objectives is to become more proficient at dealing with media. And, as Keith Reinhard noted in the quote at the beginning of this chapter, "media is the new creative frontier."

Seasonal Allocation of Media Dollars

"Fish when the fish are biting."
—Unknown

When?

Media planning is often described as the determination of the who, what, when, and where of advertising.

Discussion of the "when" of media planning, however, is often reduced to a discussion of scheduling.

The purpose for this discussion is to make the case for a more exacting method for the allocation of media dollars (or impressions) on a monthly or seasonal basis.

Advertising Should Lead Sales.

Marketing (including media) monies have historically been placed in those months when the greatest return is expected.

Most often this has translated to the allocating of media funds in direct proportion to the months when the greatest percent of sales has historically taken place.

Clearly, the goal is to build Brand awareness during the period when the potential consumer is most likely to be influenced.

Most often this requires advertising to lead sales.

Think about it. To simply allocate advertising dollars by using percent of sales to directly determine percent of media budget, on a monthly basis, is insufficient because this method does not allow advertising to lead sales. It assumes that advertising works instantly.

Advertising can be adjusted for the period of time necessary for the potential consumer to understand the advertising message.

A stronger impact could be made by allocating money just prior to the period when sales are anticipated. Naturally, this will vary by brand. An advertisement for a week-end sale at Boston Market is expected to work faster than an advertisement extolling the attributes of United Airlines with the lower fares that come from booking in advance.

A. Smoothing:

The intent of this explanation is to show how statistical smoothing can be used to allow advertising to lead into the key selling periods.

To do this, you need to know the speed at which the advertising works—or how fast the consumer learns. There are very few brands that advertise that have this knowledge.

However, a likely assumption is that the learning time would show one-third of our advertising to be motivating in the month in which it appears, one-third would take a month for the consumer to digest, and the last third would need two months to make an impact.

This lead-in to specific months of delivery is called *two-month smoothing*. It is likely that a brand employing high frequency during a four-week period would require a shorter smoothing period because awareness levels would likely be higher.

Low frequency would require a longer smoothing period. And, of course, a creative product with higher recall would shorten the smoothing period.

B. Method:

The budget that will be spent in each month can be determined by allocating the budget in percentage terms directly in line with monthly sales percentages.

In Exhibit A (page 218) the monthly sales figures are used directly for the original monthly budget percentages. In May, 8.9% of sales (index 107 to the average month) translates to 8.9% of the budget. The example calls for an annual budget of $7,500M.

The next step is to smooth the monthly budget. Based on the assumption of learning time, simply divide the budget by three and allocate that one-third of the budget to the month when the sales are expected, one-third to the prior month, and the last third to the month before that. In July, for example, we expect 9.4% of the Brand's sales.

This equates to a monthly budget of $705M.

One-third of that money ($235M) will be spent in July, one-third in June, and one-third in May. The June and May monies will be leading into the July sales period. In August, the monthly budget is $772.5M. One-third will be allocated to August ($257.5M), one-third to July (again, because July advertising will help to make sales in August), and one-third in June. And so on.

When the thirds are added again, the new allocation will show $662.5M in July. This is $42.5M less than the monthly allocation would call for and represents 8.8% of the budget (index 94 versus the original monthly budget or sales percentage).

C. **Rationale:**

This two-month smoothing method for the allocation of seasonal media (or marketing) dollars is important for three reasons:

1. Statistically accounting for the time it takes for the advertising to educate current and potential consumers both in Brand awareness and conversion to the Brand will aid the advertiser to be more precise with the use of media or marketing funds.
2. Recognition of learning time could provide the Brand with information that could impact calculation of effective frequency. This in turn could allow the Brand to determine an optimum spending level.
3. In the absence of learning time information, a two-month lead time may not be precise, but the result will likely lead to a better understanding of how consumers are influenced, and the time it takes to make that influence felt. This in turn will allow the Brand to have a clear understanding of the seasonal budget impact on sales.

D. **Conclusion:**

Smoothing can allow advertising to lead into sales instead of assuming that advertising works instantly.

The lead-in period is a function of the learning time required by the advertising and can likely be dictated by product life cycle and the impact of the creative product.

Understanding this learning period can contribute to the knowledge necessary for the amount of frequency needed to build Brand awareness and conversion to the Brand.

Smoothing will ultimately aid in market share growth for the Brand, since it provides message weight delivery proportionate to when consumers will buy and in line with how those consumers learn.

Exhibit A

Seasonal Allocation of Media Dollars
Two Month Smoothing

	Percent Sales	Seasonal Index	Percent Budget	Budget	Smoothing Third	Third	Third	Budget	Smoothed Percent Budget	Index
January	6.9	83	6.9	$517.5	$172.5	$162.5	$205.0	$540.0	7.20	104
February	6.5	78	6.5	487.5	162.5	205.0	187.5	555.0	7.40	114
March	8.2	98	8.2	615.0	205.0	187.5	222.5	615.0	8.20	100
April	7.5	90	7.5	562.5	187.5	222.5	222.5	632.5	8.43	112
May	8.9	107	8.9	667.5	222.5	222.5	235.0	680.0	9.07	102
June	8.9	107	8.9	667.5	222.5	235.0	257.5	715.0	9.53	107
July	9.4	113	9.4	705.0	235.0	257.5	170.0	662.5	8.83	94
August	10.3	124	10.3	772.5	257.5	170.0	220.0	647.5	8.63	83
September	6.8	82	6.8	510.0	170.0	220.0	190.0	580.0	7.73	114
October	8.8	106	8.8	660.0	220.0	190.0	255.0	665.0	8.87	101
November	7.6	91	7.6	570.0	190.0	255.0	172.5	617.5	8.23	108
December	10.2	122	10.2	765.0	255.0	172.5	162.5	590.0	7.87	77
Total	100.0	100	100.0	$7500.0	$2500.0	$2500.0	$2500.0	$7500.0	100.00	100

Digital Media

An invasion of armies can be resisted,
but not an idea whose time has come.
— Victor Hugo, 1852

Introduction.

The discussion of media planning must include what kinds of media vehicles do what kinds of jobs. That analysis is quite easy when the discussion is restricted to traditional media. See the exhibit on page 223.

But non-traditional, digital, and online advertising complicate the issue. The purpose for this note is to add the basics associated with the planning of digital media. For this section, I will treat the terms digital, interactive, and online advertising as synonyms.

The whole premise of advertising in digital media is to get current and potential customers to interact with the brand in a non-threatening environment. Hence the term interactive advertising. Many professionals use the term "engagement." They seek to get people to "engage" with the brand.

As a result, the advertising online must be usable. So, advertisers often test the advertising for "usability." This makes sense. Because if people find it too hard to navigate your website or advertising, they will give up.

I won't discuss the building of a website here, since I believe that virtually all businesses now recognize that this is mandatory for doing business anywhere. I also believe you are quite familiar with websites.

Even if the discussion is restricted to just advertising on digital media, there are more than a few alternatives to consider.

Mobile and in-game (i.e. X-Box, Playstation, etc) fall in the digital media banner category. I will focus the majority of our time on online because that is where the majority of ad dollars are spent at this point in time, though both categories are growing exponentially.

Online advertising.

Banners, text, video, and social networking make up the majority of online advertising.

Banners.

I went to the *New York Times* web page, nytimes.com, to see the advertising. On either side of the name of the newspaper in the traditional Old English font, are two banner ads for Continental Airlines. These are called banners.

The Continental Airlines ads are static banners because nothing moves. If there would have been any kind of animation, then they would have been flash banners. Static is just one frame and never changes

Banners appear on thousands of websites for many different advertisers. There are three types of banner ads.

Rich Media.

The Interactive Advertising Bureau (see the appendix of this book) defines Rich Media as "advertisements with which users can interact in a web-page format." They are animated and the interaction can vary significantly from playing a video, to printing a coupon, to scrolling through a catalog of recipes or registering for a contest. The unit can also be made to click through to a website.

Flash.

Flash banners are similar to Rich Media in the fact that they include animation and will click through to a website, however, they do not allow for any user interaction.

Static.

These banners are simply one static image or frame and do not include any animation or capabilities for interaction. They will only allow for a user to click through to a website of the marketers choosing.

Video Advertising.

The two most common forms of video advertising are in-banner video, which is really just a Rich Media execution as mentioned above and in-stream video. When PC and Mac have a discussion in flash on the *New York Times* website, this is an in-banner video. An in-stream video is very similar to a TV spot in that it's an advertisement that is played before, after or during something else. These in-stream units are typically referred to as pre, mid or post-roll depending on when they appear within the content. So, if you go to Hulu to watch a TV show the ad you see before the program begins is an in-stream video or a pre-roll ad.

Social Network Advertising.

Social networking has changed the way we consume any media. Many websites give you the option to post the article or content you are reading to your Facebook, Twitter, Digg, Linked In or other blog page.

Facebook is not only the largest social networking site, but one of the largest sites of any kind in the U.S. In March 2010, Facebook surpassed Google as the most visited site. Advertising on Facebook is much more developed and sells ads on both a CPM and CPC buying model. They can also provide some analytics behind how visitors used a corporate fan page. The banner advertising is standardized so creativity is limited. However, there are limitless possibilities for apps.

Twitter announced advertising in April 2010 and is still evolving, but it is likely that it will be similar to search advertising.

Oh, and don't forget the many iterations of blogs.

Search.

There are two ways to use search to help drive consumers to a website, SEO and SEM

SEM (Search Engine Marketing).

This search strategy is often referred to as "paid search." Paid search refers to the results that show up at the top of the page in the shaded box label "sponsored links" or on the right hand side of the page.

In paid search, advertisers bid against a list of keywords relevant to their brand and campaign. The list of keywords can be as short as 20-50 words, but typically will range from a few hundred to more than a thousand.

Positioning within the paid search listings is determined by a number of factors. The key factor is quality score, which is whether or not the search engine's algorithm deems the advertiser relevant for the searched upon keyword. Relevance is affected by whether or not the ad copy correlates with the intent of the search and whether or not there is content on the destination website related to that particular search.

The second factor that impacts positioning within paid listing is bid amount. If the search engine finds two advertisers bidding on the same keyword and finds both of them equally relevant to the search, the one with the higher bid will receive higher positioning.

When using paid search an advertiser only pays when a user clicks on the ad, regardless of how many times the ad is shown.

SEO (Search Engine Optimizations).

This refers to the tactic of optimizing a site on the back end within the coding so that is will naturally rise to the top of the organic listings.

In-Text Advertising.

The advertiser purchases keywords that are relevant for their brand and/or messaging from an in-text ad network. When these words appear in an article or webpage within the network they are double underlined. When the reader rolls over the word an ad will appear. Because relevancy to the adjacent content is very high these units tend to perform well.

Buying models.

There are a number of different methods to purchase digital media, however, the below three are the most commonly used among media buyers:

CPM: Cost per thousand (impressions)

CPC: Cost per click

CPA: Cost per acquisition

The buying model used is determined by what the key media/campaign objective is. For example, if it is general awareness building campaign the buy is typically bought on a CPM basis. A CPC model would be used if traffic driving to a destination website is the primary goal. For marketers who have a robust eCommerce business where consumers are able to purchase product online, a CPA model is typically used. Two advertisers who rely heavily on a CPA model are H&R Block and Dell computers.

Issues.

The issues with online advertising are just like the issues with traditional advertising. What is the best place to intercept your audience and what content is likely to influence them to engage with your brand. Engagement is the key to interactive advertising.

For more information, please also read:

1. *http://www.razorfish.com*
   This is the website of a major online advertising agency. Check the annual, "How technology is changing the way consumers engage with brands" for an update.

2. *http://www.clickZ.com*
   This is an excellent source to get up-to-date on what is happening in digital media.

Chapter Eight: Note D

Traditional Media

Indecision is the thief of opportunity.
— Jim Rohn

	Advantages	**Disadvantages**
Radio	— Target audience selectivity better than any other traditional medium. — Travels outside the home to location of purchase. — Inexpensive production costs. — High time and content flexibility.	— Listeners can use radio as background only. — Normally requires high frequency. — Audience research is quite often weak.
Newspaper	— Wide exposure to general population. — High degree of advertising options ... color, large/small, etc. — Reach audience at the convenience of the reader.	— Average person spends less than 30 minutes with a paper. — Young people do not normally read the paper. — Advertising costs have risen quickly and readers are declining.
Television	— High degree of creativity and flexibility. — Virtually any product message can be adaptable to this medium. — There is a prestige in television that cannot be found others.	— Message is perishable and easily forgotten. — Tivo, video on-demand, games, etc have reduced traditional viewership. — Advertising costs are high and rising. Declining audience magnifies this problem.
Transit	— Reach most of the population at a low cost. — Excellent method of supplementing other media. — Large bold graphics and color make it difficult to ignore.	— Messages restricted to short (6 or 7 words) messges. — Effectiveness is difficult to measure. — Limited geographic flexibility.
Direct Mail	— Highest degree to targeting among all traditional media. — Easy to test new ideas. — Timing is at the discretion of the advertiser.	— Difficult to maintain an effective mailing list. — High cost per message delivered. — Overused, many prospects medium.consider this junk mail.

The Planning Document
Chapter Nine
Below-the-line

*Next to doing the right thing, the most important thing
is to let people know you are doing the right thing.*
— John D. Rockefeller

Introduction.

Below-the-line refers to non-media advertising or promotion. The term is taken from the old commission system. Advertising agencies earned 15% commission on media placements. They did not, however, earn commission on sales promotion, public relations, events, direct, etc. These were said to be below-the-line.

ATL, BTL, and TTL.

Above-the-line (ATL) is advertising placed in traditional media. Below-the-line (BTL) includes all other methods of communicating with an audience. A newer term, through-the-line (TTL), assumes a synergistic or integrated communication approach.

Below-the-line can include both consumer and trade sales promotion. It can also include event marketing, public relations, direct, viral, and many other segments. In general, this has been an area of growing activity and expanding options.

Even though other areas have grown in importance and, often, grown in share of budget, advertising is still most often the area where initial communication strategy is developed.

There is good reason for this. Advertising is the area of marketing communications where you have virtually total control of the message. Once you figure out the most important message to deliver, it is a relatively straightforward process to modify that message for the BTL disciplines.

So, even if you end up with relatively more budgetary emphasis in BTL areas, you will, in general, be best served beginning your work on message strategy with an advertising message.

Simply put, the purpose of this part of the marketing document will be to outline the events that will work in concert with the advertising.

Sales Promotion.

Promotion and Advertising Should Work Together.

Sales Promotion is differentiated from advertising since it is a tangible motivation to do something—a bribe, or more politely, an incentive.

A fifty-cent coupon on the purchase of a McDonald's Meal is fifty cents worth of good motivation to buy french fries and a drink when you are buying a Big Mac at McDonald's.

The marketing plan is quite often evaluated on its adherence to Integrated Marketing Communication principles. That simply means everything works together for a common goal.

Synergism is the old name for it, and it is still defined by Webster. The bottom line is that the promotion plan and the execution of that plan should work in concert with the advertising.

The discipline is the same in the Below-the-line plan as it has been for every section. The objectives of the promotion plan are intended to describe what the promotion plan will accomplish. As we have discussed before, these are marketing strategies.

Two Parts: Consumer and Trade.

In the Fast Moving Consumer Goods (FMCG) category, the promotion plan is divided into two major parts: Consumer Promotion and Trade Promotion. Quite often, the same objective(s) can be used for both the consumer and the trade promotion, and quite often the two work together.

One Strategic Objective: Behavior.

Simply put, a sales promotion strategy is based on the behavior you wish to incentivize. Do you wish a new distribution channel to feature Nestlé candy bars? Do you wish to incentivize shoppers to choose those candy bars? What is the behavior? Once you know that, your next challenge is to develop an affordable program of incentives.

Example: Nestlé.

When the plan was written for Nestlé to gain new distribution in video stores, the promotion plan used to support that called for a case allowance to the video store, and consumer advertising stated that Nestlé could now be enjoyed with a movie.

A cents-off coupon for consumers was added for motivation.

The two sales promotion events worked in concert. Synergy. Integration. A clear idea of the behavior desired.

Example: Polident.

Occasionally, one promotion can serve both consumer and trade.

When Polident Denture Cleanser introduced Polident II, the promotional plan recommended including two tablets in one package.

These "two-packs" were then given, at no cost, to the trade (retailers) when they purchased a predetermined amount of regularly packaged Polident II. The trade sold the two-packs in end-aisle displays for a nickel. The consumer was delighted to try something new for such a small price, and the trade was confident that product would not sit on the shelves. The result was that one promotion was directed to both the trade and the consumer.

At a minimum, the same objectives should work for all consumer promotion, and the same objectives should work for all trade promotion.

A. Consumer Promotion:

Consumer promotion is directed at the end user, the consumer.

Examples of consumer promotion events include: coupons, rebates, contests, sweepstakes, bonus packs, samples, temporary price reductions, and premiums—on-pack, near-pack and self-liquidating.

Here is how to structure this Section:

1. Current Situation:

The written market planning document should give a little history of what has worked in the past and what has not. Cite results in comparison to previous years and to those areas that have received special promotion events and those that have not.

For example, if you are writing a marketing plan for Bisquick. You had an on-pack shrink-wrapped cookbook sales promotion event in test market, and sales were up by +7% in the test areas. A comparison chart might look like this:

	Test Period	Year Ago
Promotion	+ 7%	+ 2%
No Promotion	– 1%	+ 1%

You might make the argument that the recipe book promotion increased business in the test area by 8% because the control area was down 1% in the test period.

Even if there is no event in test market, use this space to indicate what promotion events have been used, what the competition is using, or what the current thinking is on the brand as it relates to promotion events.

Don't forget to tie this to relevant behavior—and that behavior should be tied to your objectives. In this case, the Bisquick cookbook offer would both stimulate sales by adding value *and* potentially increase usage of Bisquick. Sales results indicate that this happened.

2. **Objectives:**

The objectives are lifted directly from the marketing strategies. An example of solid sales promotion objectives might be:

To establish KCNR radio as one of the five radio stations pre-selected for use in the cars of the target audience.

It is likely that this would have a strong tie-in to the creative objective.

3. **Strategies:**

The strategies provide detail on how the objectives will be accomplished. While the objectives outline what is intended, the strategies tell how it will be done. The following strategy example might have been used by KCNR:

To convince local automobile resellers to preset the middle radio button to KCNR.

This strategy might also work well with the creative objective and strategy that outlines that KCNR (for center) wants to be the center of everything with which it comes in contact.

4. **Rationale:**

   The objectives and strategies are defended here.

   The first preference is to defend the key elements of the promotion plan quantitatively. However you decide to defend the plan, it should be done so that management is convinced that this will contribute to the volume or other number objective for the Marketing Plan in its entirety.

   There is increasing pressure being brought to bear against promotion events—they must not only provide short-term incentives to purchase, but they must also contribute to the long-term Brand image. Again, what is the relevant behavior?

5. **Tactics:**

   This is the place to describe the specific sales promotion events and how they will work in detail. Quite often there is more than one event. If this is the case, they should be named or numbered to differentiate between the events.

   A tactic from our KCNR example might be:

   To provide an incentive to the automobile resellers in the form of on-air KCNR mentions of the automobile reseller name and campaign line.

   This tactic also provides the automobile reseller an opportunity to use IMC in the execution of his or her marketing plan.

6. **Payout:**

   Each promotion event should contain a rationale in the form of justification of the budget.

   In our KCNR example, this section of the plan would show the cost of the on-air mentions for the reseller (or in this case, the lost opportunity cost), and compare this cost to the benefit of having radios turned to KCNR.

   More commonly with a packaged goods brand, the payout would show the volume needed to pay for this promotion.

   If we know that the additional margin for selling one average pizza at Pizza Hut is five dollars, then we can calculate the additional volume needed to pay for additional marketing tools. Maybe we want to recommend a more expensive commercial ... a half million dollars instead of the fifty thousand the company spent last year. Well then, how many more pizzas must we sell in order to generate the additional $450,000. With a $5 margin, the answer is 90,000 pizzas.

Companies like Pizza Hut and products like Bisquick have sales figures that are relatively easy to measure in the short term.

This could also work for the KCNR radio example, but it would be more complicated. How many more people need to tune in to the radio station in order to pay for someone to go around and tune radios in car lots to KCNR, or motivate the car lot manager to do so. That is complicated because if we get more people to tune in, we increase listenership and as a result we can increase ad rates.

Never the less, if the long-term behavioral objective is to have more drive-time listeners, we can be confident that our actions are aimed in the right direction.

A chart similar to the one shown under "Current Situation" on page 227 might be used here.

B. Trade Promotion:
The Rise of the Retailer.
Trade promotion is directed at the middle man—the "trade."

If the Brand on which we are working is a packaged good product sold in grocery stores, drug stores, or mass merchandisers, then the retailer is the trade.

The two most common trade promotions are advertising allowances and display allowances. Some manufacturers treat stocking allowances as trade promotion events.

One of the most important changes in marketing has been the increased strength of the trade.

The advent of Universal Product Code (UPC) information that can provide daily information on sales has shown the retailers exactly what is moving and what is not.

Slotting Allowances.
Retailers have become aware of their power in the marketplace and have required such things as Slotting Allowances for new products to

gain distribution. These slotting allowances can be quite significant in some cases—particularly for new products.

As a result, marketers have spent a great deal of time, energy, and money fostering trade relations.

The Trade May Have Different Motivation.
For franchise operations such as automobile dealers and fast food restaurants, the trade is a bit different—it is the franchisee.

What motivates the trade to do something may not necessarily be what motivates the parent company or manufacturer. The trade objectives and strategy must address this motivation.

The trade objectives for Promotion will be lifted directly from the Marketing Strategies and the desired behavior should be relevant and compatible.

The trade portion of the sales promotion segment of the marketing document will have the same subpoints as the consumer promotion side. Be sure to include: the current situation, objectives, strategies, rationale, and an outline of the specific events that will be used.

C. Public Relations (PR).
Public relations involves influencing a group of people, which PR professionals call a public, in the interest of promoting the Brand.

This segment will address how the public relations part of the plan can contribute to fulfilling the marketing objective. After all, that is what the strategy is all about. In most cases, the public relations part of an advertising campaign will be Marketing Public Relations (MPR), not Corporate Public Relations (CPR).

Two Key Differences.
Conceptually, your "publics" may be more wide-ranging than the target customer for the product.

Second, and this is critical, your message must be interesting to the media. Otherwise, they will not carry your story—as it is not "newsworthy." So, for example, a new ingredient in your product might be appropriate for an ad message, but it is not a story that the media would feature.

To be successful in PR, you must find a way of delivering your message in a way that is interesting to the media.

In general, your MPR should work with the advertising and the sales promotion, to maximize effectiveness ... remember the synergy.

1. **Current Situation:**

   The first step is to outline what is currently happening in the area of public relations. Some of the questions that need to be answered are:

   - What has been the history?
   - What has worked in the past?
   - Do we anticipate any news in the coming year or period covered by the plan? Don't forget to factor in lead time.

   If your product makes a great Christmas gift, you will need to be working on the PR in the summer.

2. **Objectives:**

   The second part is the objective. The Public Relations Strategy, outlined in this section, will be identical to the marketing strategy for public relations outlined in Chapter Six.

   An example of a public relations objective is:

   To enhance Nuprin positioning as the preferred analgesic for relief from sports-inflicted pain.

   While this is a marketing public relations objective relating to publicity, there could also be objectives relating to a whole host of other elements including corporate public relations.

3. **Publics:**

   Public relations address publics instead of target audiences. The two terms mean the same thing, but in public relations they are expressed as a public instead of a target.

   A public for a broad based public relations plan within an advertising based marketing plan might be stakeholders.

   Stakeholders, of course, are employees, vendors, customers, stockholders, and anyone else that has anything else to do with the Brand.

   It makes good sense to be truly integrated, and that means marketing communications need to address internal as well as external audiences.

   Think about it. In many large companies with well-paid executives and well-funded programs, it is often the lowest-paid employees that deliver the messages to consumers. Understand all of your publics.

4. **Strategies:**
Strategies are how you intend to fulfill the objective. While the public relations objective is the same generation as the marketing strategy, the public relations strategy is one lower generation.

An example of a public relations strategy is:

To influence stakeholders to support Charles Schwab online stockbrokerage due to its variety of research sources.

5. **Rationale:**
In this segment, a case must be built for why the strategy is correct. Be sure to include why this particular strategy will fulfill the marketing objective better than any other strategic direction.

Moreover, it needs to be substantive for the media to be willing to run the story. Can you make it newsworthy? Or will you have one more self-serving press release that goes directly into the waste basket?

Public relations is a way to influence public opinion by providing newsworthy information to the media. It can be a supplement to advertising, but differs from advertising because you do not have control over the final product.

D. Direct Marketing.
Direct marketing is selling the Brand directly to the consumer.

If this is a part of your business model, this segment of the marketing plan will address how direct marketing can help to fulfill the marketing objective.

1. **Current Situation:**
The segment on direct marketing is similar to other introductory segments of the advertising based marketing plan. The first step is to record what has worked in the past, what is currently working, and any other circumstances that would impact the planning.

There may be aspects of this current situation that may be of benefit to the overall situation analysis.

Some segments may not be possible in all planning documents.

For example, if you are a student group or an advertising agency pitching a new client, the current situation will not be complete.

2. **Objectives:**

   The Direct Marketing objective is next. It will be identical to the marketing strategy for direct marketing outlined in Chapter Six. There could be objectives that relate to both inbound and outboard telemarketing, direct mail, direct response, direct television, etc.

   An example of a direct marketing objective for direct mail might be:

   To establish the Lands' End catalogue as a resource for casual clothing and accessories.

3. **Target Audience:**

   Who is the intended audience? The intended target of the direct marketing should be recorded here.

   To deliver messages to a target of working women with children at home.

4. **Strategies:**

   The direct marketing strategy designed to fulfill the direct marketing objective goes here. The direct marketing objective is designed to fulfill the marketing objective. An example might be:

   To convince current and potential Lands' End customers to request a Lands' End catalogue.

5. **Rationale:**

   Defend why this will work. It is insufficient to just state that you believe the plan will work.

   It is important to provide strong support for why this plan will help to deliver the marketing objective.

   Direct marketing requires a clear understanding of where to find members of your target group. This probably means database management.

   Don't forget that about 20% of America moves every year. That means if your information is two years old, a third or more of your information is probably incorrect.

Include payout. And, if you're not sure, develop a plan to test for results before you commit to a large program.

E. Event Marketing.

Event marketing involves marketing to consumers in a special environment called an event.

This part of the campaign plan will outline how the Brand will communicate directly with current and potential customers through a specific event—or events.

There is great variety of events that are available to the Brand.

For a brand like Mobil Oil, with an objective of influencing key decision-making female community leaders, the arts may provide a fertile field for potential events.

On the other hand, a consumer product like Bank of America may want to be involved with sporting events; Apple Computer may be more comfortable with an environmental event or one that involves using their products—such as a documentary film festival.

1. Current Situation:

Again, it is important to outline key information on what has been done in the past. This segment can be detailed and include past history, current users, geography where event marketing has been used in the past, seasonality of events, and competitive information.

This could include what events competing brands have used and what success they have had.

This detailed information could also be used in pubic relations or direct marketing.

The Brand could also use an abbreviated version, only stating what has been used in the period immediately before the writing of the plan.

2. Objective:

The objective will be identical to the marketing strategy for event marketing. This in turn will fulfill the marketing objective:

To establish Mobil Oil as a community-minded business through arts involvement.

3. **Strategies:**
The event marketing strategies will help to fulfill the objective. An example might be:

To involve women 35+ with "The Nutcracker" to relay the civic and arts attitude at Mobil Oil.

More than a quarter of a century ago, David Ogilvy said "strategy is about choice." It is still true.

A brand like McDonald's may have the resources to be active in virtually every marketing communications category.

It can be surprising how many MarCom categories offer opportunities for even small brands to participate.

The choices made in those categories is what strategy is all about.

4. **Target Audience:**
This is a clear and distinct identification of the people likely to be involved in the event and those likely to be interested in the Brand:

To deliver the event to women 35+.

This Mobil Oil event may be against a marketing objective designed to give support to stock prices on Wall Street.

5. **Rationale:**
Again, the reason why this will help to increase stock prices must be clearly stated in this section. The support may be linked to any variety of reasons, but it must be clear and it must be substantiable.

Virtually every advertiser will be a presenter at a trade show at some time or another. This is also an event. The target group changes from consumer to trade, but the principles are the same.

Event marketing is different from public relations because it tends to work with consumers; public relations tends to work with the media and internal company audiences.

F. Miscellaneous.

Any other element of marketing communications for the campaign can be included here—for example, online activities. Review Note C in Chapter Eight for more detail in this area, which, in a unique way, touches on virtually all areas. It's TTL.

You should, at this point, understand that the current situation should be outlined, and that the objective for this additional element to the plan should match the marketing strategy.

A tactics section can also be added to any element of the advertising-based marketing plan.

Warning.
If you are in a class at a university, or a small business, be careful not to try to do too much. If you do, it can eat you.

Your best strategy will be to identify those marketing communications disciplines that best reinforce your marketing strategy in terms of impact and efficiency and to then limit yourself to those ideas and disciplines.

If you choose to develop work in every possible discipline, you will be developing a more balanced, more thorough plan than if you did not.

The key to this thinking is to remember that everything is a trade-off.

The first step is to develop a long list of options, calculate their cost and benefit, then choose.

For more information, please also read:

1. Daniel Pink. *Drive: The Surprising Truth about What Motivates Us.* (Riverhead Books, 2009).

2. Mark Earls. *Herd: How to Change Mass Behaviour by Harnessing Our True Nature.* (West Sussex: Wiley, 2007).

3. Chip Heath and Dan Heath. *Switch: How to Change Things When Change Is Hard.* (Broadway Business, 2010).

4. Don E. Schultz and Beth E. Barnes. *Strategic Advertising Campaigns.* 5th ed. (McGraw-Hill, 1999).
   Chapters Thirteen pertains to Sales Promotion.

5. Bud Frankel and H.W. Phillips. *Your Advertising's Great . . . How's Business?.* (Homewood,IL: Dow Jones-Irwin, 1986).
   This is a practitioner's guide to Sales Promotion.

6. Bendinger, Altman, Avery, et al. *Advertising & the Business of Brands.* (Chicago: The Copy Workshop, 2009).
   See Chapters Seven and Nine of this introductory text for more

information on Sales Promotion, Public Relations, and Direct Marketing.

7. Don E Schultz and William Robinson. *Sales Promotion Essentials*. (Chicago: NTC Business Books, 1992).
   This book is a good introduction to basic techniques.

Evaluation

Happy endings are stories that haven't finished yet.
— Jane Smith (*Mr. & Mrs. Smith*)

*How long, ye simple ones, will ye love simplicity? And the
scorners delight in their scorning and fools hate knowledge?*
— Proverbs 1:22 (KJB)

Introduction.

The Need for Evaluation.

The success or failure of the marketing plan is determined ultimately by its ability to deliver the objective. Unfortunately, this is often not a very sensitive measurement.

Occasionally, the marketing objective will be fulfilled despite the marketing plan. Other times, the marketing plan may be brilliant, but some unforeseen change in the competitive environment will prevent the fulfillment of the objective. If you sell luxury cars and the stock market crashes, this is not bad planning, it's bad luck ... but maybe we should have seen it coming.

When these situations arise, a good evaluative method will help to determine the quality of the individual elements of the plan.

The intent of the Evaluation section of the marketing planning document is to outline how this evaluation will take place.

It may be evaluated totally on how well the objective is delivered, but more than likely there will be other measures that provide information on the success or failure of the individual elements within the plan.

Interim Evaluation Measures.

Interim measures can help. A good example is evaluating the quality of the creative product by comparing attitudes of consumers on a variety of parameters toward the brand (this year versus last). This may aid the advertiser—a midyear evaluation can make the plan stronger before the end of the year.

This helps to eliminate the all-or-nothing nature of fulfilling marketing objectives. The idea is simple: try to get a midyear progress report instead of waiting for the end of the year.

Most large packaged-goods manufacturers track sales on a monthly basis in order to evaluate progress. Again, the information can be useful.

Two Kinds of Sales Information.
It is common to track sales two ways: this year versus last year and versus projection (also known as "against plan" or "against budget").

Scanning machines at retail make it possible for manufacturers to have sales information, virtually daily, by grocery store. This information probably has limited usefulness, because it provides too much detail for the manager to absorb.

The key evaluative tools that will track the Brand's progress toward the marketing objective are obviously sales and share.

Evaluating Information.
Now that you have the information, you have to determine what it means. Some of the interim tools that might help you determine what is impacting sales and share might be:

1. Copy testing
2. Attitude measurement for the Brand
3. Awareness measurement for the Brand
4. Advertising awareness measurement
5. Usage measurement
6. Purchase motivation assessment

And, of course, you need to know if your media plan is working—and to what degree.

Evaluating Media.
A media analysis might provide information on the quantity of GRPs delivered into a specific geographic area during the past six months. This in turn could let us know if the media pressure is up or down versus the previous period.

Then, to state the obvious, see if there is any relation to sales.

The same information might be available for sales promotion, publicity, or merchandising programs. This information would be developed through a detailed business analysis.

This section is not intended to provide this information. It is intended to provide a *plan* to provide (or try to provide) this information to measure consumer reaction to these elements of the marketing plan.

Example: Good Seasons.

For example, if you are the Brand Manager on Good Seasons Salad Dressing, and you knew that Little Rock had been receiving +150 GRPs a week (total is 600) in each of the advertised weeks for the past six months when compared to the control market of Birmingham (450 GRPs), then you have an opportunity to compare the impact of that extra 150 GRPs of media weight.

We could compare that impact by looking at sales or market share, but if we had a tracking study in place we could compare the results of such attitudinal measures as:

- Good Seasons tastes fresher than other salad dressings.
- Good Seasons is one of the best tasting salad dressings.
- Good Seasons is easy to prepare.
- Good Seasons is one of my favorite salad dressings.
- I would recommend Good Seasons to my friends.

If the tracking study has been set up so that respondents can evaluate these measures on a five point Likert scale, then we can start to get a measure of progress by comparing the evaluations over time.

This additional evaluation allows us to make decisions based on more than just the information that is provided by sales and share.

A. Current Situation:

How We Are Evaluating the Marketing Plan.

The section should outline what is currently being used to evaluate the marketing plan.

It will likely include both sales and share. It may also include tracking studies or any of the information-gathering techniques previously discussed.

The current situation might outline the objectives, strategy (including method), and the expected learning or benefit of any evaluation technique that is currently in place.

B. Objective:

Marketing Strategy for Evaluation.

The objective of the evaluation section of the marketing planning document is the same as the marketing strategy for evaluation. It will specify what will be evaluated and what we want to learn.

For example:

> *To determine attitudes of the target audience toward both Texaco and its advertising.*

This objective sets the stage for what information will be needed in order to track progress in the coming year. It is possible that there will be multiple evaluation objectives in a given year.

C. Strategy:
There May Be More Than One Strategy.

The strategy, as always, is written to describe how you intend to accomplish that objective. There may be several strategies for each objective.

For example in the case of evaluation for Texaco, the strategy might be:

1. To gain qualitative insight for how consumers think about Texaco, how they use gasoline in general, and what they think of Texaco specifically.
2. To conduct a quantitative attitude, usage, and awareness study during the second quarter to verify or refute information gleaned in the qualitative study.

Multiple Objectives, Multiple Challenges.

If there are multiple objectives, there will be strategies written to support each of them.

Remember, objectives are what you want to do, and strategies are how you intend to do it.

D. Tactics:
Tactics/Method.

The tactics of the evaluation segment of the plan are sometimes called the "methodology," but this word is really incorrect. It should be simply method.

Here you will list the methods for gaining the information.

With Texaco, the strategy was to acquire qualitative information.

An example of the tactics might be:

To conduct two focused group sessions in the first quarter in order to gain consumer insight to the marketing elements of Texaco.

These group sessions will be conducted in a medium BDI area and with a medium to high CDI.

The groups will seek to determine consumer attitudes toward gasoline consumption in general and about Texaco specifically.

Question Areas.

If a listing of question areas has been developed it might be included here, but more often this will be left for a specific recommendation following the approval of the marketing document.

Summary.

What You Plan to Learn.

This same process will be followed for each individual measure you hope to have for the marketing plan.

The Evaluation section of the marketing planning document outlines what is to be done in the coming year—or the period under consideration for the marketing plan.

It differs from Chapter Two, Research, since the research segment is intended to summarize what you have learned in the past that will contribute to this marketing planning document, and, in turn, for the marketing of the Brand itself.

For more information, please also read:

1. Charles E. Young and Patricia D. King. *The Advertising Research Handbook.* 2nd ed. (Ideas in Flight, 2008).
   This book may be hard to find, but has useful information.

2. Jack B. Haskins and Alice Kendrick. *Successful Advertising Research Methods.* (Chicago: NTC Business Books, 1993).
   This book may be hard to find, but has useful information.

3. Hart Weichselbaum, ed. *Readings in Account Planning.* (Chicago: The Copy Workshop, 2008), 103.
   The first two chapters of Section 3 can be helpful.

Test Marketing

The only cats that matter are the ones that take chances.
— Bill Bernbach, quoting Thelonious Monk

Introduction.

While test marketing is designed to reduce risk, it is taking a chance.

At Least One Test Market.

All good marketing plans contain at least one test market.

Exceptions to this rule should be rare.

Test Marketing, or simply testing, is altering the marketing plan in one market to find the impact of that alteration.

Testing is a way to learn the power of new marketing possibilities without risking all the geography in your franchise.

Example: New Creative Strategy.

We may have interest in a new creative strategy.

The old one has been working for many years, and sales have been solid. This was the case on Bob Evans Sausage business.

The business was good, but we believed sales could be increased by convincing current customers to use sausage more often—at lunch or dinner instead of just breakfast.

We had evidence to believe that current users would have interest in using more of the product if we showed them how.

We developed a test market to determine the impact on sales of an increased usage strategy.

The actual test was to run recipe advertising in women's service magazines in Cincinnati in order to leverage usage.

We chose Cleveland as a control market. Cincinnati was the only market to receive magazine advertising.

We reduced the quantity of television advertising going into the Cincinnati area to avoid also testing an increase in the dollar allocation to advertising.

This is a good example of test market design.

Objective, Strategy, Tactics.
It is the purpose of this segment of the marketing document to outline the test market(s) and the expected outcome(s).

The test market will be described by outlining objectives, strategies, and tactics in executional detail.

Poor Arguments Against Test Markets.
Some may maintain that if business is poor it probably needs "fixing." They state that attention should be paid to solving the problems at hand and attention should not be diverted into setting up a somewhat risky test market.

These critics of testing always point out the lack of resources for a good solid test market.

Both of these arguments miss the point.

If test markets had been in place, there is a strong probability that the business would not be in trouble, because the manager would have been learning new ways to market the Brand.

There would be at least one more piece of learning available.

Additionally, test markets do not have to be expensive and the learning can make the difference between a profitable brand and one that is not quite making it.

Recommendations.
Many marketing planning documents recommend at least one test. Some recommend many tests in order to increase learning for future years. These tests might be in many different elements of the plan.

Almost anything can be tested. David Ogilvy, in his book *Ogilvy on Advertising*, cites that Procter & Gamble is such a formidable competitor because they are disciplined. "Their guiding philosophy is to plan thoroughly, minimize risk, and stick to their proven principles." They reduce risk through testing.

Take care to select two or three markets for testing. The markets should not be contaminated by competitors' testing or unusual behavior as it relates to the category.

Selecting a Test Market.

It is unlikely that a refried bean manufacturer would test market in Buffalo. Refried beans are not consumed in Buffalo at the same levels that they are in Arizona or Texas.

The markets should be representative of the remainder of the United States (and Buffalo is a chronically depressed area, not exactly the best place to test a new product).

Pick control markets to go with the test markets so that the effect of the test can be measured against specific markets, and not just compared to the remainder of the United States. The selection of the markets for testing takes some care.

Peoria, Illinois, is a good example. It is a Midwestern market with a good mix of working, middle-class consumers. It is a relatively small DMA, which makes it more affordable than testing in Chicago or Indianapolis.

Selecting a Control Market.

Marketers may choose a test market in Peoria and compare the sales results to those in Ft. Wayne. They might choose Ft. Wayne as the control market for the test because it is about the same size as Peoria, has about the same seasonality of sales, and has about the same percentage of the market as represented by the target audience in both markets.

If the history of sales is about the same in both markets, and they have about the same brand and category development indices, then they are a good match.

Other Determining Factors.

Some marketers choose more than one test market to determine how the test will work in high development areas and in low development areas or in markets with some other skew.

Others have a requirement that a test market must represent a given percentage of the United States—one or two percent—to avoid having too small of a testing environment. Others will test in a very small environment like Alpena, Bend, or Presque Isle to avoid the high cost of larger markets, then test again in the more expensive, but more substantive markets after success has been proven in these mini-markets.

Ten Factors.

Here are ten factors from which you may want to gain actual market information in a test market environment:

1. The power of an alternative copy strategy.
2. The effect of an increase in advertising weight.
3. The impact of an increase in price.
4. The result of increasing the value of a cents-off coupon used on the Brand.
5. The acceptance of a product change.
6. The result of an alternate distribution system.
7. The consequence of implementing an ongoing publicity campaign.
8. The outcome of targeting a new audience.
9. The acceptance of moving the Brand into new geography.
10. The effect of moving marketing funds to a new season of the year.

Here is the structure for presenting Testing recommendations in your Planning Document.

A. Objective:

The objectives in the testing part of the marketing document are the same as the marketing strategies in Chapter Six.

An example of a testing objective might be:

> To determine the sales impact of a +50% increase in advertising impressions.

An explanation of how this objective will help fulfill the marketing objective will increase the chances of acceptance.

B. Strategies:

How Learning Will Take Place.

The strategies, as always, will outline how the objective will be met, or in the case of testing, how the learning will take place.

If the test is a complicated one, several strategy statements may be necessary (as it was in media), but if the market test is not complex, one strategy statement may be all that is necessary.

It might be as simple as:

> To use the television medium to carry the increased weight in a medium-development test market.

This strategy gives sufficient information about how the objective will be fulfilled, but needs more information in the tactics section to let the reader know exactly what is going to happen.

C. Tactics:

Also Known as "Method."

This section is sometimes called the method section and is used to outline precisely how the test market will be implemented.

To increase television weight in Cincinnati by +165 GRPs to a total of 495 GRPs (index 150) per flight for a one-year period.

The weight will maintain the current proportions between the daytime, early fringe, and late fringe dayparts.

A flow chart should also be attached so the reader can clearly see when the test plan will go into effect.

D. Rationale:

Management Is Entitled to a Convincing Argument.

This is the defense for why the test market will likely contribute to the marketing objective.

It is the reason to believe that the premise behind the test will provide better results than whatever is currently the standard.

There are limited opportunities for test markets, and management is entitled to a convincing argument on behalf of the value of each and every test market recommendation.

Support your point of view.

Quantitative and qualitative research and sales results will be presented here as substantiation for the test market.

E. Evaluation:

Also Known as "Payout."

This is the place to outline what the definition of success will be. Some call this section "Payout."

For example, if it will take an increase of +13% in sales in order to pay out the +50% increase in advertising, then that should be established here. It could be set up like the chart on page 227.

F. Online testing:

We could conduct a test market to determine the impact of increasing media dollars and using those dollars online. That strategy might look like:

To use "Rich Media Advertising" to carry the increased media allocation.

The problem is that this is no longer a market test because it is seen across the internet. With few exceptions, what I place on the internet in New York is also seen in Shanghai. So when Apple made a decision to use multiple advertising on the *New York Times* home page, while this may have been used as a test, it was a test of the medium across all geography.

Apple purchased several ads and they all interacted with each other. It had very high impact, but it could not be used in a test market if we define the test market geographically.

A Brief Final Warning.

It is absolutely a good idea to add this discipline to your approach.

However, remember that your competitors are watching.

If you are testing a pricing or promotional strategy for a mobile phone supplier, maybe you want to get your information another way. Don't be surprised when a competitor has jumped on your idea.

Testing is good. Just be sure that you're not providing your competition with valuable information.

For more information, please also read:

1. Marian Azzaro. *Strategic Media Decisions*. 2nd ed. (Chicago: The Copy Workshop, 2008).

2. Jack Z. Sissors and Roger Baron. *Advertising Media Planning*. 6th ed. (Chicago: NTC Business Books, 2002).

3. Jack B. Haskins and Alice Kendrick. *Successful Advertising Research Methods*. (Chicago: NTC Business Books, 1993).

4. David Ogilvy. *Confessions of an Advertising Man*. (New York: Atheneum, 1980).

5. David Ogilvy. *Ogilvy on Advertising*. (New York: Crown Publishers, 1983).

Chapter Twelve

The Presentation

Everything is about making things look and sound as good as they can.
—Richard Hsu
Wieden + Kennedy/Shanghai

Introduction.

Congratulations.

You have just finished a grueling experience—you have written your first Marketing Planning document. This is no easy task.

Most students will have invested about a hundred and fifty hours or more to get to this point. If this is a semester-long project, you will have spent about fifteen to twenty hours a week getting the marketing planning document written.

You have now completed about half of the work needed to finish the marketing planning process.

The next segment is the presentation of your work. It is easily half of the work.

At the university level, the presentation is usually a 20- to 30-minute slide show of your work.

At the professional level, the presentation can last up to two hours.

Now for the bad news.

It is more difficult to write and give a twenty-minute presentation than a two-hour presentation.

Here's the trick. You must present everything that is in a two-hour presentation, but condense it into a twenty-minute period.

This presentation segment is primarily for students. I am confident that those of you who are reading this as professionals will find some tidbits, but we will focus on student concerns.

If this is for an NSAC presentation, try to view the video of previous years' winners. You will see that teams work to a very high standard. It is what you must do.

A. Objective:

Sell Your Ideas.

Your presentation is an opportunity to sell your ideas.

Therefore, the objective of this segment of the process is to convince your target audience, probably your client, that your ideas are the best ideas available.

One of the easiest methods to convince the group that your work is the best is to have the most finished work—the best-looking presentation.

Early in my advertising agency career, someone told me that the ideas that get sold to clients may not always be the best ideas or concepts, but they are always the best executed. He meant that they were always the ideas that had the best finishing touches, the best art work, the best slides, and the most professional presentation. With computer-based graphics and presentation programs, this is truer than ever.

Whether you're in a class or a contest, or pitching new business, your objective is to win.

And that means the best presentation. Get serious about it.

B. Elements:

Strategy, Creative, and Media.

The key to the presentation is to convince the marketing people, the brand group if you like, that the creative solution you have found will fulfill the marketing objectives.

That will most likely be accomplished through a combination of the strategic thinking you developed and wrote into the planning or marketing document and the creative presentation.

1. Strategic Setup:

There are two ways to set up the creative work. One is to outline the details of the marketing plan in great detail. Usually this is given in the same order as the marketing document—Situation Analysis, Research, Problems and Opportunities, Objectives, Budget, Strategies, Creative, Media, Promotion, and Evaluation.

The degree of detail will vary based on the time available and your audience's familiarity with the material.

Testing will be inserted into that segment of the plan for which the testing is taking place. For example, a 50% increase in a media impressions test would be inserted into the Media segment of the presentation.

The second method is to just give enough information so that your audience believes the creative brief is correct. That probably includes a bit of the literature review, some pieces of the situation analysis, and some of the results of your research.

You probably want to make it clear who the audience will be and the criteria that those people use to make purchase decisions in the category.

2. **The Creative Presentation:**
   The second part of the presentation is the introduction of the creative product itself, the advertising ... and everything that supports it.

TBWA calls this support "media arts." It is a good name. When they developed the campaign for Pedigree the campaign line was "*Dogs Rule.*" They showed billboards with puppies hanging over the edge. They chalked the sidewalk leading into the Westminster Dog Show. They sold the idea as a transformation from a dog food company to a dog loving company. They even put pictures of employee's dogs on the employee's name badge.

If you go to the Pedigree website, you will first learn that Pedigree is for dogs. They support animal shelters and encourage you to help them as well. They have, as someone once said, left no stone unturned. If your idea is big enough, it will work in a hundred different ways.

It is not unusual for a presentation to begin by telling the audience what you are going to show them — including some of the creative work. Then demonstrate—that is, make it come alive—by showing how the strategy and the creative work together. Show it again. Then, at the end, tell them again what you have shown them earlier.

You have now had a frequency of three and have broken the threshold necessary for learning. Remember Michael Naples from media planning class?

C. Start Early:
Some Good Advice You Will Probably Ignore.
Everyone will give you advice to start work on the creative product and the presentation as early as possible. You, however, will ignore them because you are smarter than they are.

You are a Senior—the top of the college pecking order. You can pull it out at the last possible minute. Maybe.

A Bad Example.
One year I was coaching a team, and we were going to present at the AAF/NSAC the next morning.

After meeting with the District Coordinator, I came back to the hotel to discover that we did not have Spanish language radio yet. This was ten o'clock the night before presentation.

One of the team members recorded the commercial in the bathroom of the hotel room at two in the morning. We won the District competition, so maybe you seniors can pull it together at any late date—but you're pushing your luck.

Do Yourself a Favor.
If you start early, you'll have more opportunity to revise your presentation and make it better.

More importantly, if you just barely finish on time you'll also limit your learning. And, while winning is nice, the real value is learning skills that will help you in the business world.

One of the key learning experiences in preparing a marketing (including advertising) campaign of this nature is being able to go back and look at what you did when you are finished.

And, since you now know more than you did when you started, you can probably find some ways to make your work better. This will reinforce your learning, and enable you to have a stronger plan and develop better skills. So it's in your own best interest to start early. On the other hand, Peter Parsons used to say that work expands to fill the time allotted.

D. Write the Presentation:
Written Language vs. Spoken Language.
Writing the presentation will require slightly different language than

that in the written portion of your document. There's a good reason for this. We all speak differently than we write.

To verify this, after you write something, read it out loud.

And you might want to note the amount of time it takes to speak it.

Two Ways to Do It.
The first way is word based.

Each member of your team should write the speech for the segment of the plan that they wrote for the planning document.

When you start to write your segment of the presentation, you might want to start by setting the margins on your computer to leave at least forty percent of the page blank. This will allow you to draw in the first rough illustrations and ideas for slides—so that you can see what the presentation will look like to the audience as you are giving the verbal portion of the presentation. Both PowerPoint and Keynote have formats for notes and handouts that you might find helpful.

The second way is visually-centric.

Get some half sheets of paper. In the US this would be 5½ x 8½. In the rest of the world, it would be A5 paper. Write or draw on each piece of paper one of the points you want to make in the presentation. Spread them out on a big surface so you can see what it looks like. Bruce Rowley taught me to use masking tape and put them on the wall. It is a great idea. (See the War Room presentation at the end of Chapter 7.)

Now you can see how the presentation is working. You can see what is redundant and what is missing. Each piece of paper becomes a slide in the presentation. If you wrote headings, then you need some visuals to support it. If you drew pictures, you will have to write some headings.

TBWA has a lot of glass walls in their Shanghai office. Great idea. They can bring the stack of slides, tape them to the glass wall, and then write on the wall with dry-erase markers. It is easy to change it around and easy to see how it will flow.

When it is close, get it into the computer.

Or not.
There is more and more criticism of PowerPoint presentations. They put

people to sleep. The involvement, or engagement, by the audience is low.

When Saatchi gives presentations to Toyota dealer groups, they often just bring the notes. The information is all mounted on four-by-eight sheets of art board. This allows the dealers to all come look at the information before the meeting. Terrific. They just blew the top on the engagement meter.

Identification—Dates and Initials.
You will quickly find there is a lot to keep track of in this process.

It's a good idea to put the date and the initials of the person who authored that particular page at the bottom of each page so you will know what revision you are using.

It is likely that you'll rewrite the presentation several times before you finally get it the way you want it. You will be quite upset if you find you have been working on the version that everyone else trashed two days ago.

E. Create Slides:

If You Decide to Use PowerPoint, and Virtually Everyone Does ...
The slides are used to reinforce what you are communicating verbally at the time the slide is being shown. By the way, I prefer Keynote, but most use PowerPoint. Some use more complex platforms complete with Flash animations. But I'll assume you've gone with the default—PowerPoint. In your PowerPoint presentation, there are three types of slides you will use: type slides, creative slides, and what we'll call "miscellaneous."

1. Type Slides.

If you are talking about the objectives in the Media section, you will probably have the media objectives on a slide.

"Build" With Progressive Slides.
You might make it a set of progressive slides, where the first slide shows the first Target Audience objective in bright white Helvetica type on a black background. Like this:

The second slide might show the first Target Audience objective in grey Helvetica, and the second (geographic) objective in bright white Helvetica type.

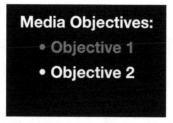

The third slide would show the first two objectives in grey and the third (seasonality) objective in bright white.

Media Objectives:
- Objective 1
- Objective 2
- **Objective 3**

And so on.

Whatever colors, type faces, or graphic devices you use, the key is that you make it easy for the audience to follow your sequence.

Support Important Points.

You may also use type slides to support a point you're trying to make.

For example, if you're giving a presentation for Dannon Yogurt you may have a slide in the Situation Analysis segment that states the following:

24.1% are over 55

This would indicate that 24.1% of all female homemakers are 55 years of age or older. You would cite verbally, that this information comes from the Spring 2009 report from MRI (now GfkMRI). You might also consider putting the source material in small type at the bottom of the slide.

This is a good slide because, like a billboard, it does not contain too much information. If you happen to have a nice photograph of a person over 55 enjoying yogurt, so much the better.

There is a danger of having too much type on the slide so that your audience spends time reading the slide and not listening to you.

It can also be difficult to present a slide that is simple.

If you have a complicated graphic slide like a media flow chart, you have to immediately explain it verbally.

A type slide can just be put on the screen with little explanation, because it is already part of the speech—it's there to reinforce what you are saying.

Graphic Slides.
The graphic slide may need explanation; the verbal portion is there to explain the graphic.

You may choose to generate unusual graphics that help to explain the strategic positioning of the Brand.

The mnemonic device (memory graphic) could be developed and used throughout the presentation to support the strategic direction.

These slides can be generated on your computer in a number of ways. PowerPoint also has chart and graphic capabilities. So does Keynote.

2. **Creative Slides:**
You can also use slides to present your Creative work. But you can add interest by presenting your work mounted on foam core.

Print Advertising.
The print advertisements you have written and designed should be put into your PowerPoint presentation whether they are in hard copy form and being presented directly or not.

If you wrote and designed the ads on the computer, then you can generate the slides of those ads the same way.

Television in PowerPoint.
When it comes to television, you can show the individual frames of your commercial on screen in PowerPoint and read or play a

prerecorded sound track of the copy.

You may be tempted to make a video commercial or a video presentation for the sales team. Good idea, but be cautious in switching from one format to another. It is one more thing that can go wrong. Video can also be an incredible time suck.

You can imbed a Quicktime video in your PowerPoint—but be sure to double check as you move from machine to machine as PowerPoint may lose track of the location of embedded/linked files. You are best served keeping everything together in the same file folder. Please use the same caution with hyperlinks.

Another reason for caution — the potential of a commercial that is only in storyboard form may be greater than the reality of a commercial produced by inexperienced people with inadequate skills and equipment. The realism of the video production can take away from the imagination of your audience.

3. **Miscellaneous:**

There will be a variety of slides you may have to take with a camera for your presentation.

For example, if you are not totally fluent in Photoshop, and if you want a slide to show the selection of magazines you are recommending, it is quite easy to buy the magazines, spread them out on a table, and take a slide.

If you or someone in your group has Photoshop skills, scan the magazines as JPEGs and place the resulting file(s) in the slide.

If you are recommending transit advertising and you want to show a bus with your work on the side, you can just take a picture of the bus and Photoshop your work onto the side of the bus.

F. The Creative Product:
Staging Your Creative.

The presentation is primarily an opportunity to show the creative work because, in general, the creative product should not be included in the marketing planning document.

The drum roll…

When presenting, there is a natural buildup that takes place—curiosity that needs to be developed before you show the creative advertising product and after management, or the judges, have had an opportunity to read the Marketing Planning Document. Once curiosity has been built up, then it's the right time to show them the creative product.

It will be easier to convince them that the executions you are recommending will contribute to fulfilling the Marketing Objective. Did I hear someone say "payout?"

Seven Good Guidelines.

This book is not a forum for what the creative product should and should not contain, but here are seven observations you should be aware of when entering student contests like the one sponsored by the American Advertising Federation.

1. **If there's a creative judge from the client, don't point out too many flaws with the current campaign.**
   Remember: one of the judges may have created it. This is a good rule for all advertising professionals. Be careful how you tell anyone that their work stinks.

2. **The best work has a good idea behind it.**
   The premise can be any variety of things, but it has to go beyond just saying the Brand name in a clever fashion. There must be a real reason for the creative idea. If it's based on a consumer insight from your research, better yet.

3. **The better your work looks, the higher the probability of winning any competition.**
   Good work looks good. Find an artist to do the finish work on your advertising. If it looks like a student project, it will be judged to be inferior to more professional-looking work.

4. **Make sure the advertising is fresh; it shouldn't look like any other advertising around anywhere.**
   Go beyond what other people have done. Be "creative."

5. **The advertising should be on strategy.**
   This shouldn't be a problem since you wrote the brief as well as the advertising. But be sure to evaluate your advertising against the strategy. Ask hard questions. The judges will.

6. **Use the campaign line on** *everything.*
Use it at the end of all the advertising—on the television, newspaper, magazine, radio, outdoor, transit, and ball caps.

If you're recommending sky writing, it should be what is written in smoke. Put it on the cover of the "leave-behind."

7. **Do something you don't think anyone else will do.**
Write original music, create a campaign in Spanish, use testimonials of famous people and get their voices on tape. Find a way to differentiate your campaign from all others.

Use Your Good Ideas.
Occasionally you will have a great idea for a magazine advertisement, but you're not recommending magazines in the media plan. Do not ignore the idea. Find a way to use it.

That may mean you have to go back and rewrite the media plan or add a test market, and find a reason to substantiate the decision to recommend magazines.

But it could also mean that you just show the work in the presentation and tell the truth. You have a great idea, but you don't know if it can be used or not.

That way, you get credit for the idea, but don't have to defend its use.

"Learn" Your Audience.
No matter what the presentation, "learn" your audience.

If you are working for an advertising agency, then your audience is your client. If you're working for a small startup company, your audience is the entrepreneur who started the business.

But if you're a team member in the AAF–NSAC, your audience is comprised of the judges. Learn as much about these people as you can.

I once had a client who was an iced tea fanatic. I found that if I brought him a cold bottle of iced tea, he was much more receptive to our ideas.

Presenting "safe" advertising can be good in some cases when the audience is conservative, but it can be deadly when your audience contains working professional creative people.

G. Rehearse:

And Rehearse Some More.

The next step is to rehearse what you have created. Practice makes perfect. Rehearse, rehearse, rehearse.

If there is someone in your group who has taken a theater class or two, so much the better. If you have an opportunity to take a theater class before the presentation, do it.

Dramatic techniques can get the attention you need.

There are many professionals who believe that they can rehearse too much. There should be, they reckon, a certain amount of spontaneity to the presentation of the campaign. That is correct — for professionals who have two hours to present their work.

Students do not, so their presentations must be rehearsed.

Present Before You Present.

Present the work as often as you can before the final day.

When I was at the University of Kansas, we had a five-hour drive to St. Louis for the AAF–NSAC District competition.

The team rehearsed the presentation ten times in the van on the way to St. Louis. That year, the team won the District against some very good competition.

Sometimes when you rehearse a presentation it begins to sound memorized. You have to go beyond that point. You have to make it a theatrical presentation; it is memorized, but it doesn't sound like it.

For more information, please also read:

1. Scott Berkun. *Confessions of a Public Speaker.* (Cambridge, MA: O'Reilly Media, 1999).
2. A current book on Keynote or PowerPoint.
   There are a number of books that are quite adequate, your team will need a useful reference to help make the most of this program.

Next Steps:

Never give up.
Never give up.
Never give up.
—Winston Churchill

Introduction.

If you read at the rate that most people do, you have read this book in a few hours. Hopefully, I've given you a few tools to craft a marketing planning document.

This is a skill that will last you a lifetime.

The Next Step.

Do it.

The next step is simple. "Just do it."

The first time you write a marketing planning document, you'll think it is an incredible task. When you are halfway through the Situation Analysis—when you have to find competitive spending information—you'll begin to believe it is not possible to gain enough information to complete this document.

You are right, and you are wrong.

Parkinson's Law is that work expands to fill the time allotted. The same is certainly true of your marketing plan.

The more time you spend on it, the better it will be, but also the longer it will take.

Get into it early on so that you can enjoy the process and so the quality will be high.

If you're an entrepreneur, the first time through the process may take six months or longer. The second time will only take a few weeks.

If you're a student finishing this document for a contest or for an Advertising Campaigns class, it clearly will take you the entire term to complete the document and give a presentation.

Don't Give Up.

Many times you will work around the clock.

Don't give up, it will be worth it.

Next time, when you are working for DDB in Chicago or Y&R in New York or P&G in Cincinnati or Adidas in Herzo-base you will finish it in a month or so.

Best of all, next time, you will get paid for it.

The AAF Contest.

Whether You Win or Lose...

If you are competing in the AAF NSAC competition, you may find that this is one of the most involving activities in your college career.

And, like any contest, you'll play to win.

And, like many contests, there will be only one winner (plus Regional winners—an honor in itself) and many who do not win.

Well, Here's a Little More Good News.

Whether you win or not, you'll find that the skills you developed preparing for this contest will serve you well.

Be Prepared.

The AAF contest prepares you for the deadlines, pressures, and high standards that are part of the competitive world of marketing—where you are not just competing for a grade or a prize, but for the very survival of your company in the marketplace.

If you work hard, you'll be preparing yourself to succeed in the real world. And that's a prize everyone can use.

The First Time is the Hardest.

I know how hard it is. Every year, I watch a new group of students wrestle with one of the most demanding tasks in business. And every year, I hear from a few former students.

So here is my last bit of good news. It gets easier.

There are Two Reasons.

So, a couple of years from now, when you're at TBWA/Singapore, McGarry-Bowen/New york, or with some brand-new company that needs your help, when you're asked to write a marketing planning document, you'll know how to do it.

And it will be easier for at least two reasons:

First, you'll know what the finished product should look like.
Second, you'll have better resources and better backup.

But even with the resources available at a large advertising agency, you wouldn't be as prepared to write the document if you hadn't been through the process first while you were still at the university.

Life on the Learning Curve.

Knowledge and information are the driving forces of our economy. Learn to use them and learn how to learn.

Work hard, learn the process, and learn the Brand.

Learn to excel and learn to lead.

If you're going to work for an ad agency, a marketer, or run your own business, you'll need everything in this book.

And a lot more that isn't.

So...good luck. I hope you reap the enjoyment and satisfaction that comes from learning to do a job well.

Glossary of Interactive Advertising Terms v. 2.0

Introduction

The IAB's Glossary of Interactive Advertising Terms has been written to help marketers, agency executives, and publishers understand the evolving language of interactive marketing. Because our industry's jargon is constantly evolving, we've created the IAB wiki in order to help populate a more dynamic database of information on interactive advertising. To be part of the discussion, please visit the IAB wiki at http://www.iab.net/wiki/index.php/Main_Page.

A

AAAA (American Association of Advertising Agencies) –
Founded in 1917, the American Association of Advertising Agencies (AAAA) is the national trade association representing the advertising agency business in the United States. See www.aaaa.org.

Abandonment –
when a user leaves a shopping cart with something in it prior to completing the transaction.

Abort –
when a Web server does not successfully transfer a unit of content or ad to a browser. This is usually caused by a user hitting the stop button or clicking on another link prior to the completion of a download.

Activity audit –
independent verification of measured activity for a specified time period. Some of the key metrics validated are ad impressions, page impressions, clicks, total visits and unique users. An activity audit results in a report verifying the metrics. Formerly known as a count audit.

Ad/advertisement –
a commercial message targeted to an advertiser's customer or prospect.

Ad audience –
the number of unique users exposed to an ad within a specified time period.

Ad banner –
a graphic image or other media object used as an advertisement. See iab.net for voluntary guidelines for banner ads.

Ad blocker –
software on a user's browser which prevents advertisements from being displayed.

Ad campaign audit –
an activity audit for a specific ad campaign.

Ad centric measurement –
audience measurement derived from a third-party ad server's own server logs.

Ad display/Ad delivered –
when an ad is successfully displayed on the user's computer screen.

Ad download –
when an ad is downloaded by a server to a user's browser. Ads can be requested, but aborted or abandoned before actually being downloaded to the browser, and hence there would be no opportunity to see the ad by the user.

Address –
a unique identifier for a computer or site online, usually a URL for a Web site or marked with an @ for an e-mail address. Literally, it is how one computer finds the location of another computer using the Internet.

Ad impression –
1) an ad which is served to a user's browser. Ads can be requested by the user's browser (referred to as pulled ads) or they can be pushed, such as e-mailed ads; 2) a measurement of responses from an ad delivery system to an ad request from the user's browser, which is filtered from robotic activity and is recorded at a point as late as possible in the process of delivery of the creative material to the user's browser -- therefore closest to the actual opportunity to see by the user. Two methods are used to deliver ad content to the user – a) server-initiated and b) client-initiated. Server-initiated ad counting uses the publisher's Web content server for making requests, formatting and re-directing content. Client-initiated ad counting relies on the user's browser to perform these activities. For organizations that use a server-initiated ad counting method, counting should occur subsequent to the ad response at either the publisher's ad server or the Web content server. For organizations using a client-initiated ad counting method, counting should occur at the publisher's ad server or third-party ad server, subsequent to the ad request, or later, in the process. See iab.net for ad campaign measurement guidelines.

Ad impression ratio –
Click-throughs divided by ad impressions. See click rate.

Ad insertion –
when an ad is inserted in a document and recorded by the ad server.

Ad materials –
the creative artwork, copy, active URLs and active target sites which are due to the seller prior to the initiation of the ad campaign.

Ad network –
an aggregator or broker of advertising inventory for many sites. Ad networks are the sales representatives for the Web sites within the network.

Ad recall –
a measure of advertising effectiveness in which a sample of respondents is exposed to an ad and then at a later point in time is asked if they remember the ad. Ad recall can be on an aided or unaided basis. Aided ad recall is when the respondent is told the name of the brand or category being advertised.

Ad request –
the request for an advertisement as a direct result of a user's action as recorded by the ad server. Ad requests can come directly from the user's browser or from an intermediate Internet resource, such as a Web content server.

Ad serving –
the delivery of ads by a server to an end user's computer on which the ads are then displayed by a browser and/or cached. Ad serving is normally performed either by a Web publisher or by a third-party ad server. Ads can be embedded in the page or served separately.

Ad space –
the location on a page of a site in which an advertisement can be placed. Each space on a site is uniquely identified. Multiple ad spaces can exist on a single page.

Ad stream-
the series of ads displayed by the user during a single visit to a site (also impression stream).

Ad transfers –
the successful display of an advertiser's Web site after the user clicked on an ad. When a user clicks on an advertisement, a click-through is recorded and re-directs or "transfers" the user's browser to an advertiser's Web site. If the user successfully displays the advertiser's Web site, an ad transfer is recorded.

Ad view –
when the ad is actually seen by the user. Note this is not measurable today. The best approximation today is provided by ad displays.

Advertiser –
the company paying for the advertisement.

Affiliate marketing –
an agreement between two sites in which one site (the affiliate) agrees to feature content or an ad designed to drive traffic to another site. In return, the affiliate receives a percentage of sales or some other form of compensation generated by that traffic.

Affinity marketing –
selling products or services to customers on the basis of their established buying patterns. The offer can be communicated by e-mail promotions, online or offline advertising.

Alternate text –
a word or phrase that is displayed when a user has image loading disabled in their browser or when a user abandons a page by hitting "stop" in their browser prior to the

transfer of all images. Also appears as "balloon text" when a user lets their mouse rest over an image.

ANA (Association of National Advertisers) –
The Association of National Advertisers leads the marketing community by providing its members insights, collaboration and advocacy. The ANA strives to promote and protect all advertisers and marketers. See ana.net for more information.

Animated GIF –
an animation created by combining multiple GIF images in one file. The result is multiple images, displayed sequentially, giving the appearance of movement.

Anonymizer –
an intermediary which prevents Web sites from seeing a user's Internet Protocol (IP) address.

Applet –
a small, self-contained software application that is most often used by browsers to automatically display animation and/or to perform user-requested database queries.

Applicable browser –
any browser an ad will impact, regardless of whether it will play the ad.

ARF (Advertising Research Foundation) –
The ARF is the premiere advertising industry association for creating, aggregating, synthesizing and sharing the knowledge required by decision makers in the field. The principal mission of The ARF is to improve the practice of advertising, marketing and media research in pursuit of more effective marketing and advertising communications. See thearf.org.

Artifacting –
distortion that is introduced into audio or video by the compression algorithm (codec). Compressed images may have stray pixels that were not present in the original image. See codec.

Aspect ratio –
the width-to-height ratio of a picture or video frame. TV broadcasts at a 4:3 (1.33:1) aspect ratio; digital TV will be broadcast with a 16:9 (1.78:1) ratio; and most feature films are shot in at least a 1.85:1 ratio. IMUs have an aspect ratio of 6:5 (330x 250; 336 x 280; and 180 x 150).

Audit –
third party validation of log activity and/or measurement process associated with Internet activity/advertising. Activity audits validate measurement counts. Process audits validate internal controls associated with measurement.

Auditor –
a third party independent organization that performs audits.

Avatar-
A graphical representation of an individual in a game or other virtual environment

B

Backbone –
High-volume, central, generally "long-haul" portion of a data network.

Bandwidth –
the transmission rate of a communications line or system, expressed as kilobits per second (kbps) or megabits per second (Mbps) for digital systems; the amount of data that can be transmitted over communications lines in a given time.

Bandwidth contention –
a bottleneck that occurs when two or more files are simultaneously transmitted over a single data line. Unless the system is able to prioritize among the files, the effect is to slow delivery of each.

Banner –
a graphic advertising image displayed on a Web page. See iab.net for voluntary guidelines defining specifications of banner ads.

Barter –
the exchange of goods and services without the use of cash. The value of the barter is the dollar value of the goods and services being exchanged for advertising. This is a recognized form of revenue under GAAP (Generally Accepted Accounting Principles).

Beacon –
See Web beacon

Beta –
a test version of a product, such as a Web site or software, prior to final release.

Bit rate –
a measure of bandwidth which indicates how fast data is traveling from one place to another on a computer network. Bit rate is usually expressed in kilobits per second (kbps) or megabits per second (Mbps).

Behavioral Targeting-
A technique used by online publishers and advertisers to increase the effectiveness of their campaigns. Behavioral targeting uses information collected on an individual's web browsing behavior such as the pages they have visited or the searches they have made to select which advertisements to be displayed to that individual. Practitioners believe this helps them deliver their online advertisements to the users who are most likely to be influenced by them.

Blog-
Generic name for any Website featuring regular posts arranged chronologically, typically inviting public comments from readers. Blog postings are generally short and informal, and blog software is generally free and very easy for individual users, making it a popular tool for online diaries as well as more professional publications.

Bonus impressions –
additional ad impressions above commitments outlined in the approved insertion order.

Bot –

Software that runs automatically without human intervention. Typically, a bot is endowed with the capability to react to different situations it may encounter. Two common types of bots are agents and spiders. Bots are used by companies like search engines to discover Web sites for indexing. Short for "robot."

Bounce –

see E-mail Bounce.

Brand Awareness-

Research studies can associate ad effectiveness to measure the impact of online advertising on key branding metrics.

Broadband –

an Internet connection that delivers a relatively high bit rate – any bit rate at or above 256 Kbps. Cable modems and DSL all offer broadband connections.

Broadband Video Commercials-

TV-like advertisements that may appear as in-page video commercials or before, during, and/or after a variety of content in a player environment including but not limited to, streaming video, animation, gaming, and music video content. Broadband video commercials may appear in live, archived, and downloadable streaming content.

Browser –

a software program that can request, download, cache and display documents available on the World Wide Web.

Browser sniffer –

see sniffer.

BtoB/B2B (Business-to-Business) –

businesses whose primary customers are other businesses.

BtoC/B2C (Business-to-Consumer) –

businesses whose primary customers are consumers

Buffering –

when a streaming media player temporarily stores portions of a streaming media (e.g., audio or video) file on a client PC until there is enough information for the stream to begin playing.

Bulk E-mail Folder –

see Junk E-mail Folder.

Button –

1) clickable graphic that contains certain functionality, such as taking one someplace or executing a program; 2) buttons can also be ads. See iab.net for voluntary guidelines defining specifications of button ads.

C

Cable modem –
a device that permits high speed connectivity to the Internet over a cable television system.

Cache –
memory used to temporarily store the most frequently requested content/files/pages in order to speed its delivery to the user. Caches can be local (i.e. on a browser) or on a network. In the case of local cache, most computers have both memory (RAM), and disk (hard drive) cache.

Cache busting –
the process by which sites or servers serve content or HTML in such a manner as to minimize or prevent browsers or proxies from serving content from their cache. This forces the user or proxy to fetch a fresh copy for each request. Among other reasons, cache busting is used to provide a more accurate count of the number of user requests.

Cached ad impressions –
the delivery of an advertisement to a browser from local cache or a proxy server's cache. When a user requests a page that contains a cached ad, the ad is obtained from the cache and displayed.

Caching –
the process of copying a Web element (page or ad) for later reuse. On the Web, this copying is normally done in two places: in the user's browser and on proxy servers. When a user makes a request for a Web element, the browser looks into its own cache for the element; then a proxy, if any; followed by the intended server. Caching is done to reduce redundant network traffic, resulting in increased overall efficiency of the Internet.

CARU (The Children's Advertising Review Unit) –
division of the Council of Better Business Bureaus that reviews advertising and promotional material directed at children in all media. See caru.org for more information.

CGI script (Common Gateway Interface) –
CGI's are used to allow a user to pass data to a Web server, most commonly in a Web-based form. Specifically, CGI scripts are used with forms such as pull-down menus or text-entry areas with an accompanying submit button. The input from theform is processed by a program (the CGI script itself) on a remote Web server.

Channel –
1) a band of similar content; 2) a type of sales outlet (also known as channel of distribution), for example retail, catalogue, or e-commerce.

Chat –
online interactive communication between two or more people on the Web. One can "talk" in real time with other people in a chat room, typically by typing, though voice chat is available.

Chat room –
an area online where people can communicate with others in real-time.

Click rate –
ratio of ad clicks to ad impressions.

Clicks –
1) metric which measures the reaction of a user to an Internet ad. There are three types of clicks: click-throughs; in-unit clicks; and mouseovers; 2) the opportunity for a user to download another file by clicking on an advertisement, as recorded by the server; 3) the result of a measurable interaction with an advertisement or key word that links to the advertiser's intended Web site or another page or frame within the Web site; 4) metric which measures the reaction of a user to linked editorial content. See iab. net for ad campaign measurement guidelines. See also, click-through, in-unit clicks and mouseover.

Click Fraud-
Click fraud is a type of internet crime that occurs in pay per click online advertising when a person, automated script, or computer program imitates a legitimate user of a web browser clicking on an ad, for the purpose of generating a charge per click without having actual interest in the target of the ad's link.

Click-stream –
1) the electronic path a user takes while navigating from site to site, and from page to page within a site; 2) a comprehensive body of data describing the sequence of activity between a user's browser and any other Internet resource, such as a Web site or third party ad server.

Click-through –
the action of following a link within an advertisement or editorial content to another Web site or another page or frame within the Web site. Ad click-throughs should be tracked and reported as a 302 redirect at the ad server and should filter out robotic activity.

Click-within –
similar to click down or click. But more commonly, click-withins are ads that allow the user to "drill down" and click, while remaining in the advertisement, not leaving the site on which they are residing.

Client –
A computer or software program that contacts a server to obtain data via the Internet or another network. Internet explorer, Outlook, and other browsers and e-mail programs are examples of software clients.

Client-initiated ad impression –
one of the two methods used for ad counting. Ad content is delivered to the user via two methods – server-initiated and client-initiated. Client-initiated ad counting relies on the user's browser for making requests, formatting and re-directing content. For organizations using a client-initiated ad counting method, counting should occur at the

publisher's ad server or third-party ad server, subsequent to the ad request, or later, in the process. See server-initiated ad impression.

Close-
Indicates that the user clicks or otherwise activates a close control which fully dispatches the ad from the player environment. May not apply to non-overlay ads.

Codec –
short for compressor/decompressor. Codecs are computer algorithms that are used tocompress the size of audio, video, and image files for streaming over a data network or storage on a computer. Apple's QuickTime, Microsoft's Windows Media Video, and MP3 are examples of common codecs.

Communication error –
the failure of a Web browser/Web server to successfully request/transfer a document.

Content integration –
advertising woven into editorial content or placed in a contextual envelope. Also known as "Web advertorial".

Contextual Ads-
Existing contextual ad engines deliver text and image ads to non-search content pages. Ads are matched to keywords extracted from content. Advertisers can leverage existing keyboard-based paid search campaigns and gain access to a larger audience.

Cookie –
a small piece of information (i.e., program code) that is stored on a browser for the purpose of identifying that browser during audience activity and between visits or sessions.

Cookie buster –
software that blocks the placement of cookies on a user's browser.

COPPA (Children's Online Privacy Protection Act) –
Congress enacted the COPPA in 1998 to prohibit unfair or deceptive acts or practices in connection with the collection, use, or disclosure of personally identifiable information from and about children on the Internet. Section 6502(b)(1) of the Act sets forth a series of general privacy protections to prevent unfair or deceptive online information collection from or about children, and directs the Commission to adopt regulations to implement those protections. The Act requires operators of Web sites directed to children and operators who knowingly collect personal information from children to: (1) Provide parents notice of their information practices; (2) obtain prior verifiable parental consent for the collection, use, and/or disclosure of personal information from children (with certain limited exceptions for the collection of "online contact information," e.g., an e-mail address); (3) provide a parent, upon request, with the means to review the personal information collected from his/her child; (4) provide a parent with the opportunity to prevent the further use of personal information that has already been collected, or the future collection of personal information from that child; (5) limit collection of personal information for a child's online participation in a game,

prize offer, or other activity to information that is reasonably necessary for the activity; and (6) establish and maintain reasonable procedures to protect the confidentiality, security, and integrity of the personal information collected.

COPPR (Children's Online Privacy Protection Rule) –
issued by the FTC in October 1999 the Children's Online Privacy Protection Rule went into effect on April 21, 2000, and implements the requirements of the COPPA by requiring operators of websites or online services directed to children and operators of Web sites or online services who have actual knowledge that the person from whom they seek information is a child (1) to post prominent links on their Web sites to a notice of how they collect, use, and/or disclose personal information from children; (2) with certain exceptions, to notify parents that they wish to collect information from their children and obtain parental consent prior to collecting, using, and/or disclosing such information; (3) not to condition a child's participation in online activities on the provision of more personal information than is reasonably necessary to participate in the activity; (4) to allow parents the opportunity to review and/or have their children's information deleted from the operator's database and to prohibit further collection from the child; and (5) to establish procedures to protect the confidentiality, security, and integrity of personal information they collect from children. As directed by the COPPA, the Rule also provides a safe harbor for operators following Commission-approved self-regulatory guidelines. See www.caru.org for more information.

Count audit –
see activity audit.

CPA (Cost-per-Action) –
cost of advertising based on a visitor taking some specifically defined action in response to an ad. "Actions" include such things as a sales transaction, a customer acquisition, or a click.

CPC (Cost-per-Customer) –
the cost an advertiser pays to acquire a customer.

CPC (Cost-per-click) –
cost of advertising based on the number of clicks received.

CPL (Cost-per-lead) –
cost of advertising based on the number of database files (leads) received.

CPM (Cost-per-thousand) –
media term describing the cost of 1,000 impressions. For example, a Web site that charges $1,500 per ad and reports 100,000 visits has a CPM of $15 ($1,500 divided by 100).

CPO (Cost-per-Order) –
cost of advertising based on the number of orders received. Also called Cost-per-Transaction.

CPS (Cost-per-Sale) –
the advertiser's cost to generate one sales transaction. If this is being used in conjunction

with a media buy, a cookie can be offered on the content site and read on the advertiser's site after the successful completion of an online sale.

CPT (Cost-per-Transaction) –
see CPO (Cost-per-Order).

CPTM (Cost per Targeted Thousand Impressions) –
implying that the audience one is trying to reach is defined by particular demographics or other specific characteristics, such as male golfers age 18-25.The difference between CPM and CPTM is that CPM is for gross impressions, while CPTM is for targeted impressions.

Crawler –
a software program which visits Web pages to build indexes for search engines. See also spider, bot, and intelligent agent.

Crowdsourcing-
Taking a task that would conventionally be performed by a contractor or employee and turning it over to a typically large, undefined group of people via an open call for responses.

CRM –
customer relationship management. Business practices that foster customer care, loyalty, and/or customer support.

CSS (Cascading Style Sheet)–
A stylesheet language used to describe the presentation of a document written in a markup language. CSS provides a more elegant alternative to straight HTML to quickly specify the look and feel of a single Web page or a group of multiple Web pages.

Cyber Cafe –
a public venue like a bar or cafe which contains computers with access to the Internet.

D

Daughter window –
an ad that runs in a separate ad window associated with a concurrently displayed banner. In normal practice, the content and banner are rendered first and the daughter window appears thereafter.

Demographics –
common characteristics used for population or audience segmentation, such as age, gender, household income, etc.

Digital signatures –
signatures for electronic documents. They establish identity and therefore can be used to establish legal responsibility and the complete authenticity of whatever they are affixed to -- in effect, creating a tamper-proof seal.

Digital Video Server –
a robust, dedicated computer at a central location that receives command requests

from the television viewer through a video-on-demand application. Once it receives this request, it then instantly broadcasts specific digital video streams to that viewer.

Display Advertising –

a form of online advertising where an advertiser's message is shown on a destination web page, generally set off in a box at the top or bottom or to one side of the content of the page.

DHTML (Dynamic Hypertext Markup Language) –

an extended set of HTML commands which are used by Web designers to create much greater animation and interactivity than HTML.

Domain name –

the unique name that identifies an Internet site. Every domain name consists of one top or high-level and one or more lower-level designators. Top-level domains (TLDs) are either generic or geographic. Generic top-level domains include .com (commercial), .net (network), .edu (educational), .org (organizational, public or non- commercial), .gov (governmental), .mil (military); .biz (business), .info (informational),.name (personal), .pro (professional), .aero (air transport and civil aviation), .coop (business co-operatives such as credit unions) and .museum. Geographic domains designate countries of origin, such as .us (United States), .fr (France), .uk (United Kingdom), etc.

DPO (Distinct Point of Origin) –

a unique address from which a browser connects to a Web site on the Internet.

Drill down –

when an online user accesses more and more pages of the Web site, i.e., he or she goes deeper into the content of the site.

DSL (Digital Subscriber Line) –

a high-speed dedicated digital circuit from a given location to the telephone company's central office, using normal copper telephone lines. DSL is the main form of consumer broadband worldwide. DSL is a general term that includes several variations: ADSL (Asymmetric Digital Subscriber Line), ranging up to 1.5 Mbps; HDSL (High-bit-rate Digital Subscriber Line), 1.5 Mbps; SDSL (Single-line Digital Subscriber Line), 1.5 Mbps; VDSL (Very high-data-rate Digital Subscriber Line), ranging up to 2.3 Mbps; and RDSL (Rate Adaptive Digital Subscriber Line), various speeds.

DVR (Digital Video Recorder) –

a high capacity hard drive that is embedded in a set-top box, which records video programming from a television set. DVRs enable the viewer to pause, fast forward, and store TV programming

Dynamic ad insertion –

the process by which an ad is inserted into a page in response to a user's request. Dynamic ad placement allows alteration of specific ads placed on a page based on any data available to the placement program. At its simplest, dynamic ad placement allows for multiple ads to be rotated through one or more spaces. In more sophisticated examples, placement could be affected by users' demographic data or usage history.

Dynamic IP address –
an IP address (assigned by an ISP to a client PC) that changes periodically.

Dynamic rotation –
delivery of ads on a rotating, random basis so that users are exposed to different ads and ads are served in different pages of the site.

E

E-commerce –
the process of selling products or services via the Web.

E-mail Advertising –
banner ads, links or advertiser sponsorships that appear in e-mail newsletters, e-mail marketing campaigns and other commercial e-mail communications. Includes all types of electronic mail (e.g., basic text or HTML-enabled).

E-mail Bounce –
An e-mail that cannot be delivered to the mailbox provider and is sent back to the e-mail Service Provider that sent it. A bounce is classified as either "hard" or "soft." Hard bounces are the failed delivery of e-mail due to a permanent reason, such as a non-existent address. Soft bounces are the failed delivery of e-mail due to a temporary issue, such as a full inbox or an unavailable ISP server.

E-mail campaign –
advertising campaign distributed via e-mail.

E-mail Inbox –
Within a mailbox provider, the default, primary folder that stores delivered e-mail messages.

E-mail Mailbox Provider –
the e-mail program, and by extension the server, that hosts the targeted e-mail address

E-mail Preview Pane –
a small window within a mailbox provider that allows the user to view some e-mail content without opening the e-mail.

E-mail Service Provider (ESP) –
a business or organization that provides the e-mail campaign delivery technology. ESPs may also provide services for marketing, advertising and general communication purposes.

Encoding –
the process of compressing and separating a file into packets so that it can be delivered over a network.

Encoder –
a hardware or software application used to compress audio and video signals for the purpose of streaming. See codec

Encryption –
securing digital information so that it is unreadable without the use of digital keys.

EPG (Electronic Programming Guide) –
an application that allows the viewer to interactively select his/her television programming.

Ethernet –
a networking technology that links computers together in local area networks.

ETV (Enhanced Television) –
a type of interactive television technology which allows content producers to send data and graphical "enhancements" through a small part of the regular analog broadcast signal called the Vertical Blanking Interval. These enhancements appear as overlays on the video and allow viewers to click on them if they are watching TV via special set-top box/software services.

Expandable banners –
a banner ad which can expand to as large as 468 x 240 after a user clicks on it or after a user moves his/her cursor over the banner. See iab.net for the IAB IMU guidelines.

Extranet –
an intranet that is partially accessible to authorized outsiders via a valid username and password.

Eyeballs –
slang term for audience; the number of people who view a certain website or advertisement.

F

Failure to transfer –
content requested by a browser can fail to transfer if the page is abandoned by the browser which requested it (see abandon) or if the server is unable to send the complete page, including the ads (known as an error or a communications error).

Family/Ad family –
a collection of one or more ad creatives. Also called ad campaign.

FAQ –
frequently asked questions.

FTP (File Transfer Protocol) –
Internet protocol which facilitates downloading or uploading digital files.

FTTH (Fiber to the Home) –
Advanced, next generation data networking infrastructure being deployed by some telcos and other companies to provide faster broadband Internet connectivity and other services.

Fiber Optic Cable –
Strands of glass used to transmit data—encoded as light—at extremely high data rates.

Fiber optics is widely deployed in backbone data networks today and is beginning to be used for "last-mile" broadband connections as well

Filtering –
the process of removing robotic activity and error codes from measurement records to make the remaining records representative of valid human Internet actions.

Filtration guidelines –
IAB voluntary guidelines for removing non-human activity in the reported measurement of ad impressions, page impressions, unique visitors and clicks. See iab. net for ad campaign measurement guidelines.

Firewall –
a security barrier controlling communication between a personal or corporate computer network and the Internet. A firewall is based on rules which allow and disallow traffic to pass, based on the level of security and filtering a network administrator employs.

Flame –
an inflammatory opinion or criticism distributed by e-mail or posted on a newsgroup or message board.

Flash™ –
Adobe's vector-based rich media file format which is used to display interactive animations on a Web page.

Floating ads –
an ad or ads that appear within the main browser window on top of the Web page's normal content, thereby appearing to "float" over the top of the page.

Fold –
The line below which a user has to scroll to see content not immediately visible when a Web page loads in a browser. Ads or content displayed "above the fold" are visible without any end-user interaction. Monitor size and resolution determine where on a Web page the fold lies.

Frames –
multiple, independent sections used to create a single Web page. Each frame is built as a separate HTML file but with one "master" file to control the placement of each section. When a user requests a page with frames, several files will be displayed as panes. Sites using frames report one page request with several panes as multiple page requests. IAB ad campaign measurement guidelines call for the counting of one file per frame set as a page impression.

Frame rate –
the number of frames of video displayed during a given time. The higher the frame rate, the more high-quality the image will be.

Frequency –
the number of times an ad is delivered to the same browser in a single session or time period. A site can use cookies in order to manage ad frequency.

G

Geotargeting-
Displaying (or preventing the display of) content based on automated or assumed knowledge of an end user's position in the real world. Relevant to both PC and mobile data services.

GIF (Graphic Interchange Format) –
a standard web graphic format which uses compression to store and display images.

Gigabyte –
one gigabyte equals 1000 megabytes.

GPRS (General Packet Radio Service)–
Digital mobile radio technology permitting moderate data rates along with voice communication. Evolution from the GSM standard; referred to as "2.5 G." See 3G.

Gross exposures –
the total number of times an ad is served, including duplicate downloads to the same person.

GSM (Global System for Mobile) –
the wireless telephone standard in Europe and most of the rest of the world outside North America; also used by T-Mobile and AT&T, among other US operators

Guerilla Marketing-
campaign tactic involving the placement of often humorous brand-related messages in unexpected places either online or in the real world; intended to provoke word-of-mouth and build buzz

GUI (Graphical User interface) –
a way of enabling users to interact with the computer using visual icons and a mouse rather than a command-line prompt/interpreter.

H

HDTV (High-Definition Television) –
a higher quality signal resolution using a digital format for the transmission and reception of TV signals. HDTV provides about five times more picture information (picture elements or pixels) than conventional television, creating clarity, wider aspect ratio, and digital quality sound.

Head end –
the site in a cable system or broadband coaxial network where the programming originates and the distribution network starts. Signals are usually received off the air from satellites, microwave relays, or fiber-optic cables at the head end for distribution.

Heuristic –
a way to measure a user's unique identity. This measure uses deduction or inference based on a rule or algorithm which is valid for that server. For example, the combination of IP address and user agent can be used to identify a user in some cases. If a server

receives a new request from the same client within 30 minutes, it is inferred that a new request comes from the same user and the time since the last page request was spent viewing the last page. Also referred to as an inference.

History list –
a menu in a web browser which displays recently visited sites. The same mechanism makes it possible for servers to track where a browser was before visiting a particular site.

Hit –
when users access a Web site, their computer sends a request to the site's server to begin downloading a page. Each element of a requested page (including graphics, text, and interactive items) is recorded by the site's Web server log file as a "hit." If a page containing two graphics is accessed by a user, those hits will be recorded once for the page itself and once for each of the graphics. Webmasters use hits to measure their servers' workload. Because page designs and visit patterns vary from site to site, the number of hits bears no relationship to the number of pages downloaded, and is therefore a poor guide for traffic measurement.

Home page –
the page designated as the main point of entry of a Web site (or main page) or the starting point when a browser first connects to the Internet. Typically, it welcomes visitors and introduces the purpose of the site, or the organization sponsoring it, and then provides links to other pages within the site.

Host –
any computer on a network that offers services or connectivity to other computers on the network. A host has an IP address associated with it.

Hotlists –
pull-down or pop-up menus often displayed on browsers or search engines that contain new or popular sites.

House ads –
ads for a product or service from the same company. "Revenues" from house ads should not be included in reported revenues.

HTML (Hypertext Markup Language) –
a set of codes called markup tags in a plain text file that determine what information is retrieved and how it is rendered by a browser. There are two kinds of markup tags: anchor and format. Anchor tags determine what is retrieved, and format tags determine how it is rendered. Browsers receive HTML pages from the Internet and use the information to display text, graphics, links and other elements as they were intended by a Website's creator.

HTTP (Hyper-Text Transfer Protocol) –
the format most commonly used to transfer documents on the World Wide Web.

Hybrid pricing –
pricing model which is based on a combination of a CPM pricing model and a

performance-based pricing model. See CPM pricing model and performance-based pricing model.

Hyperlink –
a clickable link, e.g., on a Web page or within an e-mail, that sends the user to a new URL when activated.

Hypertext –
any text that contains links connecting it with other text or files on the Internet.

I

IAB (Interactive Advertising Bureau) –
IAB is a non-profit trade association devoted exclusively to maximizing the use and effectiveness of interactive advertising and marketing. See iab.net for more information.

Image map –
a GIF or JPEG image with more than one linking hyperlink. Each hyperlink or hot spot can lead to a different destination page.

Impression –
a measurement of responses from a Web server to a page request from the user browser, which is filtered from robotic activity and error codes, and is recorded at a point as close as possible to opportunity to see the page by the user.

IMU (Interactive Marketing Unit) –
the standard ad unit sizes endorsed by IAB. See iab.net for more information.

Inbox –
See E-mail Inbox

Insertion –
actual placement of an ad in a document, as recorded by the ad server.

Insertion order –
purchase order between a seller of interactive advertising and a buyer (usually an advertiser or its agency).

Instant messaging (IM) –
a method of communicating in real-time, one-to-one or in groups over the internet. Users assemble "buddy lists" which reflect the availability (or "presence") of people with whom they communicate.

Intelligent agents –
software tools which help the user find information of specific interest to him/her. The user's profile is continually refined and improved based on the user's acceptance or rejection of recommendations over time.

Interactive advertising –
all forms of online, wireless and interactive television advertising, including banners, sponsorships, e-mail, keyword searches, referrals, slotting fees, classified ads and

interactive television commercials.

Internal page impressions –

Web site activity that is generated by individuals with IP addresses known to be affiliated with the Web site owner. Internal activity that is associated with administration and maintenance of the site should be excluded from the traffic or measurement report.

Internet –

The worldwide system of computer networks providing reliable and redundant connectivity between disparate computers and systems by using common transport and data protocols known as TCP/IP.

Interstitial ads –

ads that appear between two content pages. Also known as transition ads, intermercial ads and splash pages.

Intranet –

a network based on TCP/IP protocols that belongs to an organization, usually a corporation, and is accessible only by the organization's members, employees or others with authorization.

In-unit click –

a measurement of a user-initiated action of responding to an ad element which generally causes an intra-site redirect or content change. In-unit clicks are usually tracked via a 302 redirect. Also known as click-downs, click-ups and click-withins. See ad click; 302 redirect.

Inventory –

the number of ads available for sale on a Web site.

IP (Internet Protocol) –

a protocol telling the network how packets are addressed and routed.

IP address –

Internet protocol numerical address assigned to each computer on the Internet so that its location and activities can be distinguished from those of other computers. The format is ##.##.##.## with each number ranging from 0 through 255 (e.g. 125.45.87.204)

IRC – (Internet Relay Chat) –

1) a facility that allows people to chat in real time. The chats, or forums, are typed remarks, and they can be either public or private; 2) a protocol that allows users to converse with others in real time. IRC is structured as a network of servers, each of which accepts connections from client programs.

ISDN (Integrated Services Digital Network) –

faster-than-dial-up connections to the Internet over copper phone wires. DSL has in large part replaced ISDN. See DSL.

ISP (Internet Service Provider) –

A business or organization that provides Internet access and related services, to consumers.

ITI (Information Technology Industry Council) –
represents the leading U.S. providers of information technology products and services. It advocates growing the economy through innovation and supports free-market policies. See itic.org for more information.

iTV (Interactive Television) –
any technology that allows for two-way communication between the audience and the television service provider (such as the broadcaster, cable operator, set-top box manufacturer).

J

Java® –
a programming language designed for building applications on the Internet. It allows for advanced features, increased animation detail and real-time updates. Small applications called Java applets can be downloaded from a server and executed by Java-compatible browsers like Microsoft Internet Explorer and Netscape Navigator.

JPEG (Joint Photographic Experts Group) –
Standard web graphic file format that uses a compression technique to reduce graphic file sizes

Jump page ad –
microsite which is reached via click-through from button or banner ad. The jump page itself can list several topics, which are linked to either the advertiser's site or the publisher's site.

Junk E-mail Folder –
A folder within an e-mail client or on an E-mail Service Provider server that stores e-mail messages that are identified, either by the user or by an automated spam filter, as undesired or undesirable.

K

Keyword –
specific word(s) entered into a search engine by the user that result(s) in a list of Web sites related to the key word. Keywords can be purchased by advertisers in order to embed ads linking to the advertiser's site within search results (see "Search engine marketing."

L

Lag –
the delay between making an online request or command and receiving a response. See latency.

LAN (Local Area Network) –
a group of computers connected together (a network) at one physical location.

Large rectangle –

an IMU size. The IAB's voluntary guidelines include seven Interactive Marketing Unit (IMU) ad formats; two vertical units and five large rectangular units. See iab.net for more information

Latency –
1) time it takes for a data packet to move across a network connection; 2) visible delay between request and display of content and ad. Latency sometimes leads to the user leaving the site prior to the opportunity to see. In streaming media, latency can create stream degradation if it causes the packets, which must be received and played in order, to arrive out of order.

LBS (Location Based Service) –
Mobile data service related to an end user's immediate location. Examples include store or service locators and friend finders.

Lead Generation-
fees advertisers pay to Internet advertising companies that refer qualified purchase inquiries (e.g., auto dealers which pay a fee in exchange for receiving a qualified purchase inquiry online) or provide consumer information (demographic, contact, and behavioral) where the consumer opts into being contacted by a marketer (email, postal, telephone, fax). These processes are priced on a performance basis (e.g., cost-per-action, -lead or -inquiry), and can include user applications (e.g., for a credit card), surveys, contests (e.g., sweepstakes) or registrations.

Link –
a clickable connection between two Web sites. Formally referred to as a hyperlink.

Listserv –
a mailing list comprised of e-mail addresses.

Listserver –
a program that automatically sends e-mail to a list of subscribers or listserv.

Log file –
a file that records transactions that have occurred on the Web server. Some of the types of data which are collected are: date/time stamp, URL served, IP address of requestor, status code of request, user agent string, previous URL of requestor, etc. Use of the extended log file format is preferable.

Login –
the identification or name used to access a computer, network or site.

M

Mailing list –
an automatically distributed e-mail message on a particular topic going to certain individuals.

Makegoods –
additional ad impressions which are negotiated in order to make up for the shortfall of

ads delivered versus the commitments outlined in the approved insertion order.

M-commerce –
mobile commerce, the ability to conduct monetary transactions via a mobile device, such as a WAP-enabled cell phone.

Media Company –
A company that derives revenue from publishing content via one or more means of distribution, e.g., print publishing, television, radio, the Internet

Microblogging-
Publishing very brief, spontaneous posts to a public Website, usually via a mobile device or wirelessly connected laptop.

Micro-sites –
multi-page ads accessed via click-through from initial ad. The user stays on the publisher's Web site, but has access to more information from the advertiser than a display ad allows.

Midroll –
Form of online video ad placement where the ad is played during a break in the middle of the content video. See Preroll and Postroll.

MIME (Multi-purpose Internet Mail Extensions) –
a method of encoding a file for delivery over the Internet.

MMA- Mobile Marketing Association –
Industry trade organization dedicated to facilitating the growth of advertising on mobile phones

Minimize-
indicates that the user clicks or otherwise activates a close control which fully dispatches the ad from the player environment. May not apply to non-overlay ads.

MMORPG (Massively Multiplayer Role-Playing Game) –
Any of a variety of three dimensional, highly immersive, PC or console based video games where many players interact, competing or co-operating to achieve goals in real time.

Modem –
device which transfers digital signals to analog signals and vice versa suitable for sending across phone or cable lines.

Moore's Law –
A key observation regarding the growth in computer power experienced over the past several decades. Gordon Moore of Intel stated that the speed of semiconductor processors doubles every 18 months. So far this has remained true.

Mouseover –
the process by which a user places his/her mouse over a media object, without clicking. The mouse may need to remain still for a specified amount of time to initiate some actions.

MP3 –
Codec most commonly used for digital music online. Generic term for any digital music file, regardless of codec used to create or play it.

MPEG –
1) the file format that is used to compress and transmit movies or video clips online; 2) standards set by the Motion Picture Exports Group for video media.

MRC (Media Rating Council) –
a non-profit trade association dedicated to assuring valid, reliable and effective syndicated audience research. The MRC performs audits of Internet measurements as well as traditional media measurements.

MSO (Multiple System Operator) –
A generic industry acronym for a cable TV system operator; more correctly, any cable network operator with more than one cable TV system.

N

NAI (Network Advertising Initiative) –
a cooperative group of network advertisers which has developed a set of privacy principles in conjunction with the Federal Trade Commission. The NAI provides consumers with explanations of Internet advertising practices and how they affect both consumers and the Internet. See networkadvertising.org for more information.

Netiquette –
a term that is used to describe the informal rules of conduct ("do's and don'ts") of online behavior.

Newsgroup –
an electronic bulletin board devoted to talking about a specific topic and open to everybody. Only a handful of newsgroups permit the posting of advertising.

Non-registered user –
someone who visits a Web site and elects not to, or is not required to, provide certain information, and hence may be denied access to part(s) of the site.

Nonqualifying page impressions –
page impressions which should be excluded from traffic or measurement reports, such as unsuccessful transfers of requested documents, successful transfers of requested documents to a robot or spider, and/or pages in a frame set. See frames.

O

Off-site measurement –
when a site forwards its log files to an off-site Web research service for analysis.

On-demand –
the ability to request video, audio, or information to be sent to the screen immediately by clicking something on the screen referring to that choice.

On-site measurement –

when a server has an appropriate software program to measure and analyze traffic received on its own site.

OPA (Online Privacy Alliance) –

a group of corporations and associations who have come together to introduce and promote business-wide actions that create an environment of trust and foster the protection of individuals' privacy online. See privacyalliance.org for more information. OPA (Online Publishers' Association) – trade association representing a segment of online publishers. See online-publishers.org for more information.

Opt-in –

refers to an individual giving a company permission to use data collected from or about the individual for a particular reason, such as to market the company's products and services. See permission marketing.

Opt-in e-mail –

lists of Internet users who have voluntarily signed up to receive commercial e-mail about topics of interest.

Opt-out –

when a company states that it plans to market its products and services to an individual unless the individual asks to be removed from the company's mailing list.

OTS (Opportunity to See) –

same as page display – when a page is successfully displayed on the user's computer screen.

P

P3P (Platform for Privacy Preferences Project) –

browser feature that will analyze privacy policies and allow a user to control their privacy needs.

Packet sniffer –

a program used to monitor and record activity and to detect problems with Web transactions on a network.

Page –

a document having a specific URL and comprised of a set of associated files. A page may contain text, images, and other online elements. It may be static or dynamically generated. It may be made up of multiple frames or screens, but should contain a designated primary object which, when loaded, is counted as the entire page.

Page display –

when a page is successfully displayed on the user's computer screen.

Page impression –

a measurement of responses from a Web server to a page request from the user's browser, which is filtered from robotic activity and error codes, and is recorded at a point as close as possible to the opportunity to see the page by the user. See iab.net for ad campaign measurement guidelines.

Page request –
the opportunity for an HTML document to appear on a browser window as a direct result of a user's interaction with a Web site.

Page view –
when the page is actually seen by the user. Note: this is not measurable today; the best approximation today is provided by page displays.

Password –
a group of letters and/or numbers which allow a user access to a secured Web site

Pay-per-Click –
an advertising pricing model in which advertisers pay agencies and/or media companies based on how many users clicked on an online ad or e-mail message. See CPC

Pay-per-Impression –
an advertising pricing model in which advertisers pay based on how many users were served their ads. See CPM.

Pay-per-Lead –
an advertising pricing model in which advertisers pay for each "sales lead" generated. For example, an advertiser might pay for every visitor that clicked on an ad or site and successfully completed a form. See CPL.

Pay-per-Sale –
an advertising pricing model in which advertisers pay agencies and/or media companies based on how many sales transactions were generated as a direct result of the ad. See CPS.

PDF (Portable Document Format) –
a digital format developed by Adobe used primarily for distributing digital text files. Files with a .pdf extension can be viewed and printed consistently by anyone, regardless of platform.

Peer-to-Peer (P2P) –
the transmission of a file from one individual to another, typically through an intermediary. Individuals sharing files via P2P do not necessarily know one another, rather applications like BitTorrent manage file transmissions from those who have part or all of the file to those who want it.

Performance pricing model –
an advertising model in which advertisers pay based on a set of agreed upon performance criteria, such as a percentage of online revenues or delivery of new sales leads. See CPA, CPC, CPL, CPO, CPS, CPT.

Permission marketing –
when an individual has given a company permission to market its products and services to the individual. See opt-in.

Persistent cookie –
Cookies that remain a client hard drive until they expire (as determined by the website that set them) or are deleted by the end user.

PII (Personally Identifiable Information) –
refers to information such as an individual's name, mailing address, phone number or e-mail address.

PIN (Personal Identification Number) –
a group of numbers which allow a unique user access to a secured Web site and/or a secure area of a Web site. See password.

Pixel –
picture element (single illuminated dot) on a computer monitor. The metric used to indicate the size of Internet ads.

Platform –
the type of computer or operating system on which a software application runs, e.g., Windows, Macintosh or Unix.

PLI (Privacy Leadership Initiative) –
a partnership of CEOs from 15 corporations and 9 business associations using research to create a climate of trust that will accelerate acceptance of the Internet and the emerging Information Economy, both online and offline, as a safe and secure marketplace. See understandingprivacy.org

Plug-in –
a program application that can easily be installed and used as part of a Web browser. Once installed, plug-in applications are recognized by the browser and their function integrated into the main HTML file being presented.

Pop-under ad –
ad that appears in a separate window beneath an open window. Pop-under ads are concealed until the top window is closed, moved, resized or minimized.

Pop-up ad –
ad that appears in a separate window on top of content already on-screen. Similar to a daughter window, but without an associated banner.

Pop-up transitional –
initiates play in a separate ad window during the transition between content pages. Continues while content is simultaneously being rendered. Depending primarily on line-speed, play of a transitional ad may finish before or after content rendering is completed.

Portal –
a Web site that often serves as a starting point for a Web user's session. It typically provides services such as search, directory of Web sites, news, weather, e-mail, homepage space, stock quotes, sports news, entertainment, telephone directory information, area maps, and chat or message boards.

Posting –
entry on a message board, blog, or other chronological online forum.

Postroll –
form of online video ad placement where the advertisement is played after the content video plays. See Preroll and Midroll.

Pre-caching –
storing advertising or content in a computer's RAM or hard disk memory before it is displayed on the user's screen, rather than at the time that it plays, to reduce delays in rendering. See cache, caching.

Preroll –
form of online video ad placement where the advertisement is played before the content video plays. See Postroll and Midroll

Privacy policy –
a statement about what information is being collected; how the information being collected is being used; how an individual can access his/her own data collected; how the individual can opt-out; and what security measures are being taken by the parties collecting the data.

Privacy seal program –
a program that certifies the Web site owner complies with the site's proposed policy. Examples include TRUSTe and BBBOnline.

Profiling –
the practice of tracking information about consumers' interests by monitoring their movements online. This can be done without using any personal information, but simply by analyzing the content, URL's, and other information about a user's browsing path/click-stream.

Process audit –
third party validation of internal control processes associated with measurement. See audit.

Protocol –
a uniform set of rules that enable two devices to connect and transmit data to one another. Protocols determine how data are transmitted between computing devices and over networks. They define issues such as error control and data compression methods. The protocol determines the following: type of error checking to be used, data compression method (if any), how the sending device will indicate that it has finished a message and how the receiving device will indicate that it has received the message. Internet protocols include TCP/IP (Transfer Control Protocol/Internet Protocol), HTTP (Hypertext Transfer Protocol), FTP (File Transfer Protocol), and SMTP (Simple Mail Transfer Protocol).

Proxy servers –
intermediaries between end users and Web sites such as ISPs, commercial online services, and corporate networks. Proxy servers hold the most commonly and recently

used content from the Web for users in order to provide quicker access and to increase server security.

Publisher-
an individual or organization that prepares, issues, and disseminates content for public distribution or sale via one or more media.

Push advertising –
pro-active, partial screen, dynamic advertisement which comes in various formats.

PVR (Personal Video Recorder) –
see DVR

Q

Query –
a request for information, usually to a search engine.

R

Rate card –
the list of advertising prices and products and packages offered by a media company.

Re-direct –
when used in reference to online advertising, one server assigning an ad-serving or ad-targeting function to another server, often operated by a third company. For instance, a Web publisher's ad management server might re-direct to a third-party hired by an advertiser to distribute its ads to target customers; and then another re-direct to a "rich media" provider might also occur if streaming video were involved before the ad is finally delivered to the consumer. In some cases, the process of re- directs can produce latency. See ad serving, latency.

Reach –
1) unique users that visited the site over the course of the reporting period, expressed as a percent of the universe for the demographic category; also called unduplicated audience; 2) the total number of unique users who will be served a given ad.

Real time –
events that happen "live" at a particular moment. When one chats in a chat room, or sends an instant message, one is interacting in real time.

Referral link –
the referring page, or referral link is a place from which the user clicked to get to the current page. In other words, since a hyperlink connects one URL to another, in clicking on a link the browser moves from the referring URL to the destination URL. Also known as source of a visit.

Referral fees –
fees paid by advertisers for delivering a qualified sales lead or purchase inquiry.

Registration –
a process for site visitors to enter information about themselves. Sites use registration data to enable or enhance targeting of content and ads. Registration can be required or voluntary.

Repeat visitor –
unique visitor who has accessed a Web site more than once over a specific time period.

Return visits –
the average number of times a user returns to a site over a specific time period.

Revenue Management-
See Yield Management.

Rich media –
advertisements with which users can interact (as opposed to solely animation) in a web page format. These advertisements can be used either singularly or in combination with various technologies, including but not limited to sound, video, or Flash, and with programming languages such as Java, Javascript, and DHTML. These Guidelines cover standard Web applications including e-mail, static (e.g. html) and dynamic (e.g. asp) Web pages, and may appear in ad formats such as banners and buttons as well as transitionals and various over-the-page units such as floating ads, page take-overs, and tear-backs.

Roadblock-
Premium 100% share-of-voice rotation typically for one day or one week "aka. carpe diem"

ROI (Return on Investment) –
Net profit divided by investment.

RON (Run-of-Network) –
the scheduling of Internet advertising whereby an ad network positions ads across the sites it represents at its own discretion, according to available inventor. The advertiser usually forgoes premium positioning in exchange for more advertising weight at a lower CPM.

ROS (Run-of-Site) –
the scheduling of Internet advertising whereby ads run across an entire site, often at a lower cost to the advertiser than the purchase of specific site sub-sections.

RSS / RSS Readers-
or "Really Simple Syndication" is a process for publishing content on the Internet that facilitates moving that content into other environments. For example, top news stories on a newspaper website can be published as an RSS "feed" and pulled into and delivered via a Web portal site. RSS Readers are software programs or websites that enable users to subscribe to one or more RSS feeds, delivering content and information from multiple sources into a single user interface and environment.

S

Sample –

a subset of a universe whose properties are studied to gain information about that universe.

Sampling frame –

the source from which the sample is drawn.

Scripts –

files that initiate routines like generating pages dynamically in response to user input.

SDSL (Symmetrical Digital Subscriber Line)-

see DSL

Search –

Fees advertisers pay Internet companies to list and/or link their company site or domain name to a specific search word or phrase (includes paid searchrevenues). Search categories include:

- **Paid listings**—text links appear at the top or side of search results for specific keywords. The more a marketer pays, the higher the position it gets. Marketers only pay when a user clicks on the text link.

- **Contextual search**—text links appear in an article based on the context of the content, instead of a user-submitted keyword. Payment only occurs when the link is clicked.

- **Paid inclusion**—guarantees that a marketer's URL is indexed by a search engine. The listing is determined by the engine's search algorithms.

- **Site optimization**—modifies a site to make it easier for search engines to automatically index the site and hopefully result in better placement in results.

Search engine –

an application that helps Web users find information on the Internet. The method for finding this information is usually done by maintaining an index of Web resources that can be queried for the keywords or concepts entered by the user.

Search engine marketing (SEM)-

a form of Internet Marketing that seeks to promote websites by increasing their visibility in the Search Engine result pages

Search engine optimization (SEO) –

SEO is the process of improving the volume and quality of traffic to a web site from search engines via "natural" ("organic" or "algorithmic") search results.

Sell-through rate –

the percentage of ad inventory sold as opposed to traded or bartered.

Server –

a computer which distributes files which are shared across a LAN, WAN or the Internet. Also known as a "host".

Server centric measurement –
audience measurement derived from server logs.

Server-initiated ad impression –
one of the two methods used for ad counting. Ad content is delivered to the user via two methods – server-initiated and client-initiated. Server-initiated ad counting uses the publisher's Web content server for making requests, formatting and re-directing content. For organizations using a server-initiated ad counting method, counting should occur subsequent to the ad response at either the publisher's ad server or the Web content server, or later in the process. See client-initiated ad impression.

Server pull –
a process whereby a user's browser maintains an automated or customized connection or profile with a Web server. The browser usually sets up a unique request that is recorded and stored electronically for future reference. Examples are: requests for the automated delivery of e-mail newsletters, the request for Web content based on a specific search criteria determined by the user, or setting up a personalized Web page that customizes the information delivered to the user based on pre-determined self selections.

Server push –
a process whereby a server maintains an open connection with a browser after the initial request for a page. Through this open connection the server continues to provide updated pages and content even though the visitor has made no further direct requests for such information.

Session –
1) a sequence of Internet activity made by one user at one site. If a user makes no request from a site during a 30 minute period of time, the next content or ad request would then constitute the beginning of a new visit; 2) a series of transactions performed by a user that can be tracked across successive Web sites. For example, in a single session, a user may start on a publisher's Web site, click on an advertisement and then go to an advertiser's Web site and make a purchase. See visit.

Session cookies –
These are temporary and are erased when the browser exits at the end of a web surfing session. . See cookie.

Set-top box –
a device electronic device that connects to a TV providing connectivity to the Internet, game systems, or cable systems.

SGML (Standard Generalized Markup Language) –
the parent language for HTML.

Shockwave –
a browser plug-in developed by Macromedia (now part of Adobe) which allows multimedia objects to appear on the Web (animation, audio and video).

Shopping bot –
intelligent agent which searches for the best price.

Site-centric measurement –
audience measurement derived from a Web site's own server logs.

Skins –
customized and interchangeable sets of graphics, which allow Internet users to continually change the look of their desktops or browsers, without changing their settings or functionality. Skins are a type of marketing tool.

Skyscraper –
a tall, thin online ad unit. The IAB guidelines recommend two sizes of skyscrapers: 120 X 600 and 160 x 600.

Slotting fee –
a fee charged to advertisers by media companies to get premium positioning on their site, category exclusivity or some other special treatment. It is similar to slotting allowances charged by retailers.

Smart Card –
identical in size and feel to credit cards, smart cards store information on an integrated microprocessor chip located within the body of the card. These chips hold a variety of information, from stored (monetary)-value used for retail and vending machines, to secure information and applications for higher-end operations such as medical/healthcare records. The different types of cards being used today are contact, contactless and combination cards. Contact smart cards must be inserted into a smart card reader. These cards have a contact plate on the face which makes an electrical connector for reads and writes to and from the chip when inserted into the reader. Contactless smart cards have an antenna coil, as well as a chip embedded within the card. The internal antenna allows for communication and power with a receiving antenna at the transaction point to transfer information. Close proximity is required for such transactions, which can decrease transaction time while increasing convenience. A combination card functions as both a contact and contactless smart card.Specific to interactive television, the viewer can insert smart cards into the set-top box to trigger the box to decrypt contact programming.

SMTP (Simple Mail Transfer Protocol) –
the protocol used to transfer e-mail.

SMS (Short Message Service) –
standard for sending and receiving short (160 character) text messages via mobile handsets

Sniffer –
software that detects capabilities of the user's browser (looking for such things as Java capabilities, plug-ins, screen resolution, and bandwidth).

Social Bookmarking-
Aggregating, rating, describing, and publishing "bookmarks" – links to Web pages or other online content

Social marketing –

Marketing tactic that taps into the growth of social networks, encouraging users to adopt and pass along widgets or other content modules created by a brand, or to add a brand to the user's social circle of friends.

Social network –

An online destination that gives users a chance to connect with one or more groups of friends, facilitating sharing of content, news, and information among them. Examples of social networks include Facebook and LinkedIn.

Space –

location on a page of a site in which an ad can be placed. Each space on a site is uniquely identified. There can be multiple spaces on a single page.

Spam –

term describing unsolicited commercial e-mail.

Spam filter –

software built into e-mail gateways as well as e-mail client applications designed to identify and remove unsolicited commercial messages from incoming e-mail before the end user sees them

Spider –

a program that automatically fetches Web pages. Spiders are used to feed pages to search engines. It is called a spider because it crawls over the Web. Because most Web pages contain links to other pages, a spider can start almost anywhere. As soon as it sees a link to another page, it goes off and fetches it. Large search engines have many spiders working in parallel. See robot.

Splash page –

a preliminary page that precedes the user-requested page of a Web site that usually promotes a particular site feature or provides advertising. A splash page is timed to move on to the requested page after a short period of time or a click. Also known as an interstitial. Splash pages are not considered qualified page impressions under current industry guidelines, but they are considered qualified ad impressions.

Sponsor –

1) a sponsor is an advertiser who has sponsored an ad and, by doing so, has also helped sponsor or sustain the Web site itself; 2) an advertiser that has a special relationship with the Web site and supports a specific feature of a Web site, such as a writer's column or a collection of articles on a particular subject.

Sponsorship –

Sponsorship represents custom content and/or experiences created for an advertiser which may or may not include ad unties (i.e., display advertising, brand logos, advertorial and pre-roll video). Sponsorships fall into several categories:

- **Spotlights** are custom built pages incorporating an advertiser's brand and housing a collection of content usually around a theme;

- **Advergaming** can range from an advertiser buying all the ad units around a game or a "sponsored by" link to creating a custom branded game experience;

- **Content & Section Sponsorship** is when an advertiser exclusively sponsors a particular section of the site or email (usually existing content) reskinned with the advertiser's branding;

- **Sweepstakes & Contests** can range from branded sweepstakes on the site to a full- fledge branded contest with submissions and judging

Static ad placement/Static rotation –
1) ads that remain on a Web page for a specified period of time; 2) embedded ads.

Stickiness –
a measure used to gauge the effectiveness of a site in retaining individual users. Stickiness is usually measured by the duration of the visit.

Streaming –
1) technology that permits continuous audio and video delivered to a computer from a remote Web site; 2) an Internet data transfer technique that allows the user to see and hear audio and video files. The host or source compresses, then "streams" small packets of information over the Internet to the user, who can access the content as it is received.

Streaming media player –
a software program which decompresses audio and/or video files so the user can hear and/or see the video or audio file. Some examples are Real Player™, Windows Media and Quick Time Player.

Superstitials® –
an interstitial format developed by Unicast which is fully pre-cached before playing. Specs are 550 x 480 pixels (2/3 of screen), up to 100K file size and up to 20 seconds in length.

Surfing –
exploring the World Wide Web.

T

T-1 –
a dedicated, typically corporate, high-speed (1.54 MPS) Internet connection.

T-3 –
a very high-speed (45 MPS) dedicated, corporate Internet connection.

T-commerce –
electronic commerce via interactive television.

TCP/IP (Transfer Control Protocol/Internet Protocol) –
The software protocols that run the Internet, determining how packets of data travel from origin to destination

Target audience –

the intended audience for an ad, usually defined in terms of specific demographics (age, sex, income, etc.) product purchase behavior, product usage or media usage.

Terms & Conditions –

the details of the contract accompanying an insertion order. See iab.net for voluntary guidelines for standard terms & conditions for Internet advertising for media buys.

Text Messaging-

text messaging, or texting is the common term for the sending of "short" (160 characters or fewer) text messages, using the Short Message Service, from mobile phones. See SMS.

Textual ad impressions –

the delivery of a text-based advertisement to a browser. To compensate for slow Internet connections, visitors may disable "auto load images" in their graphical browser. When they reach a page that contains an advertisement, they see a marker and the advertiser's message in text format in place of the graphical ad. Additionally, if a user has a text-only browser, only textual ads are delivered and recorded as textual ad impressions.

Third-party ad server –

independent outsourced companies that specialize in managing, maintaining, serving, tracking, and analyzing the results of online ad campaigns. They deliver targeted advertising that can be tailored to consumers' declared or predicted characteristics or preferences.

3G –

The "Third Generation" mobile network infrastructure. As of 2007 being deployed (or already deployed) by mobile operators in most of Europe, East Asia, and North America. Supports much higher data speeds than previous mobile networks, in some cases approaching wired broadband connections.

302 Redirect –

the process of a server sending a browser the location of a requested ad, rather than sending the ad itself. Ad servers use 302 redirects to allow them to track activities such as ad requests or ad clicks.

Throughput –

the amount of data transmitted through Internet connectors in response to a given request.

Time Spent –

The amount of elapsed time from the initiation of a visit to the last audience activity associated with that visit. Time spent … should represent the activity of a single cookied browser or user for a single access session to the web-site or property.

Token –

tracer or tag which is attached by the receiving server to the address (URL) of a page requested by a user. A token lasts only through a continuous series of requests by a user, regardless of the length of the interval between requests. Tokens can be used to count unique users.

Traffic –
the flow of data over a network, or visitors to a Web site

Transfer –
the successful response to a page request; also when a browser receives a complete page of content from a Web server.

Transitional ad –
an ad that is displayed between Web pages. In other words, the user sees an advertisement as he/she navigates between page 'a' and page 'b.' Also known as an interstitial.

Transitional pop up –
an ad that pops up in a separate ad window between content pages.

Triggers –
a command from the host server that notifies the viewer's set-top box that interactive content is available at this point. The viewer is notified about the available interactive content via an icon or clickable text. Once clicked by using the remote control, the trigger disappears and more content or a new interface appears on the TV screen.

U

UMTS (Universal Mobile Telecommunications System) –
broadband, packet-based wireless transmission of text, digitized voice, video, and multimedia at data rates up to and possibly higher than 2 megabits per second, offering a set of services to mobile computer and phone users. See 3G

Unduplicated audience –
the number of unique individuals exposed to a specified domain, page or ad in a specified time period.

Unique Device-
An unduplicating computing device that is used to access Internet content or advertising during a measurement period. A count of unduplicated devices necessarily accounts for multiple browser usage on an individual computer or other computing device.

Unique Browser-
An identified and unduplicated Cookied Browser that accesses Internet content or advertising during a measurement period. This definition requires taking account for the potentially inflationary impact of cookie deletion among certain of the cookied browsers that access Internet content.

Unique Cookie-
A count of unique identifiers ... that represents unduplicated instances of Internet activity (generally visits) to Internet content or advertising during a measurement period.

Unique user –
unique individual or browser which has either accessed a site (see unique visitor) or which has been served unique content and/or ads such as e-mail, newsletters, interstitials and pop-under ads. Unique users can be identified by user registration

or cookies. Reported unique users should filter out bots. See iab.net for ad campaign measurement guidelines.

Unique visitor –
a unique user who accesses a Web site within a specific time period. See unique user.

Universe –
total population of audience being measured.

Unresolved IP addresses –
IP addresses that do not identify their 1st or 2nd level domain. Unresolved IP addresses should be aggregated and reported as such. See also domain.

Upload –
to send data from a computer to a network. An example of uploading data is sending e-mail.

URL (Uniform Resource Locator) –
the unique identifying address of any particular page on the Web. It contains all the information required to locate a resource, including its protocol (usually HTTP), server domain name (or IP address), file path (directory and name) and format (usually HTML or CGI).

URL tagging –
the process of embedding unique identifiers into URLs contained in HTML content. These identifiers are recognized by Web servers on subsequent browser requests. Identifying visitors through information in the URLs should also allow for an acceptable calculation of visits, if caching is avoided.

Usenet –
Internet bulletin-board application.

User –
an individual with access to the World Wide Web.

User agent string –
a field in a server log file which identifies the specific browser software and computer operating system making the request.

User centric measurement –
Web audience measurement based on the behavior of a sample of Web users.

User registration –
information contributed by an individual which usually includes characteristics such as the person's age, gender, zip code and often much more. A site's registration system is usually based on an ID code or password to allow the site to determine the number of unique visitors and to track a visitor's behavior within that site.

V

Video Game Console-
An interactive entertainment computer or electric device that manipulates the video

display signal of a display device (a television, monitor, etc.) to display a game. The term video game console is typically used solely for playing video games, but the new generation of consoles may play various types of media such as music, TV shows, and movies.

View-

Often used as a synonym for "impression". Any measurement and reporting of a "view" should be governed by the "impression" definition above.

Viewer –

person viewing content or ads on the Web. There is currently no way to measure viewers.

Viral marketing –

1) any advertising that propagates itself; 2) advertising and/or marketing techniques that "spread" like a virus by getting passed on from consumer to consumer and market to market.

Viral video –

Online video clips (typically short and humorous) passed via links from one person to another.

Virtual worlds –

Three-dimensional computerized environments that multiple users can explore and interact with via "avatars," characters representing themselves. Online games like World of Warcraft take place in virtual worlds, but the term is often used to define services that are open-ended and geared for socializing, as opposed to the more goal- oriented environments of online games.

Visit –

A single continuous set of activity attributable to a cookied browser or user (if registration-based or a panel participant) resulting in one or more pulled text and/or graphics downloads from a site.

Visit duration –

the length of time the visitor is exposed to a specific ad, Web page or Web site during a single session.

Visitor –

individual or browser which accesses a Web site within a specific time period.

VRML (Virtual Reality Modeling Language) –

programming language designed to be a 3D analog to HTML.

W

WAN (Wide Area Network) –

connectivity between a number of computers not located at the same physical location.

WAP (Wireless Application Protocol) –

a specification for a set of communication protocols to standardize the way that wireless devices, such as cellular mobile telephones, PDAs and others access and browse Internet-based content.

WASP (Wireless Applications Service Provider) –
an organization that provides content and applications for wireless devices.

Web beacon –
a line of code which is used by a Web site or third party ad server to track a user's activity, such as a registration or conversion. A Web beacon is often invisible because it is only 1 x 1 pixel in size with no color. Also known as Web bug, 1 by 1 GIF, invisible GIF and tracker GIF.

Web site –
the virtual location (domain) for an organization's or individual's presence on the Web.

Web bug –
see Web beacon.

Webcasting –
real-time or pre-recorded delivery of a live event's audio, video, or animation over the Internet.

Widget –
A small application designed to reside on a PC desktop (Mac OS X or Windows Vista) or within a Web-based portal or social network site (e.g., MySpace or Facebook) offering useful or entertaining functionality to the end user

Wi-Fi –
Any of a family of wireless LAN data standards (IEEE 802.11) used fairly ubiquitously for corporate and home connectivity. Also available as "hotspots" in public areas such as cafes and airport terminals, either for free or for a one-time use charge or subscription fee.

WIMAX –
A wireless WAN standard (IEEE 802.16) designed to provide portable (eventually mobile) wireless broadband access. Single WIMAX antennas can provide coverage over large physical areas, making deployment potentially very cost effective. Although not widely available as of 2007, sometimes considered a potential competitor to cable modems and DSL for residential broadband.

X

XML (eXtensible Markup Language) –
a richer more dynamic successor to HTML utilizing SGML or HTML type tags to structure information. XLM is used for transferring data and creating applications on the Web. See SGML and HTML.

y

Yield –
the percentage of clicks vs. impressions on an ad within a specific page. Also called ad

click rate.

Yield Management-

Yield and Revenue Management is the process of understanding, anticipating and influencing advertiser and consumer behavior in order to maximize profits through better selling, pricing, packaging and inventory management, while delivering value to advertisers and site users.

Team Members

Schedule

Notes &
Resources